A Systems View of Education

Concepts and Principles for Effective Practice

1-24, 36-50, 77-91, 131-166, 174-175

A Systems View of Education

Concepts and Principles for Effective Practice

Bela H. Banathy

EDUCATIONAL TECHNOLOGY PUBLICATIONS
ENGLEWOOD CLIFFS, NEW JERSEY 07632

Library of Congress Cataloging-in-Publication Data

Banathy, Bela H.
A systems view of education : concepts and prinicples for effective practice / Bela H. Banathy.
p. cm.
Includes bibliographical references and index.
ISBN 0-87778-245-8
1. Education. 2. Social systems. 3. Systems analysis.
I. Title.
LB1028.35.B37 1992
371.3'078—dc20 92-7928
CIP

Printed in the United States of America.

Library of Congress Catalog Card Number: 92-7928.

International Standard Book Number: 0-87778-245-8.

First Printing: May, 1992.

TO MY WIFE, EVA

AND TO THE CREATION OF JUST SYSTEMS

FOR FUTURE GENERATIONS

Preface

"Systemic" is the buzz-word of high currency in both the public and private domains. We are seeking "systemic" solutions to "systemic" problems. If we are ambitious, we combine "systemic" with "long-term" as we contrast it with short-term, piecemeal, disjointed efforts. Recently, the notion of "systemic" has become a core concept in a search for educational reform.

When we probe into the meaning of the term, often we get such answers as: "things are connected," "there is no single cause of the problem," "things are complex," etc. Of course, these answers are all valid. But there is much more to it. "Systemic" enfolds large sets of concepts that constitute principles, common to all kinds of systems, that are manifested in multiple connotations; such as: the way we can think (systems thinking), the way we understand phenomena (having a systems perspective) and characterize an entity (systems description), the way an entity behaves (systems behavior), and the way we might do things (systems practice).

Having and acting upon a "systems view" embrace all the above. Having a systems view of education, for example, means that we can think about education as a system, we can understand and describe it as a system, we can design education so that it manifests systems behavior, and we can engage in educational inquiry by using approaches and methods of systems practice.

This book is meant to be used as a workbook. Those who wish to understand basic systems concepts and principles, who wish to view and characterize education as a system, and wish to learn the basics of systems practice can see their wishes come true by "working-with" this book and completing the activities in it. This "working-with-it" requires first reflective thinking; willingness to give up—at least suspend—old ways of viewing and thinking and becoming open to new ways of seeing and projecting. Then, it requires creative thinking and action, as one applies the systems view to the reconceptualization and redefinition of education as a system, and to its redesign as a system that nurtures learning and aims at the full development of human potential.

Table of Contents

Introduction

The genesis of this work is a small workbook I developed almost twenty years ago under the title, DEVELOPING A SYSTEMS VIEW OF EDUCATION: A SYSTEMS MODELS APPROACH (Lear Siegler/Fearon, 1973). The development of the workbook marked a major milestone in my own professional development, as I "leaped out" from the closed systems confines of instructional systems design into an open systems perspective of education as a social system. Earlier, my instructional and curriculum design work culminated in the publication of INSTRUCTIONAL SYSTEMS (Fearon, 1968) and A DESIGN OF FOREIGN LANGUAGE CURRICULUM (D.C. Heath, 1972). But once in my educational R&D work at the Far West Laboratory, where I confronted education as a social system, I realized that the closed systems engineering type of thinking of instructional design was not only useless in the social systems arena, but also it was dangerously counterproductive. Fortunately, getting involved in social systems research, and working with—and using the resources of—the international systems science community, I was able to develop an open, whole systems view and learned to use and develop intellectual technologies applicable to working with social systems.

The systems workbook has been used for the last two decades in many R&D projects I have directed at the Far West Laboratory. It was a learning resource in graduate education programs at San Jose State University and U.C. Berkeley during the seventies, and for my Ph.D. students at the Saybrook Graduate School since the early eighties. It is interesting to note that while the systems view book was extensively used in educational R&D projects, in the graduate courses I had very few students from the educational community. This is not surprising. The professional educational community is probably the last—among all the other professions—to "get interested in the systems idea." It has failed to embrace systems thinking and has resisted viewing the educational enterprise as a social system. While there has been a proliferation of graduate programs in instructional systems technology, which is conceptualized on closed systems and systems engineering notions, one can seldom find courses on systems thinking—much less on systems theory or methodology—in the catalogues of schools of education.

The realization of this state of affairs led me to focus my work with increasing intensity on ways by which the open/social systems notion, systems thinking, and the dynamics of systems change might be institutionalized in the educational community. I have committed myself to the idea of building a culture of systems thinking and systems practice in the educational arena. This book is one of the means by which people can learn and apply basic systems concepts and principles in meaningful real-world situations. I selected concepts and principles that are most relevant to education as a human activity system, and organized and arranged them in the form of three systems models: a system-environment model, a functions/structure model, and a process model. The three models incorporate insights, understanding, and knowledge about complex open/social systems which I have gained in the course of the last two decades. In the text, the models are first developed in a context that is generic to social systems, and then they are applied to characterizing, describing, and assessing educational systems.

The systems ideas and the three systems models presented in this work can be used in two specific ways. First, to describe and understand existing educational arrangements as systems and make an assessment of their environmental and systemic adequacy. Second, in the case where a new system is designed, it can be described with the use of the same three systems models. The comparison of the two sets of models will show us the difference between where we are now and where we want to be.

The presentation of the three systems models in Chapters Two, Three, and Four constitutes the main body of the work. In Chapter One, the systems view is discussed and the strategy of developing it by the use of the three models is set forth. In Chapter Five, the extended application and activation of the systems view is demonstrated. A glossary of systems terms is added as a conclusion.

It is recommended that those who work with and want to apply the material in the text use a notebook in which they respond to the various activities in the text. By completing these activities, the user of this book can develop a systems view of education and apply the systems view to educational activity systems of his or her choice.

BHB

January, 1992

The Use of Arrows in Figures

Key characteristics of entities conceptualized and described as "*systems*" are "relationships," "interactions," "mutual causality," and "recursiveness." These notions are represented in the figures in the text by arrows, that depict the above systemic features. In addition, arrows depict the flow of process in the system. In the figures (of the text) arrows have two heads. The marking of the heads depicts two kinds of relationship.

A. An arrow in which both heads are filled, such as:

indicates mutual causality of the interaction. It shows a two-directional process of equal significance. It stands for recursiveness and "mutual shaping."

B. In most cases, only one of the heads is filled, such as:

The direction indicated by the "filled head" signals the primary flow of influence. The head not filled indicates active search of feedback-interaction, confirmation of adequacy, or verification of appropriateness or lack of it. Thus, it still indicates "mutual shaping."

A Systems View of Education

Concepts and Principles for Effective Practice

pp. 3-24

CHAPTER ONE

Exploring the Systems View

In this chapter, I set the stage for the development of a systems view of education by exploring five questions: Why a systems view? What is the genesis of the systems view? What is its conceptual foundation? How can it be developed? And how is the systems view applied in education? In conclusion I'll map the road for the journey toward the acquisition of the systems view.

WHY A SYSTEMS VIEW?

The second half of the twentieth century is marked by massive changes affecting all aspects of our lives. We have experienced a major societal transformation from the industrial machine age to the postindustrial information/knowledge age. These changes and transformations have shaped our thinking and recast the way we view ourselves, the systems of which we are part, the environments in which we live, and the way we view the world. This "view of the world" has many dimensions. These dimensions include the sociocultural, the sociotechnical, the socioeconomic, the organizational, and the scientific. These dimensions interact and mutually influence each other. What emerges from their interaction is a world view that is very different from the one which characterized the previous era: the era of the industrial society. A world view is framed by its dimensions and becomes a window on the world. Or it is a lens through which we perceive the landscape of life that becomes our reality. Those who look through the lens of the previous era see their own reality very differently from those who use the lens that the new era has crafted. This change between the two world views is often called a "paradigm shift."

When a new stage emerges in the evolution of society—as was the case around the midpoint of this century—the continued use of the old paradigm, the old world view lens, creates increasingly more problems. A case in point: Societal systems, such as our educational activity systems, that still operate based on the design of the bygone era, and use the world view lens of the industrial machine age, are losing their viability. They operate in a continuous crisis mode, and eventually face termination unless they frame a new mind set, learn to use the new lens of the new era, and acquire new thinking that is based on the new world view.

In the Introduction I discussed the implications of the still prevailing use of the old design in our educational systems and introduced the rationale for the development of a new world view. In my recent book, SYSTEMS DESIGN OF EDUCATION: A JOURNEY TO CREATE THE FUTURE (Educational Technology Publications, 1991), I explored the educational implications of the emerged new world view. In this work, I focus on the emerged new scientific paradigm: systems inquiry and its manifestation; and the systems view and its development and application in education.

WHAT IS THE GENESIS OF THE SYSTEMS VIEW?

"Man is a prisoner of his own thinking." ... his "brain has been programmed to deal with a vanished world. This old world was characterized by the need to MANAGE THINGS—stone, wood, iron ... The new world is characterized by the need to MANAGE COMPLEXITY... Complexity is the very stuff of today's world. But our concepts belong to the much less complex old world, not to the much more complex today's world." (Stafford Beer)

A good way to begin to grasp the differences between the mind sets of disciplined (scientific) inquiry of the old and the new eras is to explore the key concepts that mark the two mind sets. The mind set of the industrial era has its roots in classical science—often associated with Newton—that emerged some three hundred years ago, as the mechanistic/deterministic world view. Its technological manifestation culminated in the industrial revolution, which greatly extended our PHYSICAL POWERS through machine technology: we learned to "MANAGE THINGS." The mind set of the postindustrial era is very different from the industrial era. It is shaped by cybernetic/systems science that emerged as the new paradigm of disciplined inquiry some four decades ago. Its practical applications—in high technology—greatly extended our COGNITIVE POWERS. This new mode of disciplined inquiry and its associated intellectual technologies enable us to "MANAGE COMPLEXITY," which is the dominant characteristic of the new era. Let me explain.

Over the last four to five decades, we have been faced with increasingly more complex and pressing problem situations, embedded in interconnected systems that operate in dynamically changing and turbulent environments. In addressing these problem situations and working with their relevant systems, we have learned to recognize the limitations of the perspectives, methods, and tools of traditional scientific orientation. More specifically:

* The technologies of MANUFACTURING THINGS worked well in managing the organized simplicity of the closed systems production of the "THINGS WORLD" of the machine age. But those technologies became useless, once we were faced with the organized open systems dynamics of the "WORLD OF COMPLEXITIES" of the new era. In today's world the methods of CREATING, ORGANIZING, and USING INFORMATION and KNOWLEDGE are the requisite intellectual technologies. Classical science defined complexity in terms of the multiple parts of a system, while systems science defines it based on multiple interactions with the environment and interactions among parts within the system.

* Inspired by the Cartesian-Newtonian scientific world view, disciplined inquiry during the last three hundred years has sought understanding by taking things apart, seeking the "ultimate part," and groping to see or reconstruct the whole by viewing the characteristics of its parts. This REDUCTIONIST orientation was not able to grasp "wholeness," which EMERGES from the interaction of parts, where the part gets its meaning from the whole and by its interaction with all other components of the whole. Thus, today we realize that the reductionist method of ANALYSIS had to be complemented with SYNTHESIS and with EXPANSIONISM, aimed at understanding larger and larger wholes in which our systems of interest are embedded.

* The CERTAINTY of DETERMINISM and the confidence in PREDICTIONS—markers of classical science—have been found less and less useful even in physics, where Heisenberg's UNCERTAINTY principle and Einstein's RELATIVITY have humbled our expectations for predictions. In human activity systems this insight has led us to aspire to UNDERSTANDING rather than predicting, and problem management rather than problem solution. Most significantly, we know NOW that we cannot predict the future. But we also know that systems science has given us the conceptual power and intellectual technology to shape our future by purposeful design. In human activity systems, determinism has been replaced by PURPOSE SEEKING as a mode of thinking and action. The principle of uncertainty has also helped us to understand that

the observer cannot be separated from what is observed. This insight became obvious even in physics, and much more so in social science.

* The unidirectional CAUSE-AND-EFFECT thinking—a key marker of traditional science—is defeated in the face of our understanding of the "counter-intuitive" nature of complex, dynamic systems. These systems—such as human activity systems—have too many interactive variables to be treated with a single linear causational notion. We know now that in such systems the dynamics of MULTIPLE, MUTUAL, AND RECURSIVE causation operate.

* The reductionist, single causality orientation of traditional science was unable and unwilling to consider PURPOSE and MEANING. In the emerged view of disciplined inquiry, purpose, meaning, and ethical and moral considerations have a guiding role. There is now a search for establishing a grand alliance of science, philosophy, art, and religion.

* Classical science saw systems to be basically closed, having only limited and highly controlled interaction with their environment. Accordingly, goals are set, such as setting the reading on a thermostat, and action is taken only when there is a deviation from the set goal. (The system operates based on negative feedback.) However, living systems, such as social systems, are open systems. They have intensive interactions with their environment. This interaction often results in changing goals and ways of doing things. Thus, change occurs not only to reduce the deviation from the set goal (negative feedback), but also—influenced by interactions with the environment as well as actions within the system—we may change goals and INCREASE the deviation from previously set goals. (The system operates also on positive feedback.)

ACTIVITY # 1

Review the characterizations of differences between the two orientations, presented above. Think about how those differences are manifested in systems you can observe. Enter your findings in your notebook. Raise questions that you want to explore.

Figure 1.1 portrays an overview of the contrast between the world views of classical science and systems science. The figure also is a MODEL, an abstract/conceptual representation, showing differences between the two kinds of scientific orientation. Bring-

FIGURE 1.1 KEY DISTINCTIONS BETWEEN THE TWO ORIENTATIONS

	PERSPECTIVES OF CLASSICAL SCIENCE	PERSPECTIVES OF SYSTEMS SCIENCE
FOCUS ON	SINGLE VARIABLES, PARTS, LINEAR RELATIONSHIPS	MULTIPLE/DYNAMIC INTERACTIONS, THE WHOLE, PATTERNS OF RELATIONSHIPS
MODE OF INQUIRY	ANALYSIS, REDUCTIONISM	ANALYSIS AND SYNTHESIS, EXPANSIONISM, EMERGENCE
REASONING	CAUSE-EFFECT DETERMINISM	NONDETERMINISTIC, PURPOSE, MEANING
RULE	OBJECTIVITY, OBSERVER DETACHMENT	OBSERVER INVOLVEMENT AND INFLUENCE
GOAL	PREDICTION	UNDERSTANDING
CONTROL	GOAL-DRIVEN, NEGATIVE FEEDBACK, ADJUST FOR ERROR	GOAL-DRIVEN (ADJUST FOR ERROR) AND POSITIVE FEEDBACK, CHANGE OF GOALS

ing this contrasting presentation into our exploration of the systems view, we may summarize as follows:

What emerged in the course of the last several decades as the new scientific orientation is the disciplined inquiry of systems science. The internalization of this new type of inquiry in our thinking manifests itself in the SYSTEMS VIEW, and its activation in education will lead to practical systemic action.

The few characteristics of the new scientific orientation discussed above seem to be adequate to show why their understanding becomes imperative in working with social systems and particularly with educational activity systems in today's world. Unfortunately, the mind set of the classical scientific orientation described here still prevails in both educational scholarship and practice. (See Note 1.)

We study "education" in a variety of fragmented disciplines. This separating-into-disciplines approach can provide only partial interpretation of the system studied and sets forth descriptions based on disparate theoretical frameworks. We study the sociology of the classroom, the psychology of instruction, the economics of education, the anthropology of school culture, the economics of educational administration, and the politics of government. Such compartmentalized inquiry, with the use of widely differing orientations, methods, and languages of the separate disciplines, results in unintegrated and incomplete knowledge and characterization of what education is as a whole system. A particular discipline can address only a narrow aspect of the whole. Educational scholarship typically focuses on only a few variables, studied in isolation by the experimental methods of classical science. Thus, we cannot consider the complex interactions and systemic connectedness of the various components that integrate into the whole. We cannot adequately portray the mutually interacting and recursive dynamics of the processes of our complex educational systems.

Unfortunately, the "mind set" of the fragmented and classical scientific orientation—described above—is the dominant conceptual framework that has guided the educational improvement movement of the last decade. It manifested itself in a piecemeal and incremental, disjointed, "tinkering with parts" approach to educational improvement. It has failed to connect and integrate the various so-called "solution ideas" that have emerged into an internally consistent system of solutions. It has focused on the existing system and stayed within its boundaries. At best, it stipulated changes at the margin. It has failed to recognize the complexities of current issues surrounding education as a social system; a system interacting with other societal systems, a system which is embedded in the rapidly and dynamically changing larger society.

ACTIVITY # 2

Based on your experience with observing/participating in educational improvement programs, describe in your notebook examples that reflect either systemic or fragmented efforts of renewal.

For all the reasons portrayed above it is suggested that the educational community faces the reality that the old ways of thinking and viewing do not work anymore and that we have to be willing to consider the application of systems thinking, systems inquiry, and the use of the systems view in BOTH educational scholarship and educational practice.

Systems inquiry has demonstrated its capability in dealing effectively with highly complex and large-scale problem situations and has orchestrated the efforts of various disciplines within the framework of systems thinking. The systems view has been applied to the analysis, design, development, assessment, and management of systems of all kinds. The application of the systems view and the introduction of systems inquiry in education are long overdue.

In this book steps are taken toward the introduction of the use of systems thinking in education, and the demonstration of the development and application of the systems view in contexts that are of immediate interest to those who work in the educational arena.

WHAT IS THE CONCEPTUAL FOUNDATION OF THE SYSTEMS VIEW?

In answering this question, first systems inquiry and its constituents are defined. Next the various types of systems are described, with special attention to social (human activity) systems. Third, the characteristics of human activity systems are discussed. The consideration of these questions will open up for us the landscape of systems inquiry.

SYSTEMS INQUIRY

The systems view is a world view that is based on the discipline of systems inquiry. Central to systems inquiry is the concept of SYSTEM. In the most general sense, system means a configuration of parts or components connected and joined together in a web of relationships. By this joining and integration, they are creating emerging properties that are properties of the whole system rather than its parts. SYSTEMS INQUIRY is a system itself. As a conceptual system, it has three interrelated and internally consistent aspects: systems theory, systems philosophy, and systems methodology. Furthermore, systems inquiry embraces two kinds of disciplined inquiry. Its conclusion-oriented inquiry produces systems knowledge. Its decision-oriented inquiry mode uses systems knowledge by the application of systems methods that address real-world situations and arrangements. (Note 2.)

In classical science, each scientific discipline has developed its own theoretical scheme. Systems science, on the other hand, transcends disciplinary boundaries and seeks alikeness (or isomorphy) of concepts, principles, and laws that exist in the various realms of experience and cuts across all the domains of scientific disciplines. The organized arrangement of these "general" concepts, principles, and laws constitutes a GENERAL THEORY OF SYSTEMS: an exposition applying to all systems. Within the framework of systems theory, we can integrate the findings of the various disciplines pertinent to a particular field or application. That is the unique power of systems theory. This power is needed so that we can understand and work with complex systems, enabling us to integrate within the framework of the theory the insights and knowledge generated by those disciplines that are relevant to our domain of inquiry.

SYSTEMS PHILOSOPHY asks the questions: How can we understand systems? How can we inquire about them? What is the best way to think about them? In contrast to the analytic, reductionist, linear, single cause-and-effect view of the philosophy of classical science, systems philosophy brings forth a reorganization of ways of knowing and thinking about perceived reality. It creates a new world view of disciplined inquiry. This view is manifested in synthetic, expansionist, dynamic, and multiple/mutual causality modes of thinking and inquiring. With the perspectives of systems philosophy, we look at the world in terms of facts and events in the context of wholes, and we understand them as integrated sets purposefully arranged in systemic relations.

SYSTEMS METHODOLOGY has two domains of inquiry: (a) the study of methods by which we pursue systems scholarship and produce systems knowledge, and (b) the identification and description of approaches, methods, and tools for applying systems theory and systems thinking in the analysis, design, development, and management of complex systems. More specifically, the task of those using systems methodology in this second sense—which is our present interest—is threefold:

* To identify, characterize, and classify the system of interest, the system of problems embedded in that system, and other relevant systems in the environment of the system of interest.

* To select, identify, and characterize the system model and the general approach by which the system problem or a system of problems can be addressed.

* To select, identify, and characterize specific strategies, methods, and tools appropriate to use by those who are involved in addressing the problem situation.

The brief discussion above highlights the difference between systems inquiry and the inquiries of the disciplines. The methodology of a particular discipline is clearly identified and is to be adhered to. The methodology is the hallmark of the discipline. In systems inquiry, on the other hand, one selects from a wide range of types available those approaches, methods, and tools that best fit: (a) the type of system of interest, (b) the purpose and the nature of the investigation, and (c) the specific problem situation. In the discussion that follows, I categorize and briefly describe the various systems types. In contemplating educational activity systems, the identification of the type of system we select is a crucial issue.

TYPES OF SYSTEMS

There are two major types: NATURAL SYSTEMS and DESIGNED SYSTEMS. NATURAL SYSTEMS range from subatomic systems to living systems of all kinds, our planet, the solar system, the galactic system, and the universe. The genesis of these systems is the origin of the universe and the result of the forces and events of evolution. The other main types are DESIGNED SYSTEMS. These are our creations and include three major types: (a) designed physical systems (man-made artifacts and hybrid systems that combine construction and nature, e.g., a hydroelectric plant); (b) designed conceptual systems (such as theories, philosophies, mathematics, logic, etc.) and abstract or conceptual representations in the forms of books, records, and descriptive or prescriptive models; and (c) human activity systems. For our present purposes, human activity systems and their relevant abstract systems and representations are of special interest. (Note 3.)

HUMAN ACTIVITY SYSTEMS are our purposeful creations. They are less tangible than natural and designed physical systems. They are manifested in sets of activities carried out by people who select and organize these activities to attain a purpose. These activities often involve various natural and designed physical systems and/or abstractions of the way we think about and reason these activities, such as theories of action. Human activity systems range from families and small groups (organized for a purpose) to organizations, communities of various size and complexity, nations, regional/international associations, and the global system of humanity.

We can speak of various types of human activity systems. We can define and describe these types based on such considerations as: the degree to which they are closed or open, their mechanistic vs. systemic nature, their unitary or pluralistic position as to their purpose, and their degree of complexity. (Note 4.) Based on these considerations we can differentiate various types, such as:

* RIGIDLY CONTROLLED systems, such as man-machine systems or assembly-line work groups, are rather closed and have only limited and well-guarded interactions with their environment. They have few components and a limited degree of freedom, and they have singleness of purpose and behave rather mechanistically.

* DETERMINISTIC systems are more open than rigidly controlled systems but they still have clearly defined goals, and some degree of freedom in selecting means of operating (less mechanistic). They might have several levels of decision-making; thus they are more complex than the rigidly controlled systems. Examples: bureaucracies, centralized (national) educational systems, small business operations.

* PURPOSIVE systems—such as corporations, public service agencies, our public education systems—are still unitary (have their goals set), but have freedom in selecting operational objectives and methods. They are considered to be somewhat open in that they are to react to environmental changes. They are often very complex.

* HEURISTIC systems—such as new business ventures, R&D agencies, nontraditional (experimental) educational programs—formulate their own goals under some broad policy guidelines (thus, they are somewhat pluralistic). They are open to changes

and interact intensively—even coevolve—with the environment. They are complex and systemic in their functions/structures. Examples: R&D agencies, innovative educational programs, new corporate ventures, etc.

* PURPOSE-SEEKING systems are ideal-seeking, guided by their vision of the future. They are open and are able to coevolve with their environment. They are complex and systemic. Being pluralistic, they define their own policies/purposes and constantly seek new purposes and new niches in their environments. Examples: corporations seeking social service roles, communities seeking to establish comprehensive systems of learning and human development and to integrate their social service functions, and societies/nations establishing integrated regional systems.

A key consideration in making distinctions among various types of systems is the issue of: how much freedom does the system have to select purpose, goals, methods, tools, etc., and how widely is the freedom to select distributed (or concentrated) in the system?

ACTIVITY # 3

"Type" and describe in your notebook your selected system with the use of the characterizations introduced in the text above. Keep in mind that a particular system may have characteristics that cut across the various types. Furthermore, a system which is a purposive type will have components that are deterministic (e.g., the finance office of your school) or rigidly controlled (e.g., when you work with a computer, the rules you follow are controlled by the software).

In considering the renewal of our educational systems, the issue of what type of system education should become in our rapidly changing and transforming society is a crucial one. Most likely, we shall identify with either the heuristic or purpose-seeking types.

THE CHARACTERISTICS OF HUMAN ACTIVITY SYSTEMS

I shall now provide a characterization of human activity systems that is more comprehensive than what has been offered heretofore. The statements that follow comprise an internally consistent definition and characterization. A HUMAN ACTIVITY SYSTEM:

* Is an assembly of people and other resources organized into a whole in order to accomplish a purpose. The people in the system are affected by being in the system, and by their participation in the system they affect the system. People in the system select and carry out activities individually and collectively that will enable them to attain the collectively identified purpose.

* Maintains sets of relations sustained through time among those who are in the system. The maintenance of these relations is of primary importance. The process by which these relationships are maintained is the system's regulation—the rules of the game—and the limits within which these rules can be sustained are the conditions of the system's stability through time. It is here where commitment (to the shared purpose) and motivation (to carry out activities) play such an important role.

* Is open to and interacts with the environment: depends on it and contributes to it. The nature of its relationship with the environment is mutual interdependence. This interdependence imposes constraints and expectations on both the system and the environment. The system is expected to carry out its commitment to the environment responsively. The environment is expected to provide the resources and support that are required by the system.

* Acts as a whole toward itself and by itself—by its internal relations and internal integration—by which it can also sustain itself. Thus, while we view the system as a whole, at the same time we consider it as part of and embedded in its environment.

What is portrayed in these brief paragraphs characterizes human activity systems that are the purposive, the heuristic, or purpose-seeking types. This portrayal can be depicted in an image, presented in Figure 1.2.

The description and Figure 1.2 are helpful to further our understanding of human activity systems. An insight of what the system is and does emerges from an understanding of the dynamics of the purpose-seeking and purpose-fulfilling relational interaction and integration of people in the system, and interaction with the environment of the system. Purpose, process, interaction, integration, and emergence are the salient markers of this understanding. Furthermore, we should think about and define human activity systems always at three levels. A system serves the purposes of its collective entity, it serves the purposes of its members, and it serves its environment or the larger system in which it is embedded. How often we neglect to address the purposes of those who are in the system and those of the environment!

FIGURE 1.2 A SYSTEMS MODEL OF A HUMAN ACTIVITY SYSTEM

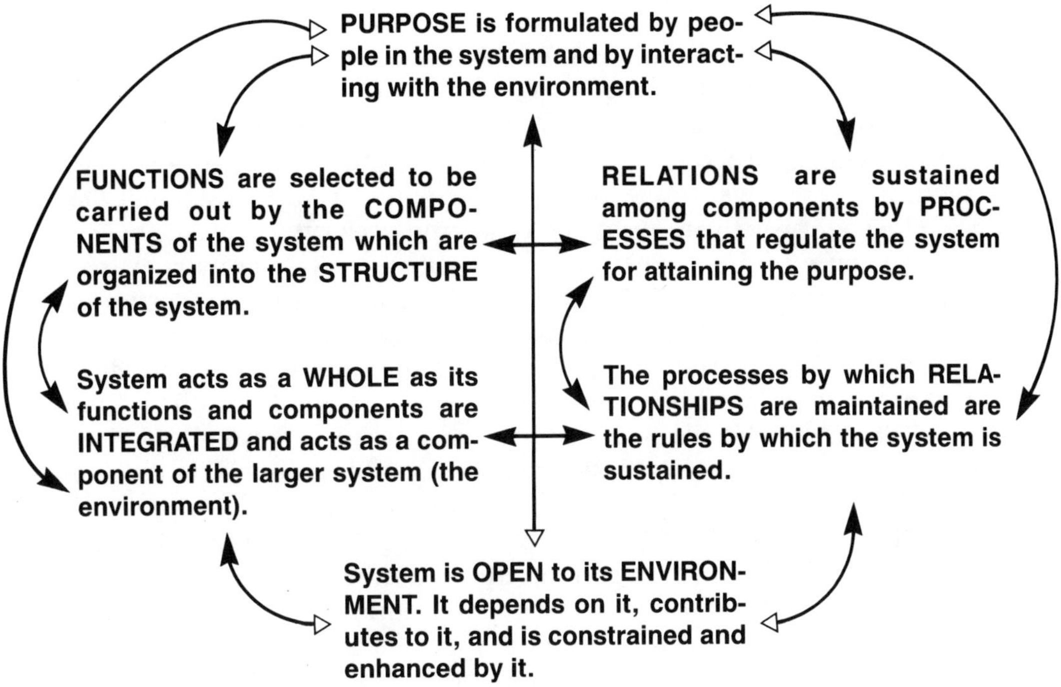

ACTIVITY # 4

Using the characterization of human activity systems introduced in the above section, describe your specific educational system as a human activity system.

In this section we opened up the landscape of systems inquiry as we considered its three main components (systems theory, systems philosophy, and systems methodology); as we explored systems types; and described the general characteristics of human activity systems which are our specific interest in this book. We can move on now to discuss the development of a systems view.

HOW CAN WE DEVELOP A SYSTEMS VIEW?

The systems view is a "certain" way of looking at ourselves, at the environments we live in, at the systems that surround us, and at those we are part of. I described this "certain" way in the sections above. But having a description of systems inquiry, or even an understanding of systems concepts and principles or types of systems, does not YET mean having a systems view. The systems view is a way of thinking, it is a world view we can possess. And there are ways by which it can be developed. I propose here that we can develop the systems view in two stages.

By observing various types of systems and studying their behavior, we can recognize characteristics that are common to all systems. Once we have identified and described a set of CONCEPTS that are common to systems, and observed and discovered among some of them certain relationships, we can construct from them general systems PRINCIPLES. Thus, a systems principle emerges from an interaction/integration of related concepts. Next, we are in the position to look for relationships among principles and organize related principles into certain conceptual schemes we call SYSTEMS MODELS. This process of starting from observation and arriving at the CONSTRUCTION of systems models constitutes the FIRST STAGE of developing a systems view.

The SECOND STAGE is the process of INTERNALIZATION/APPLICATION: the integration of those concepts, principles, and models into our own thinking AND their application in real-life contexts: in systems and situations of interest and importance to us. This process of internalization and application constitutes our journey toward the development of a systems view. A description of the two stages follows.

STAGE ONE

In this book my first contribution is to present the first stage by constructing three systems models: a systems-environment model, a functions/structure model, and a process model; all of which are applicable to understanding and working with human activity systems. I prefer to call these models "lenses." As I use the systems-environment lens, I can see and understand the relational arrangements and dynamics between the system and its context. The functions/structure lens helps me to see the system at a given moment in time. I understand what it is; it projects a snapshot of the system. The third lens shows motion: the behavior of the system through time. None of the lenses give me a whole picture of the system. Only as I superimpose the images can I capture a comprehensive view. The main task for the user of this book will be to use the three lenses, look at the system of his or her choice, and describe what is observed. Thus, users create three systems models of their system of interest. This process of using the lenses and describing a system provides the first experience of internalization and application of the systems view.

STAGE TWO

At this point I provide an example of a transformation of the general models as I present models of educational activity systems. My portrayal will be of a general model of educational activity systems. The user now is asked to use my transformation and description as reference in going through a second internalization/application in the context of his or her selected system and situation and to make adjustments in the three models he or she created. My general description includes a set of questions that is useful in making an assessment of the adequacy of a human activity system from the vantage point of the three perspectives.

A CLARIFICATION. There are various levels of comprehensiveness, detail, and depth (I do not like to use the notion of sophistication, but it might help) at which a systems view can be developed. In this workbook I aim at an introductory level. I have selected limited sets of the most common and most significant systems concepts and principles that will enable users to make practical, situational, and meaningful use of them, by the transformation of the general models in the context of a system of their choice.

THE APPLICATION OF THE SYSTEMS VIEW IN EDUCATION

What can we expect to attain by the development of the systems view? I suggest that the systems view helps us to understand the true nature of education as a complex, open, and dynamic human activity system that operates in ever-changing multiple environments and interacts with a variety of societal systems. Beyond such understanding, once we develop the systems view, we have developed ways of knowing, thinking, and critical reasoning that empower us to organize a system of comprehensive, disciplined inquiry capable of addressing all issues of educational practice.

As I mentioned in the introduction, during the past two decades we have applied systems thinking and systems inquiry in education and other societal systems. As a result of these applications, we now have available to us models and methods of systems inquiry that enable us to work creatively with the dynamic and complex nature of education as a purpose-seeking social system. I have organized these models and methods in four complementary domains of organizational inquiry (Note 5):

* The ANALYSIS and DESCRIPTION of educational activity systems, by the application of the three models presented in this work and by the use of systems process analysis (Note 6).

* SYSTEMS DESIGN, conducting design inquiry with the use of design models, methods, and tools appropriate to educational activity systems and the specific type of system chosen (Note 7).

* IMPLEMENTATION of the design by SYSTEMS DEVELOPMENT and the INSTITUTIONALIZATION of the new system (Note 8).

* SYSTEMS MANAGEMENT, the management of systems operations, and the management of change (Note 9).

Figure 1.3 depicts these four domains of organizational inquiry. In the center of the figure is an integrating cluster. In this cluster we articulate sets of core ideas, core values, and organizing perspectives that collectively guide our inquiry. Furthermore, for

FIGURE 1.3 A COMPREHENSIVE SYSTEM OF EDUCATIONAL INQUIRY

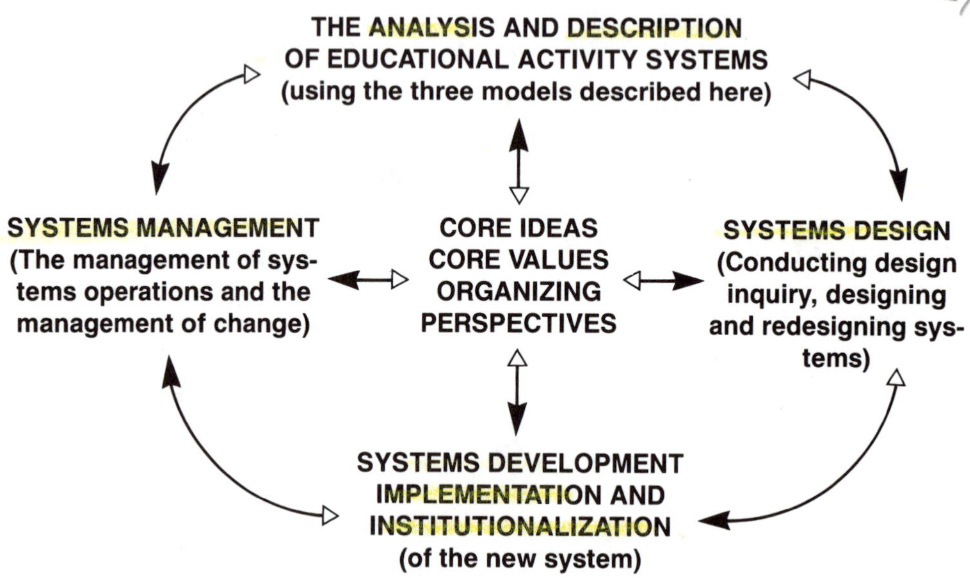

(Note: the three models introduced in this book are used in both analysis and design.)

the users of this book, it is important to know that the systems view they acquire can be used not only in describing and assessing educational activity systems, but it is the basis of all aspects of organizational inquiry in education. It is embedded in a larger conceptual system of practical reasoning and action. (Note 10.)

The figure shows where and how the three models presented here fit into the context of organizational inquiry in education. The four domains of the inquiry, mentioned above, are in recursive relationship. They mutually affect each other. Each domain can become the source of initiating/activating an inquiry process.

The inquiry system depicted in the model of Figure 1.3 is not yet applied in the "mainstream" practice of the educational community. Nor is this kind of organizational inquiry yet part of our professional development programs. The lack of such programs and the lack of competence in using the kind of program described here are shortcomings that offer a partial explanation for the inadequacy and even failure of the recent educational reform movement. The present work is seen as a major step toward overcoming this shortcoming.

A JOURNEY TOWARD THE ACQUISITION OF THE SYSTEMS VIEW

The five sections in the figure above have guided us in developing an appreciation for the contribution that the systems view can make toward engaging in a comprehensive organizational inquiry in the educational arena. In this closing section of Chapter One, I map out the road we can take to acquire a systems view. This road maps a journey that will take us through a process of working with the three systems models. First, I will discuss the term "model" and the sense in which it is used here. Then, an approach to working with the three models is mapped. In conclusion a brief description of the three models is presented.

MODELS AND THEIR USEFULNESS

The term model, as it is used here, is a descriptive/abstract representation used in two senses. First, the "general" models are mental images of general systems concepts and principles, organized into a scheme. Second, the user will apply these concepts and principles to represent a mental image, a description of a perceived real-world educational system. In this sense the user's model will be a product of his or her experience with that system. Such a model also can be a mental image, a normative description and representation of a future system that we have created by design. THE ORGANIZED DESCRIPTION OF AN EXISTING OR A DESIGNED FUTURE SYSTEM IS THE MODEL OF THAT SYSTEM.

Models are useful as frames of reference that we can use to examine and talk about the system the model represents. We work with models all the time. When we exchange ideas about something, we usually do so by using conceptual models. In a discourse, it is helpful to have a common model, or a common frame of reference, so that we have some assurance that everybody is talking about the same thing. Because our purpose here is to talk about education as a system, it is important for us to create a common frame of reference for our discourse—to build systems models of education. In an earlier section of this chapter, I described the two stages of how to develop a systems view. In the following material, I map the journey for the user of this book and personalize the acquisition of the systems view.

MAPPING THE ROAD FOR THE USE OF THE THREE MODELS

Concepts and principles that are manifested in social systems can be organized in systems models. These systems concepts and principles, then, can be transformed into the context of educational activity systems, and can be organized and displayed as systems models of education. In systems research we develop models that represent one or more classes of systems. The more classes of systems represent the models, the more general the model is. Our present examination focuses on a single class of systems—social systems or human activity systems. I have selected this class as a focus because education is representative of this class. Once I present a model—which is a generalization of this class—the user is asked to transfer this general model of social systems into a specific model of the educational activity system of the user's choice. The user will thus build system models of a particular educational activity system.

Still another step follows. I develop—as the next stage of the journey—a general model of educational activity systems. The user, then, is asked to examine this model and explore its applicability to the specific model he or she developed. The question is: does this general model represent, in a general sense, the educational activity system the user has portrayed in his or her model? Figure 1.4 portrays the use of the models as described here.

FIGURE 1.4 THE DEVELOPMENT OF A SYSTEMS VIEW

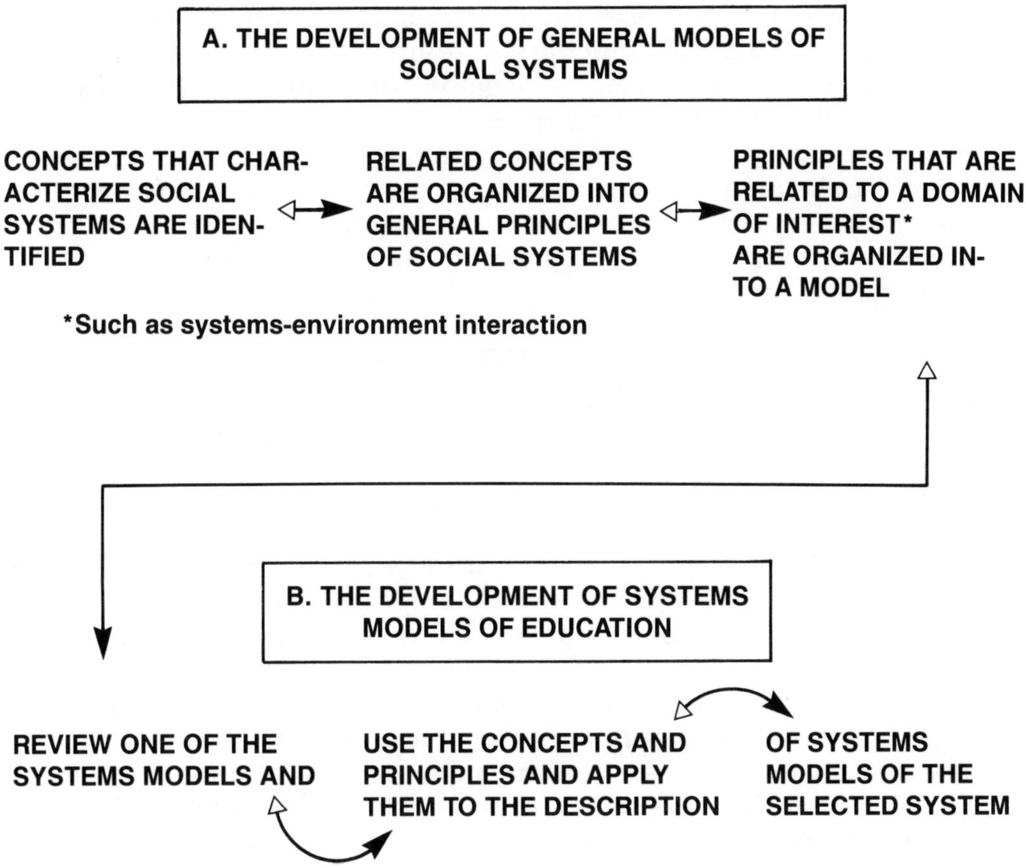

AN INTRODUCTION TO THE THREE MODELS

As already mentioned, I constructed three models that are general representations of social systems that represent systems concepts and principles pertinent to: (a) systems-environment relationships, (b) the functions/structures of social systems described in a given moment of time, and (c) the behavior of systems through time. These models are lenses that can be used to look at an educational activity system and understand, describe, and analyze it as an open, dynamic, and complex social system. The three models are briefly described next.

The use of the **SYSTEMS-ENVIRONMENT MODEL** enables us to describe an educational activity system in the context of the community and the larger society. It is a lens that projects a "bird's-eye-view" of the landscape in which the system is embedded. The concepts and principles that are pertinent to this model help us to define "the rules of the game" that guide systems-environment relationships, interactions, and mutual interdependence. A set of inquiries—presented in the general description—guides the user to make an assessment of the environmental adequacy and responsiveness of the educational activity system and, conversely, explore the adequacy of the responsiveness of the environment toward the system.

The **FUNCTIONS/STRUCTURE MODEL** provides us the lens through which we can focus our attention on what the educational activity system IS at a given moment of time. It projects a "STILL PICTURE" image of the system. It enables us to (a) describe the goals of the system (that elaborate the purpose(s) that emerged from the use of the environmental lens); (b) identify the functions that the system carries out in order to attain the purpose(s) and goals; (c) specify the relational arrangements of those functions; (d) define the components and parts that engage in attending to those functions; and (e) describe how the components are organized in relational arrangements and how they are integrated into the structure of the system. The application of this model will guide the user to produce a "snapshot" model of the educational activity system. The description of the general functions/structure model includes the description of a set of inquiries that can guide the user to probe the function/structure adequacy of the selected educational activity system.

The **PROCESS MODEL** provides the user with a lens that helps to concentrate inquiry on what the educational activity system DOES through time. It projects a "MOTION PICTURE" image of the user's system. It helps to understand how the system behaves as a changing living social system in the context of the community and the larger society. How it (a) receives, screens/assesses, and processes input; (b) transforms input for use in the system; (c) engages in operations that attend to the purpose(s) and goals of the system and produce the expected outcomes; (d) continuously assesses and guides the transformation operations; (e) processes the outcomes and assesses their adequacy, and (f) makes adjustments and changes in the system and, if indicated, transforms the system based on the assessment as well as information (feedback) coming from the environment. The general model includes a description of inquiries that the user can apply in evaluating the adequacy of the selected educational activity system from a "process perspective."

What is important for us to understand is that no single model or lens can provide us with a true representation of an educational organization as a complex social system. Each lens portrays certain characteristics, but not all, that we need to describe an educational activity system as a whole system. Only if we consider these three descriptions jointly, as if overlaid upon each other, do the lenses help us to provide a comprehensive image and reveal the real story of an educational organization as a system.

REFLECTIONS

This chapter sets the stage for a journey on a road that can guide the educational community toward understanding educational activity systems as complex, open, and dynamic social systems that coevolve with and make contributions to our ever-changing larger society. The stage is set by introducing to the user of the book some basic systems concepts and principles, organized in relational arrangements in the form of three "systems models" that can be used as "lenses" which capture a systems-environment view, a functions/structure view, and a process view of the user's educational activity system. The expectation is that by using these lenses, a first step is taken toward the development of a systems view which, then, can be activated in the analysis, design, evaluation, development, and management of educational activity systems.

NOTES

(1) For details see Chapters One and Two in: Bela H. Banathy (1991). *Systems Design of Education: A Journey to Create the Future.* Educational Technology Publications, Englewood Cliffs, NJ.

(2) For more on systems inquiry, see: Bela H. Banathy (1988, June). "Systems Inquiry in Education," *Systems Practice.*

(3) For details on Human Activity Systems, see: Peter Checkland (1981). *Systems Thinking, Systems Practice.* Pergamon Press, London.

(4) A comprehensive description of systems types is found in Bela H. Banathy (No. 1, 1988). "Matching Design Methods to Systems Types," *Systems Research.*

(5) See Chapters Two and Ten in reference (1) above.

(6) For a description of systems process analysis, see: Bela H. Banathy (1988, June). "Systems Inquiry in Education," *Systems Practice.*

(7) For details see: Parts Two and Three in reference (1).

(8) For institutionalization, review: Bela H. Banathy (1986). "A Systems View of Institutionalizing Change in Education." The NAAS/ASSS Symposium: Future Educational Delivery Systems. The National Association of Academics of Science, Columbus, OH.

(9) Various ways of managing change are described in Chapter Eight in reference (1) above.

(10) Discussed in C. West Churchman (1971). *The Design of Inquiring Systems.* Basic Books Inc., New York.

CHAPTER TWO

The Systems-Environment Model

In this chapter, we join in developing a systems-environment model of education. First, in SECTION ONE, from sets of general concepts and principles of human activity systems, I will build a systems-environment model of those systems. Then, you will study the model in order to understand the meaning of those concepts and principles and examine their relevance to educational activity systems. The purpose is NOT merely to learn some systems terms but to understand the concepts represented by the terms and gain insight from the principles—and test their power—to represent the environmental relationships of human activity systems. In SECTION TWO, you are asked to use what you have learned and transform the model into an educational activity system of your choice and use the ENVIRONMENT LENS to view your selected system and describe what you see. Most likely, this description will be brief. In SECTION THREE, I will use the environment lens to transform the general model into a general (systems-environment) model of educational activity systems. By this transformation, I will explore the application of the general concepts and principles in more detail, and expand the scope of the use of the environment lens. In SECTION FOUR, you will explore my description and you are asked to transform my general description into the specific functional context of the educational activity system of your choice. In this activity, in fact, you will synthesize your model—developed in SECTION TWO—with my general model of education. In SECTION FIVE, I present a line of inquiry, in the form of a set of questions, which probes into the systems-environment adequacy of the educational activity systems in general. You will be asked to use the questions and examine and probe into your selected system and describe your findings. Figure 2.1 depicts the five sections as cumulatively expanding spirals of developing a systems view in the context of systems-environment relationships.

You can see from the above description that what you are involved with here is a process of ever-expanding development of

FIGURE 2.1 THE DEVELOPMENT OF A SYSTEMS-ENVIRONMENT VIEW

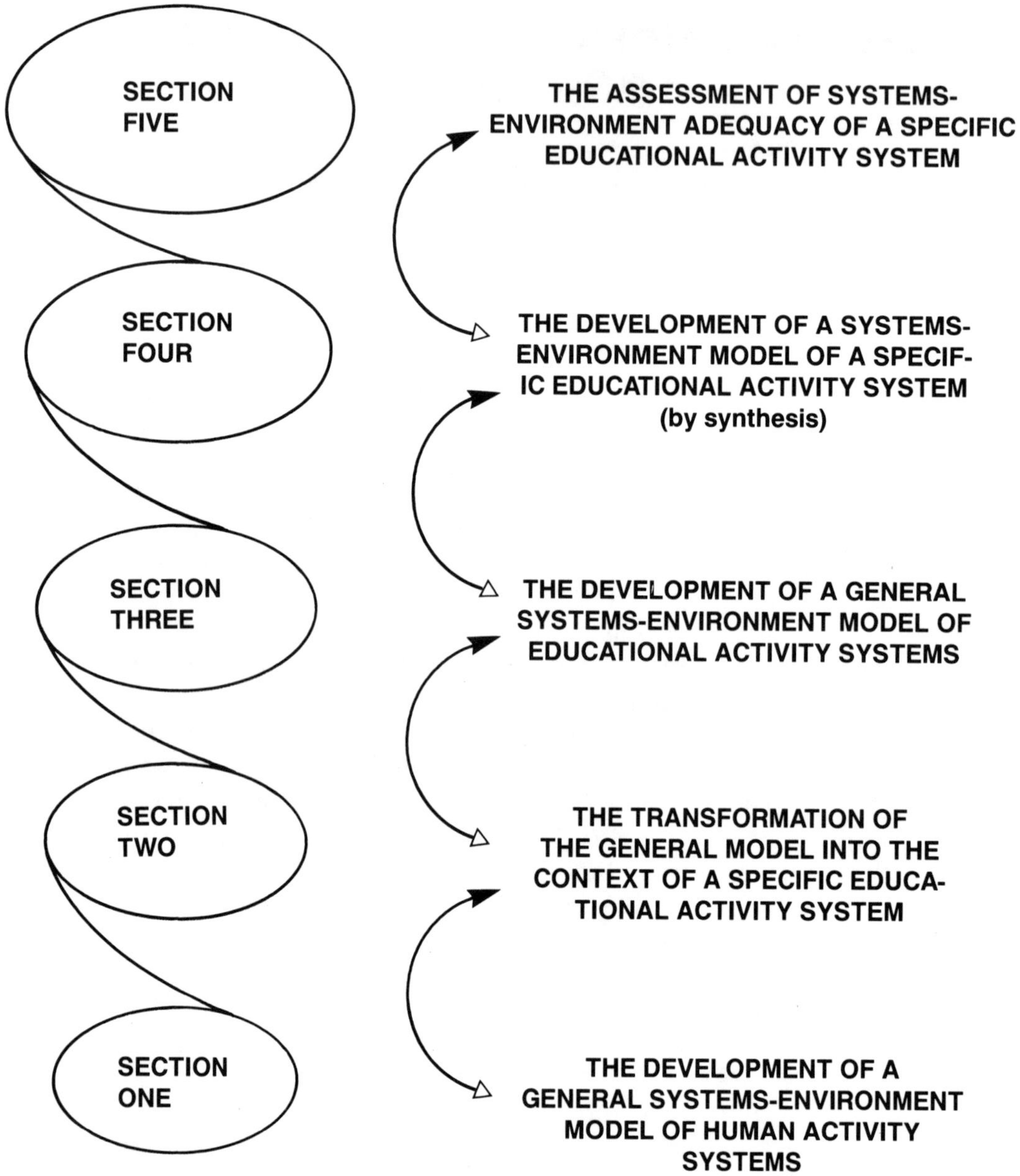

YOUR systems-environmental view of educational activity systems. It is expected that the series of activities you will go through will lead you: (1) to gain new insights about the true nature and characteristics of human activity systems in general and educational activities in particular; (2) to learn to look at systems with a "new eye," and to think about them differently; and (3) to apply the insights and the new way of thinking in BOTH evaluating and designing educational activity systems.

In advancing from one section to the other you will gain an ever more clear understanding of systems concepts and principles, and—most significantly—will apply what you have learned in a situational context which is meaningful and useful to you.

SECTION ONE

A GENERAL SYSTEMS-ENVIRONMENT MODEL OF HUMAN ACTIVITY SYSTEMS

In this section, I focus the systems-environment lens on human activity systems (HAS's) of all kinds and select a (limited) set of concepts that characterize the interaction and relationship between HAS's and their environment. Next, I merge related sets of concepts and construct principles from them, after which I organize these principles into a model. For example, I select the following concepts: OPENNESS (of the system) and INPUT. From the relationship of these, the following principle can be constructed: THE MORE OPEN THE SYSTEM IS, THE MORE KINDS OF INPUT IT HAS TO COPE WITH. From this example we can see that a systems principle is essentially a law that governs the system. It is from principles relevant to systems-environment interactions and relations from which I construct the general model of a HAS.

As you work with the description of general system concepts and principles, ask yourself these questions: How do the statements in the text apply to your selected educational activity system? How can my generalized statement be interpreted in a way that will help you to define the relationship of your selected system to its environment? Try to avoid substituting this book's general statements with general statements of your own. TRANSFORM the general description into the specific context of your system. Reformulate the ideas expressed in the text in a way that meaningfully characterizes relationships and interaction between your selected system and its societal environment.

PORTRAYING HUMAN ACTIVITY SYSTEMS IN THEIR ENVIRONMENT

Human activity systems (HAS's) exist in SPACE and TIME. The overall SPACE of a HAS is the SOCIETY in general, and a definable area of it is the specific context in which HAS's exist. HAS's also exist in TIME. They exist in the present, they have their own past, and they move toward their future. What is common to these three time dimensions is CHANGE; change that may mean GROWTH (change in quantity), DEVELOPMENT (change in quality), DECLINE (in quality), and possibly EXTINCTION or TERMINATION of the system. It is important for us to understand and contemplate the distinction between growth and development.

The ENVIRONMENT is the context within which a HAS exists. It is composed of all things that surround the system, and it includes everything that may affect the system or that may be affected by the system. The notion of the degree and intensity of "affect" helps us to differentiate between the GENERAL ENVIRONMENT and the SYSTEMIC ENVIRONMENT. The sentence above: "It is composed of..." characterizes the general environment. The SYSTEMIC ENVIRONMENT is that part of the general environment where the degree and intensity of the "affect" relationship is higher and is regularly ongoing. How and where to draw the boundary between the general and systemic environments is a matter of judgment. Furthermore, the boundary, in most cases, will be "FUZZY." One way to help the selection of what is considered as the systemic environment is by asking the question: Which part, of the general environment, is that with which the HAS in question routinely interacts?

A critical judgment that the observer of a HAS—or people of the HAS—can make is defining the BOUNDARIES that DELIMIT the SYSTEM SPACE and setting aside from the environment all those entities, their attributes and relationships, that belong to the system. A helpful question in defining the system space is: What are entities and aspects over which the HAS has direct control? Still, the boundaries of HAS's are not drawn sharply. First, boundaries cannot isolate the system from its environment, and they are often changing. We can speak of a great variety of boundaries. The "space" type is the geopolitical and the physical. Others include economic, social, sociobiological, psychological, cultural, ethical, temporal, technological, etc. Making BOUNDARY JUDGMENT is a significant task of people in the system.

There are also BREAKS in the boundaries through which the system interacts with its environment, and through which the system receives its INPUT and sends its OUTPUT into the environment. The INPUT is a collective concept that refers to everything that the system receives from its environment. For HAS's we can speak of three major types of input. The first is the "definition" type. The environment establishes the system—or the system establishes itself in the environment—in order to satisfy certain environmental expectations, demands, and requirements. These EXPECTATIONS, DEMANDS, POLICIES, and REQUIREMENTS make up one part of the "definition" type of input. The other part constitutes CONSTRAINTS and RULES under which the system is to operate. The second type is constituted of the various RESOURCES that the system needs in order to function. These include people, information, knowledge, money, materials, facilities, etc. The third type of input is a large and unorganized collection of "undefined" input. We often call this type "NOISE." We always have to deal with this type in HAS's.

OUTPUT is another collective system concept that operates through the breaks on the boundaries. This stands for whatever the system sends back to the environment. Output is also of three major types. The first is, again, the definition type. It constitutes the OUTCOME of what the system does. It is the tangible realization of stated expectations, demands, and requirements that the environment or the system defined as one type of input. The second type, resources, also matches the other input type (resources). It is formulated in terms of requests, requirements of resources that the system needs in order to produce the expected output. The third type is again undefined; it includes unexpected output, waste, noise, etc. We can now construct another system principle: "In order to produce output, the system requires input from the environment." A simple drawing can depict a representation of an initial systems-environment model that offers a summary, a broad stroke picture of system and environment. Figure 2.2 portrays this picture.

In addition to projecting an initial model, the figure also shows us an image of what we call EMBEDDEDNESS or NESTEDNESS. The HAS is embedded in its systemic environment and the sys-

FIGURE 2.2 AN INITIAL SYSTEMS-ENVIRONMENT MODEL

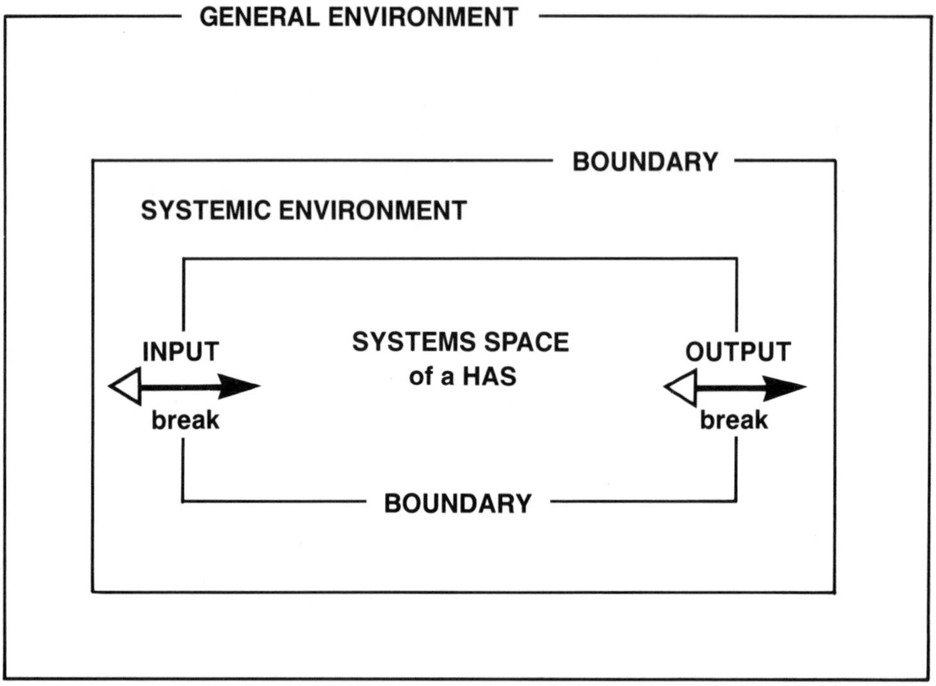

temic environment is embedded or is nested in the general environment.

RELATIONSHIPS

Generally we can speak of RELATIONSHIPS between HAS's and relationships within a particular HAS. The first kind relates to embeddedness. Let me explain. The systemic environment of a HAS often can be considered to be its SUPRASYSTEM, whenever it can be defined as a system in itself. For example, a city—which can be considered to be an organized human activity system—is the suprasystem of its fire protection system. A suprasystem is made up of a set of systems; thus, it also may be thought of as a MULTI-SYSTEM. Systems within a suprasystem are PEER SYSTEMS. In a city, law enforcement and social service systems (such as education) are peer systems. Relationships among peer systems can be two kinds: centralized and egalitarian. In a CENTRALIZED relationship, one system plays a central or PRIMARY role and other systems are related to it and arranged around it. In an EGALITAR-

IAN relationship, none of the peer systems has a dominant or central role. Within a particular system we can speak of SUBSYSTEMS that, through their interaction, serve the purpose of the system of which they are parts. In MULTILEVEL SYSTEMS subsystems have components that play the same role as the subsystems do in relationship to the system in question. Thus, here we can define a HIERARCHICAL arrangement and relationship.

Further examination of relationships between the system and its environment brings into focus other characteristics: the open or closed nature of systems. A system is CLOSED if it is sealed off from its environment by its boundaries and if there is no interchange between the system and its environment. A system is OPEN if its boundaries are not closed and have breaks that enable the system to interact with its environment. The larger these breaks, the more open the system, and the more kinds of input and output it deals with. For practical purposes, as we consider HAS's, we cannot speak of completely open or completely closed systems. Openness or closedness are matters of degree. In a situation when there are large-scale changes or transformations in the societal environment of a HAS, there is a tendency in certain HAS's to "close-off" and "protect" themselves from the effect of those changes. Such closure may create situations where the system will no longer meet the expectations and requirements of the environment, it does not act responsively toward it, and, therefore, will lose the resource support of its environment. Such unwarranted closure will greatly impede the operation of the system and might lead to its termination. On the other hand, a totally open system is exposed to a totally unstable, unregulated, and random input. In such systems, much of the input might be the "noise" type. This creates a difficulty with interpreting and understanding expectations, requirements, and constraints; getting the required resources; and, in general, defining what the system is about. HAS's cannot be closed, but neither can they be completely open. HAS's have to cope with certain RANDOMNESS of input, but they always have a specific purpose and specific expected output. HAS's cope with this randomness by regulating the breaks on the boundary through which the input flows in; they have the ability to adjust the breaks and regulate the input/output.

The more open the system, the more varied and complex the input. Thus, the more COMPLEX the system, the more complex is the output. The principle stated here explains one of the dimensions of complexity. Another dimension is the complexity of the environment. In its interactive relationship with its environment, a system has to match that variety (complexity) of the environment which is RELEVANT to the system. This principle is called: REQUISITE VARIETY.

SELF-REGULATION

Self-regulation has wide-ranging implications for systems-environment relations as well as for the life of the system within its system space. The notion of SELF-REGULATION flows directly from what I discussed in the previous paragraphs. HAS's have to be sensitive to changes in their environment that are relevant to the system. They do this by modifying or redefining themselves both in relationship to and in interactions with the environment as well as in their internal operations, so that they will produce the kind of output expected by themselves and by their environment. There are two kinds of approaches to self-regulation: ADAPTATION and COEVOLUTION BY TRANSFORMATION.

ADAPTATION

ADAPTATION implies the system's capability to RESPOND to systems relevant changes in the environment. This is predominantly uni-directional. In order for a system to survive, it needs to be adaptive. If the system fails to produce the expected output and fails to be responsive to the environment, there are three options: (1) The system ADJUSTS itself in order to produce the expected output. (2) The environment changes its expectation to ACCOMMODATE the system. (3) If none of the above, the system may face TERMINATION.

Self-regulating adaptiveness is triggered by: (1) sensing system-relevant changes in the environment, (2) receiving information from the environment on changed requirements, and (3) the process of FEEDBACK, by which information is introduced into the system about the inadequacy of the output. Adjustment can be made on the basis of this information and is accomplished through self-regulation. Through feedback, the ACTUAL STATE of the output is continuously compared with its EXPECTED STATE. Feedback enables us to correct for differences between what is actually produced by the system and what was expected to be produced. This correction and adjustment aim at REDUCING the DEVIATION between the two states. In systems inquiry we call this NEGATIVE FEEDBACK, meaning that we leave the expectations and—correspondingly—the output as stated, and make changes only if those are not accomplished. This kind of feedback dominates in relatively stable environments, when adjustments and piecemeal improvements in an existing system could bring it in line with slow and gradual changes in the environment.

COEVOLUTION BY TRANSFORMATION

In time of environmental turbulence, accelerating and dynamic changes, and discontinuities—that characterize the current era of societal developments and transformations—small adjustments and piecemeal changes in a HAS will not enable the system to keep in sync with its environment. The system has to change so that it will become compatible with its environment. This situation calls for INCREASING the DEVIATION. Positive changes are called for that match new expectations and requirements, and introduce new functions, components, and operations in the system. In this case, POSITIVE FEEDBACK indicates the need for a NEW SYSTEM STATE. Through self-regulation, the system responds to the positive feedback and learns to COEVOLVE with its environment and TRANSFORMS itself into a new state. The relationship between the system and its environment is harmonized by SYSTEM-ENVIRONMENT CO-ACTION. In this case, we have mutual accommodation. The environment affects the systems and the system transforms itself. The new system affects the environment and brings about a new systemic environment that will have the resources to support the new system. Such recursive mutuality becomes true COEVOLUTION. The massive societal changes and transformations that have marked the postindustrial, information/knowledge era call for a continuous coevolution in—and the transformation of—all our social systems.

SUMMARY OF THE SYSTEMS-ENVIRONMENT MODEL

Systems exist in their environment, from which they are set apart by their boundaries. Some systems are rather closed and are isolated from their environment, but HAS's are not. They are the open kind. They have breaks on their boundaries that enable them to interact with their environment through input-output interactions. These kinds of systems are self-regulative and maintain compatibility with their environment by meeting environmental expectations, while expecting that the environment will meet their requirements. Need for change in HAS's is indicated by feedback that is a mechanism for self-regulation. In the case of minor environmental changes, the system has to learn to adapt to the environment. In the case of major environmental changes and transformations, it has to learn to coevolve with the environment, to introduce major changes, in fact, to transform itself in a new system state by design. Figure 2.3 presents a new sketch of the systems-environment model.

FIGURE 2.3 A REVISED SYSTEMS-ENVIRONMENT MODEL

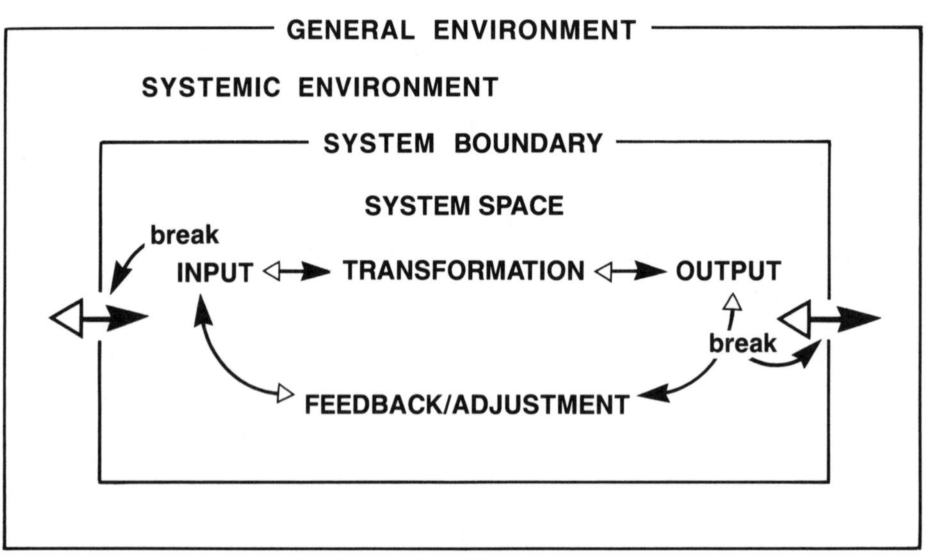

REFLECTIONS

In SECTION ONE of this chapter we took a bird's-eye-view of human activity systems as they exist in their environment. The focus of this section was on understanding the relationship between the HAS and its environment. The concepts and principles I have highlighted are relevant to all kinds of human activity systems and have helped us to understand their systemic characteristics as they live in and coexist and coevolve with their environment. In the section that follows you will be asked to apply these concepts and principles to an educational system of your choice.

SECTION TWO:

YOUR SYSTEMS-ENVIRONMENT MODEL

In SECTION ONE, I presented a general systems-environment model of social systems. You are now asked to transform my general model into a systems-environment description of your selected educational activity system, by using the concepts and principles I introduced in the general model of human activity systems. Make sure you place those concepts and principles into the specific functional context of your selected system. The purpose of this activity is NOT merely to learn some systems terms but to enable you to APPLY what you have learned in SECTION ONE in real-life context as you see it. Only through applications will those systems concepts and principles become your own. This first attempt to develop your model may be a brief one. You will get more in depth use of a systems-environment lens in the course of the next three sections. At this point, prior to moving on to the next section, describe the systems-environment model of your selected system in your notebook.

SECTION THREE:

A SYSTEMS-ENVIRONMENT MODEL OF EDUCATIONAL ACTIVITY SYSTEMS (EAS's)

In the section above, you worked with a set of concepts and principles, organized into a general systems-environment model, and transformed them into the context of your own system. Thus, you formulated a systems-environment model of your own. In this section you will work with my formulation of systems-environment characterizations of educational activity systems (EAS's) and use my characterization in order to develop an extended description of your own system. In a sense, you synthesize your first description with my characterization. My description has not been developed in a specific context. It attempts to portray GENERAL EDUCA-

TIONAL ACTIVITY SYSTEMS-SOCIETY relationships. It elaborates the concepts and principles you worked with in SECTIONS ONE and TWO, and introduces some additional concepts and principles that are relevant to EAS's. As you work with the text below, make notes that will help you to develop your extended characterization in SECTION FOUR. Activities in this section will enable you to work with some of the systems ideas. Integrate the findings you develop in working with the activities into the description of your synthesis statement in SECTION FOUR of this chapter.

A general systems-environment model of EAS's is developed by (1) examining the EAS in the context of its environments, (2) exploring relationships in that context, and (3) considering the two major means by which relationships are lived, namely, adjustment or total systems change and transformation.

EDUCATIONAL ACTIVITY SYSTEMS (EAS's) IN THEIR ENVIRONMENT

EAS's exist in space and time. The society in general and a given community in particular are the enfolding SPACE, the context, or the environment of EAS's. In the TIME dimensions, EAS's operate in the present, they have their own past, and they move toward their future. In this context we speak of the dynamics of growth, development, decline, and possibly termination. All of these indicate some form of change. These concepts have important implications for EAS's. GROWTH means change in size or quantity. It does not mean a better EAS. Growth often means a DECLINE in quality. Decline might lead to the TERMINATION of the EAS. DEVELOPMENT means purposeful increase in quality. Growth, development, and decline indicate CHANGE. Inasmuch as EAS's are to carry out societal functions, change in the society calls for change in EAS's. Societal change may be slow and gradual. But in the course of the last forty years the major change has been in the rate and intensity of change itself. As a rule, EAS's have not responded adequately to recent major societal changes. A lack of attention to these changes has created the current crisis situation in education. It is of the utmost importance for us to understand and contemplate the distinction between growth and development, as well as to consider the educational implications of major societal changes and transformations that have emerged in the course of the second half of this century. I will come back to this issue later.

ACTIVITY # 5

Speculate about ways in which you would make a "valuation" of the development of quality in your selected EAS. Enter your ideas in your workbook.

The community and the larger society constitute the functional ENVIRONMENT that not only surrounds the EAS, but also creates it and in turn is affected by its creation. This environment is comprised of other societal systems and systems in the private and public sectors that may affect the EAS and are affected by it. These systems constitute an "endless mass of surrounding space" and point to a major and difficult issue of thinking about EAS-environment relationships. In order to cope with the "endless mass" we shall: (1) work with the notion of embeddedness, (2) differentiate between general and immediately relevant "systemic" environment, (3) discuss the notion of hierarchy, and (4) learn to draw system boundaries.

The GENERAL ENVIRONMENT of the EAS is the larger society that can be seen as ever expanding from the immediate community into a county, a region, or a state, then into a nation, and finally into the global community. These larger and ever larger ENFOLDING environments are EMBEDDED or NESTED in each other. To make the expanding space of environments manageable we shall differentiate between three embedding environments of EAS's. (1) The "outer field" is the larger society that extends into the global community. (2) The "intermediate field" is the geopolitical environment of an EAS. (3) The "immediate field" is comprised of social systems, ranging from the family to the community. Numbers (2) and (3) jointly comprise the SYSTEMIC ENVIRONMENT, that part of the general environment with which the EAS regularly interacts. Let us see these one by one.

We consider the LARGER SOCIETAL ENVIRONMENT as the GENERAL ENVIRONMENT of the school. We explore this environment in order to understand the educational implications of emerging societal changes and transformations that represent emerging societal expectations and requirements that EAS's are to consider and satisfy. Awareness of what these changes and transformations are and understanding how they might affect the EAS are important considerations for EAS-society relations; they guide the educational community to formulate the broad purposes of education. Examples: movement from the industrial society to the information society; from representative democracy toward participative governance; from competition toward cooperation; from conspicuous consumption toward conservation; from "high-volume" economy to "high-value" economy (Note 1). These and other changing societal characteristics have (or should have) major influences on: defining the societal function and purposes of education; selecting the content of learning; and determining where, when, and how we should provide arrangements and resources for learning and human development.

ACTIVITY # 6

As you work with the above paragraph, provide your own list of emerged societal characteristics that, in your judgment, should have an effect on your selected EAS.

In a particular setting, the larger GEOPOLITICAL ENVIRONMENT and within it a specific COMMUNITY jointly comprise what we might call the directly relevant or "SYSTEMIC" ENVIRONMENT of the EAS. Systemic means a systemically (and not randomly) connected state. The GEOPOLITICAL ENVIRONMENT includes those political, social, and economic systems that deal with or influence educational policy and educational requirements. They play a role in determining resources that are available to the EAS. This environmental domain thus includes federal, national, state, and regional systems and agencies.

ACTIVITY # 7

In the context of your selected EAS describe the relationship of those external systems that are systemically connected to your selected EAS. What is the functional effect of those connections on the EAS?

The other part of the SYSTEMIC ENVIRONMENT is all of the COMMUNITY. The community has a direct and ongoing influence on the EAS and is connected with it by high intensity interactions. It is the community from which students enter into the EAS, upon which the system depends for most of its support, and into which it sends students who have learned: (a) how to realize their potential, (b) how to make valuable contributions to the community and the society, and (c) how to become competent and participating citizens. Interactions and relationships between the EAS and its systemic environment are well defined and regulated and comprise a system of relations and interactions. (That is why we call this environment "systemic.") But it is still "environment" because it is not under the control of the EAS, even though it is influenced by it. On the other hand, the systemic environment does have control over the EAS.

ACTIVITY # 8

Describe the interaction between your EAS and its community, with particular attention to the notion of control. What are the form and substance of this control?

Figure 2.4 portrays the notion of embeddedness and presents an image of types of environments in which the school is nested. In Figure 2.4 we may also capture the image of HIERARCHICAL LEVELS. The systemic environment of the EAS, the EAS as a system, and the parts that comprise the EAS constitute a systems hierarchy, operating at three levels. (See the horizontal lines, indicating these levels in Figure 2.4.) In working with societal systems—such as an EAS—it is of utmost importance that we consider at least three hierarchical levels simultaneously and interdependently. In this trilevel relationship, the EAS: (1) serves the purposes of its societal and systemic environments, (2) serves its own self-defined purposes, and (3) serves the purposes of its constituents, such as its students and staff.

ACTIVITY # 9

Describe—in the context of your EAS—stated purposes (if any) at the three levels OF THE HIERARCHY and speculate about some of the potential conflicts that may arise from attending to purposes at those levels.

In the figure, I designated the EAS as one which operates as the PRIMARY SYSTEM LEVEL. The various systems above the EAS are designated as the embedding environments. The subsystems below the EDUCATIONAL ACTIVITY SYSTEM are embedded in the particular EAS that operates as the primary system level.

ESTABLISHING BOUNDARIES is the fourth and the most significant means in coping with—what we called—the "endless mass" of the expanding environment. The boundaries of an EAS delimit its system space and set aside—from the environment—all those entities with their attributes and relationships that comprise

FIGURE 2.4 THE EMBEDDEDNESS OF EAS's

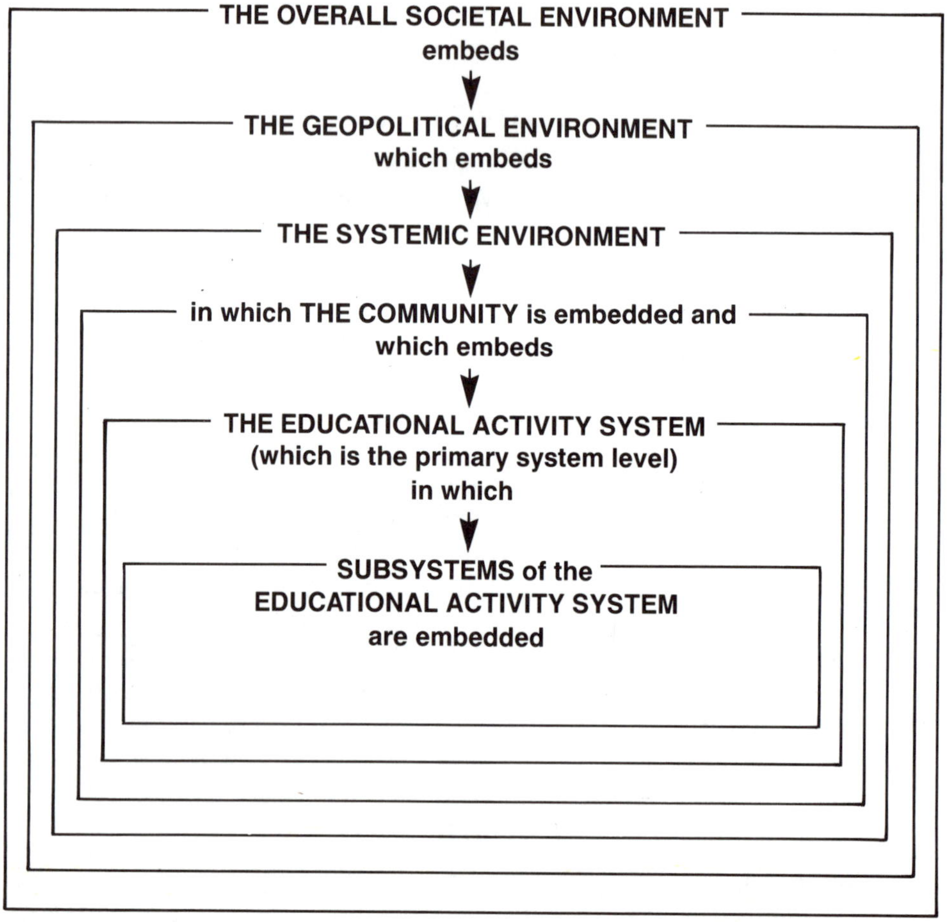

(or belong to) the EAS. The boundaries of a societal system—such as an EAS—are of various kinds. For an EAS, boundaries can be identified and described in such categories as: physical, geopolitical, economic, social, sociobiological, psychological, temporal, cultural, ethical, and technological. The physical boundaries of the EAS are multiple. One definition of the physical boundary is the limits of the collection of the physical plant and related facilities. A larger boundary is the geographical area which has been defined for the EAS as its service area. A third boundary dimension is the resources that the EAS uses to provide for learning experiences as well as whatever is considered to be the "learning territory." A joint consideration of these three types of boundaries will demonstrate to us that drawing or establishing boundaries is an issue of "perception" and "judgment." Boundaries—of societal systems—are "in the eye of the beholder." In Note 2, I refer to a reference in which I provided an example of the implications of setting boundaries in a way that includes a larger learning territory and a richer resource base than that which the typical school has today.

Economic boundaries can be defined in terms of fiscal and other types of resources available to the EAS as well as the economic conditions and climate that prevail in the community or the geopolitical environment of the EAS. Psychobiological boundaries indicate student characteristics, such as age, socioeconomic background, aptitude, etc. Psychological boundaries refer to feelings, attitudes, dispositions, and perceptions about the EAS of all those who are within it and who are in its systemic environment. Sociocultural boundaries are dominant in setting standards, expectations, and valuation.

ACTIVITY # 10

Describe the nature, characteristics, and significance of the various boundaries of your EAS. As you describe those boundaries, you will realize how much setting boundaries is a question of judgment, and what the implications are of setting boundaries.

For the type of (societal) system that an EAS is, boundaries are not drawn in a way that would isolate the system from its environment. There are BREAKS in the boundaries: gates, or entry and exit openings, through which the EAS interacts with the community and the society. It is through these breaks that the EAS receives its input and through which it sends its output to the society.

The EAS receives multiple INPUTS from the society. In fact, all the various boundaries that we discussed earlier are markers for various inputs. Thus the term input is a collective term. It refers to everything that the EAS receives from its systemic and larger environment. We can differentiate three types of input. The first is the "definitional" type. The society establishes an EAS—or an EAS establishes itself in the society—in order to satisfy certain societal needs, expectations, or requirements, as well as to satisfy its own aspirations, expectations, and needs. These NEEDS, EXPECTATIONS, and REQUIREMENTS make up one part of the "definition type" input. Its other part constitutes CONSTRAINTS that the systemic environment of the EAS sets, under which the EAS has to operate. One common characteristic of the above type of input is that it enters the school in the form of INFORMATION.

Another large type of input is comprised of RESOURCES, such as people, funds, materials, and energies that all come from the systemic environment of the EAS as its contribution to the operation of the EAS. All this input enables the functioning of the EAS. In turn, the EAS uses the input provided to it by the systemic environment, and transforms it into outcomes that are of value to the community and the larger society. The third type is a collection of unorganized and UNDEFINED INPUT, often called "noise." The EAS has to evaluate "noise" for its possible relevance. Irrelevant noise will be screened out so that it does not interfere with the operation of the system.

OUTPUT, which also operates through the boundary breaks, stands for whatever the system sends back to the environment. Output is also of three major types. The definition type is output that is the tangible realization of expectations, demands, and requirements that the EAS sends into the society. This type includes, first and foremost, learners who have been educated, the knowledge that has been developed, and other services of value to the community and the society. This also includes information provided to the systemic environment about the performance of the EAS, the achievements of its students, and the operation of the EAS. The second type of output is formulated in terms of requests and requirements that pertain to resources and facilities that the EAS needs in order to operate. The third type is the "waste" that the EAS sends into the environment. Most unfortunately, this waste today includes a large number of students—at certain places as many as half of those who enter schools—who have dropped out, been weeded out as undesirable, or cannot perform as expected. What a waste of human potential! The extent of this waste is a measure by which the systemic environment makes judgment about the adequacy of the EAS. In recent years, this judgment has been expressed by saying that the nation is "at risk" on account of the poor performance of our schools; that we are at the bottom range in educational performance among the developed nations, etc. Another type of output that is undefined includes unintended or nontargeted information.

ACTIVITY # 11

Develop a description of the various types of input and output that you have observed in your EAS, and name parts of the various types.

RELATIONSHIPS

Describing relationships in the context of EAS's, we can speak of vertical and horizontal relationships between and among systems, and relationships within a specific educational activity system. The vertical relates to embeddedness. At times, a given EAS is embedded in a larger EAS. In this case the larger system is called SUPRASYSTEM. For example, in the case of an EAS that is operated by a religious institution, the institution acts as its suprasystem. In the current organization of public education, a school district is the suprasystem of one of its schools. In our exploration we continue to consider the community as part of the systemic environment rather than the suprasystem of the EAS. Today there is organic relationship between a given school and its school district, but such relationship does not exist between the community and a particular school. In the current system, an elected school board acts as the gatekeeper of the interaction between the school and the community. Suprasystems are made up of several constituent systems, which in relation to each other are called PEER SYSTEMS. In a given community, a specific EAS has such peer systems as other educational agencies or institutions (a community college, a university, a private school), business, industry, government and social agencies, religious institutions, community agencies, the media, etc. The EAS interacts with these peer systems; it influences them and is affected by them. The nature of the relationship between various systems, operating in a given environment, can be of three types: egalitarian, centralized, or hierarchical. In current practice an EAS seems to have EGALITARIAN relationships with its peer systems, such as those described above. In case a community-wide educational system is established—such as the one I referred to earlier (see Note 2)—the EAS would play a CENTRALIZED role. A HIERARCHICAL relationship indicates that one system is subordinated to another. In discussing embeddedness, we have already considered HIERARCHY. As with most social systems, an EAS is comprised of constituent parts, called SUBSYSTEMS. Subsystems of EAS's may have the same type of relationship as the three types described above (egalitarian, centralized, hierarchical). In considering vertical and horizontal relationships, there are two useful concepts that help us to order and guide thinking: the notion of system level and system in focus. SYSTEM LEVEL is designated (in a hierarchy) as a level at which a particular system is organized. There are levels above it and below it at which systems operate in relationship to that particular system. To avoid confusion, it is of utmost importance to designate the system level at which our SYSTEM OF INTEREST is organized as the PRIMARY LEVEL. For example: we may say that our system of interest is the "Sunrise Elementary School," which, then, becomes the primary system level of our exploration. The district which embeds this school is at the suprasystem level and parts of the school are at the subsystem level. In this particular exploration, Sunrise School also becomes the SYSTEM IN FOCUS in relationship to other elementary schools in the district. Next month the "Sunset Elementary School" may occupy the SYSTEM IN FOCUS position as our district-wide assessment of school effectiveness continues. The issue of PRIMACY OF LEVEL and SYSTEM IN FOCUS will become a major item of consideration in our next chapter when we discuss functions that the school is to carry out.

ACTIVITY # 12

In order to help you to develop the systems-environment model of your selected system, describe here the web of relationships that exist in your EAS, with the use of concepts introduced above.

OPENNESS AND CLOSEDNESS

An examination of the relationship between the system and its environment, between the EAS and the community, brings into focus another significant issue: the open and closed nature of systems. A system is CLOSED if it is sealed off from its environment by its boundaries and if there is no exchange between the system and its environment. The consequences of closure are that the system will not receive information, energy/material from the environment, and it will "run down." But educational activity systems should not be closed toward their environments. In rapidly changing and turbulent environments—characteristics of our current era—there is a temptation in the educational community to "protect'' the system against those external forces. Such a move, however, is a closing-down move which may decouple EAS's from their environments and may decrease their relevance to the environment.

Educational systems are OPEN systems. They have ''breaks'' in their boundaries that enable them to interact with their environment and receive information, energy/matter which are essential inputs, enabling the EAS to function. The more numerous and larger the breaks in the boundaries, the more open the system and the more types and kinds of input (and output) it has to process. A completely open system—one without boundaries—would not be, and could not be, considered to be a system in that it could not have any orderly interaction with its environment. It would have no control over inputs and no definitions of itself. A totally open system implies a random and uncontrolled input and output, in essence a non system. In social systems, such as an EAS, we cannot speak of completely open or closed systems. Openness and closedness are a matter of degree.

We consider EAS's to be open systems, but they are not completely open. Their inputs are regulated, their constraints identified, and their outputs specified. The more varied and complex the input, the more COMPLEX the EAS and the output it produces. The less varied the input, the less varied the output and the more closed is the EAS. In our current turbulent, rapidly changing, and COMPLEX society we are indeed aware of the complexity of the environment of EAS's as well as the complexity of the input they receive (e.g., multiple and increasing demands), and the complexity of the output EAS's are expected to produce. EAS's have to cope with a certain degree of randomness of input, but still have specific purposes identified—formulated by external and internal expectations and requirements—and thus they produce an expected output. As with other social systems, an EAS exercises CLOSURE BY CONTROL. This means that an EAS has the ability to define its boundaries, adjust the breaks on its boundaries, and regulate its input and output. The extent of this closure and what kind of closure are always issues of judgment. Such control should enable the EAS to regulate its input, but it should not lead to a situation where EAS-environment relations and interaction are hampered or blocked.

ACTIVITY # 13

It is your turn now to work with the ideas, concepts, and principles introduced above; to describe the open/closed nature of your EAS and characterize the aspects by which it can be considered open or closed; and to make judgments on "closure by control."

SELF-REGULATION

The overall attention of an EAS is directed at the attainment of expected outputs: the education of its pupils. But such expectations are changing as the environment and the EAS itself are also changing. EAS's work with changing conditions and expectations by self-regulation. SELF-REGULATION has had wide-ranging implications for EAS-environment relations as well as for the life of the system. Self-regulation flows directly from what I discussed in the previous paragraphs. EAS's have to be able to adjust themselves to external and internal changes by modifying their functions and components, their operations, and their structure. They have to maintain compatibility with their environments. An EAS in environment "A" has to operate differently from an EAS existing in environment "B." An EAS operating in the inner city of a metropolis, for example, faces requirements that are quite different from those in rural areas. The EAS should be able to work creatively with differences in environmental demands and produce the output specified by its environment. By so doing, the EAS manifests its responsibility to the society and maintains its compatibility with it. There are two kinds of adjustments: ADAPTATION and COEVOLUTION BY TRANSFORMATION. These two are distinctly different manifestations of SELF-REGULATION.

ADAPTATION

ADAPTATION implies a capability to RESPOND to environmental changes that are relevant to the life of an EAS. This is primarily unidirectional. In order to continue its life, the EAS is to meet certain expectations, demands, and requirements. If an EAS fails to meet these—as is the case in most educational communities today—the EAS is faced with three options. (1) The EAS CHANGES itself so that it will meet expectations. (2) The environment of the

EAS changes—lowers—its expectations. (3) If none of the above, the EAS may face termination. In the current climate of an educational "crisis," option (2) is not viable, and unless option (1) is exercised, option (3) becomes reality.

ADAPTATION is a process by which we correct for errors and introduce modifications to bring the EAS in line with small changes in the environment and in educational expectations. But we live in an age of massive societal changes, when we have to go beyond adaptation, when we have to transform our EAS's.

COEVOLUTION BY TRANSFORMATION

Yes, we live in an age when we have to go beyond adaptation and small adjustments in our educational activity systems. Trying to improve existing EAS's—grounded in the societal image of the 19th century—will not do any more. In view of the massive societal changes and transformations that have occurred in the course of the last half century, EAS's find themselves in a position where they have to reconceptualize what they are about. In view of the emerged societal characteristics, they have to understand the educational implications of these characteristics, create a new educational image, and—based on the image—design new systems of learning and human development. Recalling what I said earlier, namely, that in this new era the intensity and rate of change have also changed, the challenge of EAS's is to learn to COEVOLVE with their environment and TRANSFORM themselves.

ACTIVITY # 14

You should now take another look at your selected system and in view of the two systems ideas of adaptation and coevolution describe which one of these is operative in your EAS.

The approach to adaptation and coevolution is SELF-REGULATION. Self-regulation is exercised by the EAS through FEEDBACK. We recognize in open systems, such as in EAS's, two kinds of feedback. One kind serves the function of CORRECTING FOR ERRORS. We call this NEGATIVE FEEDBACK. The function of the other is to TRANSFORM THE SYSTEM. We call this POSITIVE FEEDBACK. Negative feedback introduces information about the adequacy, e.g., the state, the characteristics, the quality of the output. Adjustment can, then, be made based on this information.

Through this type of feedback the ACTUAL STATE of the educational output is continuously compared with the EXPECTED STATE. Thus, feedback enables us to CORRECT for differences between the two states; to correct for errors. We call this type of feedback NEGATIVE FEEDBACK. Negative feedback control begins with the process of collecting—for example—student performance data, comparing these data with the PERFORMANCE or OUTPUT MODEL, which we devise based on educational goals. The results of the comparison are analyzed, interpreted, and fed back into the system for use in making CORRECTIONS in the system. Through the use of such self-regulating, control-based feedback, the EAS can remain in a STEADY STATE condition. By adjusting some operations IN the EXISTING SYSTEM it can realize desired educational outcomes. In this case, the EAS can expect that the society will ACCOMMODATE it and provide the resources and the support it needs in order to be able to function. Adjustment and accommodation are harmonized as mutual recursive and complementary operations. This type of negative feedback driven EAS-environment interaction is operative at times when societal changes are slow and gradual.

In times of accelerating and dynamic changes and discontinuities—that characterize the current environment of EAS's, as described earlier—small changes and piecemeal adjustments, that are guided by negative feedback, will not suffice. Negative feedback aims at reducing DEVIATION from stated norms and expectations. But when these norms and expectations change—as they do today in response to massive environmental changes and transformations—efforts to improve the existing outdated system become counter-productive. We cannot transform a horse and buggy into a spacecraft, regardless of how much we try and how much money we invest in trying. We have to be willing to ask: Do we need a DIFFERENT EAS? We may need to change not only the output but also the whole system: its purposes, its boundaries, its systemic environment, and also the way we think about education. When EAS's find themselves "out-of-sync" with the environment, in order to match new expectations and requirements, we may have to design new EAS's. The mechanism that operates here is POSITIVE FEEDBACK, which leads to rethinking education, redefining its societal functions, re-visioning its image, and recreating it by design. Positive feedback enables the EAS to go beyond adaptation and to COEVOLVE with the environment and TRANSFORM it by design. In such evolving system creation, the emerging new EAS—in coordination with the environment—redefines the systemic environment that is necessary to support the new system, and reformulates the boundaries, the functions, and the purposes of the EAS. Through these, the relationship is harmonized between the EAS and the society by co-action, leading to mutual accommodation. This recursive mutuality becomes true COEVOLUTION.

Coevolution by transformation implies a fluid state of continuous change. As new expectations and purposes emerge, the system attempts to influence the environment or find new environments, explore or create new niches in the environment so that the new environment will accommodate or support those new purposes or expectations. This type of system-environment interaction and behavior is manifested in general in societal evolution. The history of the evolution of societal systems tells us that they have often been driven by positive feedback, reorganizing themselves at a higher level of complexity, and in so doing, attaining a very different system state. (See Note 3.) Such behavior is clearly manifested in the evolution and behavior of purpose-seeking societal systems. These systems have the capacity and can develop the capability to direct their own evolution by purposeful design. The challenge of EAS's today is to become such purpose-seeking systems that are capable of designing and directing their own future.

Education in the emerged, post-industrial information age might move toward seeking a new system state at a higher level of complexity. It might transform itself. The image of a community-based societal model of education described in the referenced piece (Note 4) might project an image of such a new system.

ACTIVITY # 15

Your task now is to review your description of the self-regulation paragraphs of the systems environment model you developed in Section Two and synthesize your statement with my statement above. Pay particular attention to this question: How would positive feedback and coevolution with the environment work in your EAS?

SUMMARY OF THE EAS–ENVIRONMENT MODEL

EAS's exist in the environment of the society and are marked by boundaries that set them aside from their immediate systemic environments and the overall societal environment. Through breaks in the boundaries, EAS's interact with their environment. From it they receive input: information on expectations of learning outcomes and resources they need to produce those outcomes (output). Thus, EAS's are open to their environment. In order to meet expectations, EAS's are capable of regulating their operations by feedback that indicates changes to be made. Negative feedback works when deviations from the expectations are minor and can be reduced by adjustment. But there are times when there is a major discrepancy between the EAS and the society, indicating the need for major changes in the EAS, or even the need for a new educational design. The self-regulative mechanism that senses the need for and guides such major change is positive feedback. When a gap opens up between the rapidly changing and evolving society and its educational systems, EAS's have to learn to coevolve with the society, close the evolutionary gap, and transform themselves by design.

SECTION FOUR:

THE RE-VISIONED SYSTEMS-ENVIRONMENT MODEL OF YOUR EAS

Your task now is to re-vision/re-conceptualize and describe the systems-environment model of the EAS of your choice. At this point, you are asked to consider and work with all the text that is available to you in this book as well as with the description you developed in Section Two. The challenge is not just to elaborate your earlier version (in Section Two) by REVISING it based on my description of a general systems-environment model of EAS's, but to step back from the texts and RE-VISION your model. The activities you have completed in working with Section Three have developed new insights that will help you in this re-visioning. Questions have surely arisen as you worked with my text and the activities. Try to answer those on your own, based on the larger context of understanding systems in the course of your work with Chapters One and Two. If questions are still left, it means that you have to continue developing a systems view of human activity systems and a systems view of educational activity systems.

SECTION FIVE:

ASSESSMENT OF SELF, THE MODELLED SYSTEM, AND THE MODEL

The purpose of working with the systems-environment model in the previous parts of this chapter was to foster the development of a systems view of how a system lives in its environment and how we—who live in that system—can use the understanding that we can gain from a systems-environment view to enhance our lives, the life of the system, and the life of the society. In this section we are taking another look at the issues of understanding and living at the three systems levels as stated here. I introduce next some perspectives that allow us to assess ourselves (our readiness to think systemically), the systems-environment adequacy of the selected system, and the adequacy of the systems-environment model we have jointly developed.

SELF-REFLECTIVE ASSESSMENT

In the previous sections we embarked on the journey to develop and internalize a systems view in our thinking and actions. It is appropriate now to reflect upon the question: Is there any disposition we now have that would hinder us in acquiring a systems view of education? The development of a systems view is often blocked by certain dispositions, which—if present and persistent in our thinking—will make it difficult for us to embrace a systems perspective and use the systems lenses introduced in this work. The recognition and understanding of these dispositions are important for us. Unless we become aware of their existence, we cannot deal with them.

People generally prefer to operate in closed systems. Even when a system is open by design, we often make it less so by narrowing the breaks in the system's boundary in order to decrease the interaction between the system and its environment. We are concerned about the dynamics of change, turbulence, uncertainty, and ambiguity that might flow into the system from an ever-changing environment. We prefer stability, certainty, and clarity; we feel more secure when we operate on well-known ground, surrounded by familiar landmarks. We are comfortable with adjustments that are guided by only negative feedback. (It is interesting to note that the concept of feedback is limited in the educational community to its use in the negative feedback sense. Positive feedback—if used—usually implies just the opposite of what it means; namely, that everything is OK.) The intensive improvement movement of the eighties clearly demonstrated the prevalence in the educational community of the disposition described here. In order to overcome this disposition we have to learn to do several things.

The systems view places a high premium on a continuous and intensive interaction between the EAS and its environments, the community and the larger society. In times of massive societal changes we have to INCREASE and INTENSIFY the EAS-environment interaction rather than trying to close our boundaries and "protect" our EAS. Thus, rather than being locked into it, we have to learn to LEAP OUT from our existing system in order to UNDERSTAND the educational implications of emerging characteristics of the societal environments in which we are embedded. In times of a newly emerging societal landscape we have to learn to "map into" that changing landscape an educational landscape by RE-CREATING rather than restructuring the existing one. This re-creation means a willingness to change our thinking about education, reconceptualizing its societal functions and its purposes, as well as redefining what should be LEARNED when, where, and how. It is this leaping out and re-creating metaphor that might well explain the notion of positive feedback. All this means that we have to learn to welcome change, uncertainty, and ambiguity, which is a formidable task when we—as a rule—have valued stability, certainty, and constancy. We have to learn to "strive on chaos" as many management experts tell us today.

Each one of us should reflect upon the question: What can we—what should we—do to overcome the well-rehearsed disposition of protecting ourselves—and our EAS—from change? There are several things to do. We should learn to LEAP OUT from our existing EAS. Leap out, SEE the larger landscape of our changing society, and UNDERSTAND it. Based on that understanding, CREATE a NEW IMAGE of education and REALIZE that image by DESIGN.

ACTIVITY # 16

This activity aims at helping you to clarify in your own mind if you indeed have dispositions that hinder you from embracing the systems view. It is not easy to do this. Try to recall instances in working with the various sections when you felt ill at ease about certain propositions I have made about the systems view. Make notes about your findings in your notebook.

THE ASSESSMENT OF THE MODELLED SYSTEM

In the preceding sections, you worked with concepts and principles that constitute a general systems-environment model. You have transformed that model into an EAS-environment model of your own. You then worked with my interpretation of a general EAS-environment model and, based on it, re-visioned a systems-environment model of your selected educational activity system. Working with these sections has put you on the road to the acquisition of a systems view as it relates to systems-environment interaction.

Now we join forces in reaching another important milestone on your journey to attaining a systems view of education. You are asked to work with a set of questions that I developed for the assessment of the environmental adequacy of an EAS. The questions are representative rather than all-inclusive. As you work with them, and APPLY them to the ASSESSMENT of your SELECTED SYSTEM, you might find it useful to add other questions or modify my questions. The sequence of the questions follows, in general, the sequence of my presentations. You have already confronted the issues that the questions reflect while working with the various activities in Section Three. The questions now offer a summary assessment of the systems-environment adequacy of an EAS. Respond to each question by introducing your observations in your notebook.

1. How is the environment of your selected system defined? Is it well-described and documented? Is it known to people in the system (as a functional systemic environment) in the sense implied in this chapter or is it only a superficially or vaguely identified environment? How would somebody

in the system—who has not worked with this book—describe the environment of the system?

2. What constitutes the boundaries of the system? To what degree of specificity are boundaries defined and described? What are boundaries which in your judgment are not considered or defined? Is there a "boundary awareness" by people in the system? Who makes the boundary judgments? How are they made?
3. Are entities (systems) in the environment identified that may affect your system AND might be affected by it? What appears to be unidentified entities (systems)?
4. Are the relationships and interaction patterns between the system and its environment well-defined and described? How are they defined? Who defines them? Considering the systems ideas developed up to this point, how well is this issue handled?
5. What constitutes the input entities of the system? How well are these accounted for? Given the range and types of input described in the text: Are there—in your judgment—some unidentified input entities that should be—but are not—considered?
6. How well is the output defined? How well are the output entities accounted for? Given the range and types of input described in the text: Are there—in your judgment—some unidentified output entities that should be—but are not—considered? For example, are there outcome expectations stated at all three systems levels: the environment, the system itself, and people in the system?
7. How well defined are the ordering relationships of the various systems that are involved in the system complex? Is the nature of these relationships well-defined as subordinate, centralized, or egalitarian?
8. What definitions, descriptions, or other evidences are available to show the degree to which the system is open or closed? Is there evidence that the notions of openness and closedness are understood? Is a disposition for closure in evidence?
9. To what degree is the system able to adjust to its environment? Is there any sign that people in the system recognize and attend to the massive societal changes that have emerged? Is there any sign that people contemplate changes in the societal functions that their EAS should attend to, in the learning content offered, and in how and

where it is offered? Is there any sign that would indicate the desire to coordinate with other social and community agencies?

10. Is there an awareness of the difference between correction for error vs. systems change? Is the process of adjustment and self-regulation handled differently by the use of negative vs. positive feedback? (It is not important what people call these regulative operations, but it is important to make sharp distinctions between the two operations.)

ACTIVITY # 17

If you have followed my recommendation, you have responded to the questions above and introduced your comments in your notebook. Using your notes, develop a summary description—a narrative—of your assessment of the overall systems-environment adequacy of the EAS you selected for description and evaluation.

ASSESSING THE MODEL

In this closing section you will explore the adequacy of the systems-environment model we have jointly developed. Assisting you in conducting this exploration, I introduce next a criterion that you might use. The adequacy of the model can be tested in two ways. The concepts and principles that constitute the model can be assessed as to their usefulness and explanatory power in the context of an operational educational activity system and the insight they generate by the user of the model. While we do this type of assessment we can also identify concepts and principles that are not yet part of the model. An assessment may address the following question: Does the model represent adequately such aspects as the following:

* Systems entities that exist in the space and the environment of educational activity systems.
* The attributes and states of these entities.
* Relationships among these entities.
* The characteristics of these relationships.
* The processes in which entities engage.

ENTITIES of the systems-environment scene were identified in the description of the model as one set of concepts. These include: (1) the space and time dimensions in which systems exist, (2) the environment and its various component entities of which the system is a part, (3) systems and (4) their subsystems, (5) boundaries, (6) breaks in the boundaries, through which (7) input entities enter the system, and (8) output entities leave the system.

ACTIVITY # 18

You can now consider the following questions: In the analysis of your selected system, did you discover entities that we did not account for in the model? If you did find any, can you make generalizations about them (relevant to various kinds of human activity systems) and include those in the model? On the other hand, did you find some entity concepts—described in the general model—that did not fit into the characterization of your selected system? Report your findings in your notebook.

ATTRIBUTES and STATES of entities comprise a large set of concepts and principles. These can be described as: open, closed, controlled, self-regulating, adaptive, adjusting, coevolving, ordered, variant, invariant, vague, well-defined, stable, unstable, uncertain, ambiguous, changing, sharply drawn, isolating, recursive, etc.

ACTIVITY # 19

You may enlarge this inventory of attributes from your findings of your characterization of your selected EAS. On the other hand, you might question the attributes assigned to certain entities in the description of the general systems-environment model. Describe your comments on attributes and states in your notebook.

RELATIONSHIPS emerge from the interaction of entities that operate in the various spaces of EAS's. Concepts that describe relationships in the systems-environment domain include: interrelatedness, adjustment, accommodation, coevolution, dependence, independence, interdependence, cause-and-effect, and multiple or recursive causality. Characteristics of the relationships were described as: hierarchical, centralized, egalitarian, dominating, subordinate, responsive, unresponsive, sensitive, etc.

ACTIVITY # 20

Did you find these relationships and their characteristics well exhibited in the system you described? Did you find relationships (and their characterizations) that were not displayed in the model? Describe your findings in your notebook, and include your discovery in the description of your model.

PROCESSES of the systems-environment scene include interaction, communication, correlation, control, negative and positive feedbacks, adjustment, adaptation, coevolution, accommodation, etc. Some of these also stand for the characterization of relationships as well as attributes of entities.

ACTIVITY # 21

Most likely you will be able to add to the above list some other processes that you identified as you described your selected EAS. Enter your findings in your notebook. Keep in mind, however, that only processes relevant to systems-environment interaction should be considered here.

REFLECTIONS

You might use the findings of your assessment of the system and the model discussed in this section for the purpose of revising the description of your system. Such revision will conclude the creation of a systems-environment model of your selected system. Creating a systems model of one's own is a giant step toward the acquisition of a systems view.

NOTES

(1) The significance of the difference between the "high-volume" economy of the industrial age and the "high-value" economy of today—and the educational implications of this difference—are clearly articulated by Robert B. Reich (1991). *The Work of Nations*. Alfred A. Knopf, New York.

(2) An image of a community-based system of learning and human development is described in Chapter Six of B.H. Banathy (1991). *Systems Design of Education: A Journey to Create the Fu-*

ture. Educational Technology Publications, Englewood Cliffs, NJ.

(3) A characterization of societal evolution is outlined in B.H. Banathy (Volume 23, 1-2 1987). "The Characteristics and Acquisition of Evolutionary Competence." *World Futures*.

(4) A societal-based characterization of education was presented by B.H. Banathy. "The School: An Autonomous or Cooperative Agency?" In Louis Rubin, Ed. (1980). *Critical Issues in Educational Policy*. Allyn and Bacon, Boston, MA.

CHAPTER THREE

The Functions/Structure Model

In this chapter we join forces again in developing the second systems model: the functions/structure model of educational activity systems (EAS's). In SECTION ONE, I build a general functions/structure model of human activity systems. I build this model from concepts and principles that characterize various types of human activity systems. In SECTION TWO, you will work with my model and use those concepts and principles to create a functions/structure characterization of the specific educational activity system you worked with in the previous chapter. Most likely, your description will be rather brief. In SECTION THREE, it will be my turn to build a functions/structure model of EAS's. This model is a general EAS model. I use the functions/structure lens to view EAS's in general and portray a STILL PICTURE of what an EAS is at a given moment in time. It is an "IS" picture in contrast with the third model which—in Chapter Four—portrays what an educational activity system "DOES" through time, by projecting a MOTION PICTURE image. In SECTION FOUR, you will consider my description as well as the description you developed in SECTION TWO, and describe a more detailed functions/structure systemic characterization of your selected EAS. In fact, in this section you synthesize my description of an EAS with your characterization of a specific EAS. In SECTION FIVE, I introduce a line of inquiry—in the form of sets of questions—which probes into the functions/structure adequacy of EAS's and the adequacy of the functions/structure model. You will work with these questions and make your own assessment. Figure 3.1 depicts the relationship of the five sections of the chapter as cumulatively expanding spirals of developing a systems view of educational activity systems in the context of their functions/structure systemic characteristics.

You can see from the description above that what you are involved with here is a process of an ever-expanding development of your systems view of EAS's. It is expected that the series of activities you complete will lead you: (1) to gain additional insights into

FIGURE 3.1 THE DEVELOPMENT OF A FUNCTIONS/STRUCTURE VIEW

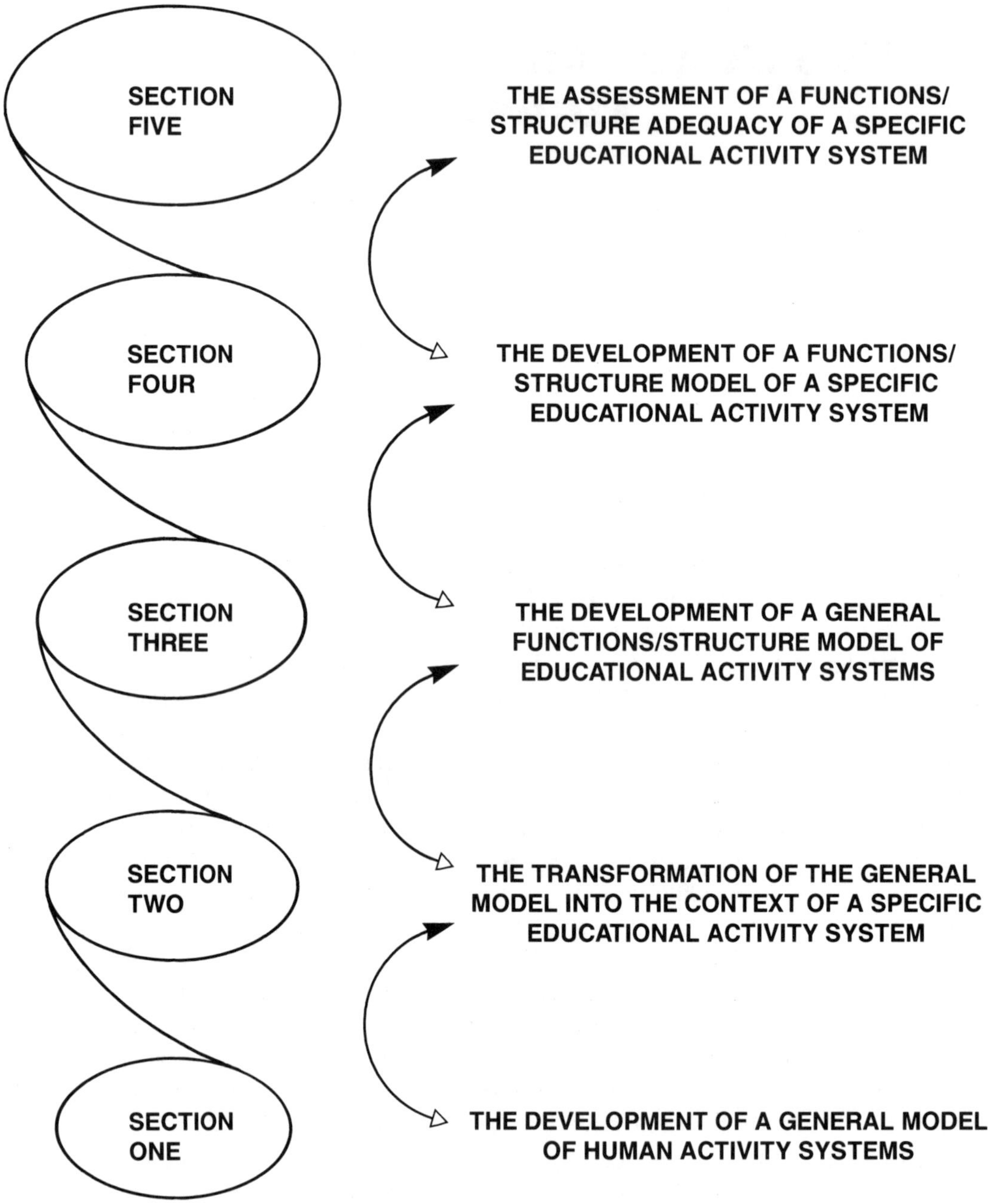

the systemic characteristics of human activity systems in general, and educational activity systems in particular; (2) to learn to look at systems with a "new eye," and think about them differently; and (3) to apply the insights and the new way of thinking in working with, assessing, and designing EAS's.

In advancing from one section to the next, you will gain a clearer understanding of systems concepts and principles, and—most significantly—you will apply what you have learned in a functional context that is meaningful and useful to you.

SECTION ONE

A GENERAL FUNCTIONS/STRUCTURE MODEL OF HUMAN ACTIVITY SYSTEMS

In this section, I focus the functions/structure systems lens on human activity systems (HAS's) of all kinds and select a limited set of concepts and principles—constructed from related concepts—that characterize HAS's. The selected concepts and principles will be organized into a model that defines the system based on: (1) whatever emerged from the systems-environment interaction as input, (2) generalizations about HAS's involving their purposes, functions, components, their relationships, and their structure. As a result of the exploration of these generalizations, a new SPATIAL, FUNCTIONS/STRUCTURE MODEL WILL EMERGE. This model will display what the system is like, what it does, with what it does it, and how it is organized. It will not explain how the system behaves through time, but only what it does in a given moment in time. The description of the general model is organized in five parts:

* Defining or creating the IMAGE of the HAS.
* SYSTEMS DEFINITION: purpose(s) and systems specifications.
* Identifying the FUNCTIONS that have to be carried out.
* Designating the COMPONENTS that carry out the functions.
* Defining the relational arrangements: the STRUCTURE.

These five are bound together by SYSTEMIC RELATIONSHIPS and INTERACTIONS and constitute the FUNCTIONS/STRUCTURE MODEL of the system.

Next, two examples show how I construct general principles of a HAS from selected related general concepts. Relating the concepts of EXPECTATIONS of the STAKEHOLDERS (in the environment), the DEFINITION (of the system), and CORE VALUES AND IDEAS (of people in the system), the following principle emerges: the purpose of a human activity system is formulated from the stated expectation of the stakeholders in the systemic environment and the core values and core ideas of people in the system. Another example: from the relationship of such concepts as DEFINITION, FUNCTIONS, and COMPONENTS, the following principle emerges: functions that the system should attend to are identified in order to attain whatever the system wants to achieve, and components are selected based on their potential to carry out these functions.

As you work with the general concepts and principles identified in this section, you should ask yourself the questions: How do the statements in the text apply to the specific EAS you selected? How can you interpret my generalized statements and transform and describe them in order to reflect and explain the functions/structure characteristics of your selected system? In developing your own model, reformulate the ideas you find in the text in a way that will be meaningful and useful to you and others who are in your selected system.

DEFINING THE IMAGE OF THE SYSTEM

Human Activity Systems (HAS's) are guided by images as they seek and fulfill their purposes. As used in this text the concept of IMAGE stands for the most general designation of: (1) what is the HAS about? and (2) what system type is it? (In Chapter One I outlined types of systems and the way we can differentiate them.) Two examples might be useful to show the degree of generality I speak of in defining the image.

EXAMPLE ONE. One health agency might see itself (its image) as a HAS that promotes the physical, mental, and spiritual health and wellness of all people in the community by education and by providing health services. Health education and health service professionals see themselves to be partners of people in the community. They jointly share responsibility in promoting health. If this image is realized, the whole community may become the context for developing physical, mental, and spiritual wellness for all its members. A system that is designed on the basis of this image can be designated as a purpose-seeking system. It seeks to envision new purposes and ways and means of serving the wellness of all members of the community.

EXAMPLE TWO. In sharp contrast to the "collectively seeking wellness image," the prevailing image of most health agencies is a focus on treatment of disease. The services of health professionals are used by people in need. The terrain of the system, as institutionalized today, is limited to the doctor's office, the hospital, and the pharmacy. On the purpose-seeking and rigidly controlled continuum of systems types, this type of health agency can be designated as deterministic or at best purposive. (I discussed the designation of systems types in Chapter One.)

There are two sources from which an image of the system is EMERGING. One is an UNDERSTANDING of the overall society and the EXPECTATIONS of the systemic environment. The other source is people who constitute the HAS. I discuss these two sources and how they are used to create the image.

The FIRST SOURCE of defining the image is an understanding of the characteristics and the systems-relevant expectations and needs of the systemic and the general environment in which the system is embedded. Those involved in the creation and guidance of a HAS will consider: (a) the IMPLICATIONS of the characteristics of the larger society for the existence of the system, and (b) the expectations of the systemic environment; and, based on (a) and (b), make a JUDGMENT as to what these imply for determining what the system is about. The meaning of these characteristics and expectations is NEGOTIATED with STAKEHOLDERS and potential CLIENTS in the systemic environment. From a consideration of all of the above will emerge some aspects of the image of the system.

The SECOND SOURCE of defining the image is people in the system: (1) their expectations of what the system should be about, (2) what CONTRIBUTIONS it should make to the society, (3) how it should SERVE and WORK WITH the environment and people in the system, and (4) how it should express and manifest their WORLD VIEW, their VALUES and IDEAS about their COLLECTIVE LIFE in the system.

ACTIVITY # 22

Review the two examples of image description presented above. Take example one and ask the question: What information was taken from what sources that determined the image? Be specific in considering various possible sources for creating the image. Formulate the world view (values, core ideas) upon which the image was created. Then, take example two and do the same. Take one more step, and describe contrasting images of educational services in the fashion in which I contrasted the two health services images. You are free to speculate! Enter your descriptions and ideas in your notebook.

I continue the discussion of the use of the two sources. Whichever of the sources is the DOMINANT one determines the system's DEGREE of FREEDOM to define what it is about. HAS's that are ESTABLISHED by the SOCIETY for the explicit purposes of SERVING the society will be defined primarily—but not exclusively—based on the first source: the EXPECTATIONS and NEEDS of the society. Even in this case, however, the more FREEDOM people (in the system) have to SHAPE the image of the system, the more likely they will COMMIT themselves to it. The types of systems we speak of include: public education systems, community agencies, social service systems, health service agencies, etc.

Systems that DEFINE THEMSELVES—rather than be defined by the environment—will depend more on their own judgment, and have more freedom. Still, to the extent to which they REQUIRE RESOURCES from the environment, they will have to listen to it. Examples: a private school, a volunteer youth agency, a service club, religious institutions, business and industry, etc.

The definition of the IMAGE will EMERGE from a SYNTHESIS of the statements that emerge from the two sources described above. The IMAGE then becomes the BASIS upon which the PURPOSE of the HAS will be formulated.

ACTIVITY # 23

Once you have transformed the text above on IMAGE formation into a text that reflects the formulation of the images in educational activity systems, you should also define the current image of your system of choice and, if you wish, your own choice of an image. Enter your interpretation of image formation and your designation of the image—as you see it or as you wish to see it—in your notebook.

THE CORE DEFINITION OF A HAS

A core definition has two components: (1) a STATEMENT of PURPOSE(s) and (2) SYSTEMS SPECIFICATIONS that describe the characteristics that the system should have in order to attain the stated purpose(s). These two components will be described in turn. A CORE DEFINITION should be formulated in such detail that it becomes adequate as a BASIS to determine the FUNCTIONS that the system should carry out in order to correspond to the core definition.

PURPOSES

Purposes interpret the image in more detail. The image responded to the overall question: What is the system about in general? In identifying purposes of a HAS we have to elaborate the image at a higher level of resolution. Formulating purposes of a HAS, first I discuss purposes that are GENERIC to all kinds of HAS's. These generic purposes are inherent in the general nature of HAS's. But there are purposes that are SPECIFIC to a particular HAS. These specific purposes are grounded in the UNIQUENESS of a HAS: (1) having a unique environment, (2) being unique on its own, and (3) having people in it who are unique individuals. (A lack of consideration of such uniqueness is a major shortcoming of the so-called "social engineering approach.")

GENERIC PURPOSES are those which are characteristics of HAS's in general. In considering HAS's in general, we can envision purposes that reflect the ideas of ancient Greek philosophers who identified four pursuits as being individually necessary and collectively sufficient for the development of man and society: truth, plenty, goodness, and beauty. (1) The pursuit of TRUTH might be reflected in facilitating the production of information and knowledge that are needed to develop increasingly more effective and efficient means for conducting the affairs of a HAS individually and collectively. (2) The pursuit of PLENTY can be reflected by a purpose that aims to facilitate the acquisition of resources required for the life and operation of a HAS individually and collectively. (3) The pursuit of the GOOD is the ethical-moral dimension of a HAS, which can be reflected by purposes that define the ethical and moral responsibilities of members of the HAS and that of the collective of the HAS both toward the environment and toward each other in the system. (4) The pursuit of BEAUTY is the aesthetic purpose: the purpose of attaining the highest possible inner quality of life of individual members as well as the collective of the system. (See Note 1.)

I formulated a definition of GENERIC purposes of HAS's that reflects a DEGREE of SPECIFICITY that goes beyond the one described above. (See Note 2 for reference.) The set of general purposes described next addresses the MULTIDIMENSIONAL REALITY of individual and social EXPERIENTIAL LIFE. It pertains to all social systems, from the family to the global system of humanity. I suggested that purposes formulated for HAS's should address:

* A SOCIAL ACTION dimension, aimed at increasing and maintaining social justice and cooperation and interaction among individuals in the HAS and with other social systems in the environment of the HAS.

* An ECONOMIC dimension, with a focus on economic justice and integrated and indigenous (unique to the potential of the particular HAS) development of the system. (This dimension relates to the pursuit of plenty discussed above.)

* A MORAL dimension of our lives. It would particularly focus on self-realization, and social and ecological ETHICS. (This reflects the moral/ethical pursuit mentioned above.)

* The nurturing of the PHYSICAL, MENTAL, EMOTIONAL, and SPIRITUAL HEALTH and well-being of members of the HAS and the collective of the system; and the nurturing of the full development and the reaching of the FULL POTENTIAL of members of the HAS as well as the system itself.

* The SCIENTIFIC and TECHNOLOGICAL dimension mobilized for selecting or developing means for the operation of the HAS and for promoting the attainment of sociocultural and technological intelligence in making individual and collective judgments and making choices affecting the life of the system. (This was also mentioned among the four pursuits above.)

* The AESTHETIC dimension for the pursuit of aesthetic values and the enrichment of the inner quality of life of members of the HAS and the system itself. (Also mentioned among the four pursuits.)

* The GOVERNANCE and GUIDANCE dimension which integrates all other dimensions and connects the HAS with other systems in a cooperative relationship for the improvement of human conditions.

I suggested that these seven dimensions are all NECESSARY for a HAS to be or BECOME a FUNCTIONAL WHOLE in providing the wholeness of human experience. Furthermore, the purposes described above are NOT separate and independent dimensions.

They are to be viewed and formulated as a SYSTEM of INTERRELATED and INTERNALLY CONSISTENT PURPOSES. It is this SYSTEM of PURPOSES around which the overall SYSTEM is BUILT.

ACTIVITY # 24

Consider the ideas implied by the four-pronged pursuits and the seven dimensions of the GENERIC purposes above and formulate purposes for your EAS. You might add to or modify the generic ideas. Enter your findings in your notebook.

SPECIFIC PURPOSES are those that are unique to a particular HAS. We shall focus on stating purposes that will tell us what the system is going to do for: (1) the LARGER SOCIETY, (2) the SYSTEMIC ENVIRONMENT, (3) OTHER SYSTEMS, (4) the CLIENTS and STAKEHOLDERS of the system, (5) PEOPLE who serve the system, and (6) how it wants to see ITSELF as a system. The example that follows was generated based on the image of the health service system described earlier. The WELLNESS ACTIVITY SYSTEM proposes to:

* Be a societal institution that makes purposeful contributions to human betterment by establishing, demonstrating, and maintaining a community-wide wellness activity system.

* Offer programs, resources, and arrangements by which individuals, families, social groups, and the community as a whole can learn to attain and maintain to the fullest their physical, mental, and spiritual well-being; enrich their inner quality of life and the quality of their environment.

* Develop the community as a "wellness society" in which learning to become and stay healthy is an individual and collective purpose. Establish community-wide conditions and regulations for attaining that purpose.

* Establish and maintain coordinated inter-organizational linkage and coordination of social and human service systems in the community in order to offer integrated arrangements and resources for learning to be healthy, taking responsibility for one's health, and for providing health services.

* Ensure a high quality of working life for all who are in the system, encourage and reward cooperation among individuals and groups who serve the system, and facilitate personal and professional development.

* Be a self-directing and self-organizing HAS that can learn as an organization, can give direction to its continuing development through design, and manage itself by the widest possible participation of its members, its clients, and the community at large.

A statement of purposes formulated for a specific HAS should be such that it ENDOWS everyone in the system and in the community that embeds the system with a sense of COMMITMENT. It should provide GUIDANCE to the life of the system as it becomes its focus and enable the CREATION and MAINTENANCE of INTERNAL COHESIVENESS and clear IDENTITY. It should also INFORM those who are OUTSIDE the system about the purposes of the system. Thus, a statement of purposes should be both INSPIRING and INFORMING. Furthermore, the specific purposes should be seen as a SYSTEM of INTERRELATED and INTEGRATED PURPOSES that have INTERNAL CONSISTENCY.

ACTIVITY # 25

Your task now is to formulate a statement of purposes of your selected EAS. One statement should reflect the purposes of the existing system. If you wish, you can formulate another set of purposes that reflects your ideas and ideals as to how the system should be. Enter your descriptions into your notebook.

The formulation or clarification of purposes is one of the most crucial tasks in describing the functions/structure model of the system. The more SPECIFICALLY we state purposes the more likely we can ASSESS their ATTAINMENT. Such specificity is both ENVIRONMENT and SYSTEM SERVING. The environment will know what to expect and, if the expectations are met, the environment will SUPPORT the system more willingly. But specifying purposes is truly instrumental in identifying the functions of the system. The HIGHER the DEGREE of SPECIFICITY, the EASIER it is to IDENTIFY the FUNCTIONS that have to be considered in order to ACHIEVE the PURPOSES. The downside of over-specifying is that it might lock the HAS into a state where it might lose FLEXIBILITY and hinder change that is indicated by internal insights and requirements, and/or emerge from a continuous system-environment interaction and coevolution.

In this chapter I have used the term "purpose" as a designation of what the system is about. Working with human activity systems—which are of the societal service type—we often use the concept of "mission" as a general dedication of intent and "purpose" that is stated at the next level of specificity. Building a general model, I have stayed with one designation: purpose.

SYSTEMS SPECIFICATIONS

In building a general functions/structure model of HAS's, the continuing task is to build a knowledge base for defining the functions that the system carries out to attain the purposes. This task now leads us to frame questions the answers to which will be instrumental in the selection and definition of the functions of the system. The questions that follow provide an example of the kind of inquiry that guides the formulation of specifications.

* Who are the clients of the system? What services are offered to them? What characteristics do these services have? Where, when, and how are these services offered?

* Who "owns" the system? How is ownership distributed? What rights and responsibilities do owners have?

* What is the system's responsibility towards its clients, its members, the community, and the larger society? How are these responsibilities handled?

* How is the system related to the various levels of government? How are these responsibilities handled?

* What kind of relationship does the system have to the community, community organizations, the private sector, and other relevant systems?

* What are environmental constraints that the system has to consider? How do these constraints impact on the definition of the system? How do these potentially affect the functions of the HAS?

* What is the specific "world view"—an image or model of the world—that guides the thinking and action of members of the system individually and collectively and provides the "meaning" of the life of the system?

The above sets of inquiries are the "generic" types that exemplify aspects that help us to designate or identify systems specifications. There are others that emerge as we consider the specific context and the uniqueness of the system we are describing.

ACTIVITY # 26

Consider the seven clusters of questions introduced above and, in view of the purposes you stated for your existing system, try to identify its specifications. Next, based on what you formulated in Activity # 25 as purposes that reflect your own ideas and ideals, describe the specifications you wish your system to have. Enter your findings in your notebook.

FUNCTIONS OF HAS's

A human activity system is established in order to attain purposes. Purposes are attained by carrying out functions. PURPOSES and FUNCTIONS are the primary markers of a system. Once purposes are determined, the issue becomes: What are functions that we have to attend to in order to achieve the purposes? Only then do we ask the questions: What COMPONENTS/PARTS have to be involved, and in what ARRANGEMENTS that have the CAPABILITY to attend to the functions? Thus: FORM FOLLOWS FUNCTIONS. This is a key systems principle. Often we go about describing HAS's the other way around, by focusing on the parts/components and their structure (organizational chart), and only then consider whatever those parts/components do. As a rule, we "model" the structure first, putting the cart before the horse.

The relational arrangement of functions provides us with the first systems MODEL of a HAS. The FUNCTIONS MODEL is the systemic arrangement of all the activities that the system must accomplish in order to be the kind of system identified in the core definition. This model is built from VERBS that denote action. The functions (model) can be described at several LEVELS OF RESOLUTION. The key or major functions are described (in a systemic arrangement) at the lowest level of resolution. Each major function can be shredded out into sub-functions (each organized in a systemic arrangement) at a higher level of resolution. Then, each sub-function is described in terms of its component functions, stated at an even higher level of resolution. Corresponding to the earlier characterizations, we can speak of two kinds of functions. The first kind is those that are attended by all HAS's. We call these GENERIC SYSTEMS FUNCTIONS. Those functions that reflect the uniqueness of the system and that are necessary for the attainment of the specific purposes and specifications of the system are labeled SPECIFIC-TO-THE-SYSTEM FUNCTIONS. These designations make no distinction in the importance of the two kinds of functions. In order to attain the purposes of the system, both the generic AND the specific-to-the-system functions must be employed.

GENERIC SYSTEMS FUNCTIONS

Generic systems functions denote activities that can be observed in all human activity systems. In Chapter Two, many such functions were identified as we considered system-environment interactions and relations. These included: interacting, identifying and receiving input, establishing boundaries, providing output, monitoring input and output, (re) entering feedback, exercising control, making adjustments, accommodating, providing resources, coevolving, integrating, transforming, producing, transmitting or exchanging information, exploring implications, etc. All of these are functions that operate through time and will be discussed in detail in the process model (Chapter Four). Others will be identified as we discuss the functions/structure model in this chapter. A crucial generic function, for example, is SYSTEMIZATION. Systemization is the function that brings together and integrates activities and components or parts and makes them increasingly more system-like and purpose serving. Another key general function of HAS's is MAINTAINING RELATIONSHIPS among people within the system as well as with others in the systemic environment. Vickers considers this the single most important systems function. (Note 3.)

SPECIFIC SYSTEMS FUNCTIONS

Functions that respond to the specific purposes of the system and attend to its unique specifications are formulated by carefully analyzing these purposes and specifications and describing the activities that are to be carried out to attend to them. The best way to explain specific-to-the-system functions is by providing an example. The example of specific-to-systems functions described next is derived from the example of the purposes of the wellness system introduced earlier. The example is speculative, but might help you to make use of it in your functions/structure description of your specific educational activity system. Primary functions of a "community-based wellness system" (CBWS) might include the following:

A. Maintain continuous interaction with systems of the society that are relevant to wellness and the systemic environment of the CBWS in order to provide continuous input to the system.

B. Define—on a continuous basis—the meaning of CBWS, the desired outcomes of the system, and what wellness means in operational terms.

C. Define CBWS-relevant systems (in the community) and wellness-relevant programs, resources, and arrangements.

D. Establish and maintain linkage and interorganizational coordinated arrangements with all CBWS-relevant systems.

E. Establish and maintain programs, resources, and arrangements required to operate the CBWS and attain desired outcomes.

F. Provide easy and quick access to individuals, groups, and the community in general to CBWS programs, resources, and arrangements.

G. Use CBWS programs, resources, and arrangements.

H. Develop and maintain programs for ensuring high quality of working life of those in the CBWS.

I. Monitor, guide, and manage functions, and ensure continuous organizational learning.

Figure 3.2 provides an image of a system of primary functions that should be considered as the first model of a CBWS.

ACTIVITY # 26

You again have two tasks. First, identify the existing specific functions of the system you are considering and organize them into a system of functions. Second, based on the example presented above, develop specific functions that you believe your system should carry out and organize them into a system of functions. Enter your findings into your notebook.

SYSTEMS COMPONENTS

COMPONENTS (or PARTS) of a HAS are selected and employed on the basis of their potential to carry out FUNCTIONS that are necessary in order to attain the PURPOSES of the system. The relationship among components, functions, and purposes is clear and is defined as the following systems principle: PURPOSES determine the FUNCTIONS in which the HAS has to engage, and functions determine the CAPABILITIES that the system's COMPONENTS should have. Thus, the PURPOSE-FUNCTION-COMPONENT sequence is obligatory.

In this context, another systems principle can be stated: A system is more than the sum of its components. What makes it more is: (1) the RELATIONSHIPS of the components to each other and (2) the DESIGNED INTERACTIONS that fuse these components into a system of components. It is through these two that components become system-like. Components of HAS's are connected by PATTERNED relationships that form the system. These connections are the relationships, and the pattern is the STRUCTURE of the system. Connections and relationships can be static or dynamic.

FIGURE 3.2 AN IMAGE OF A MODEL OF A SYSTEM OF FUNCTIONS

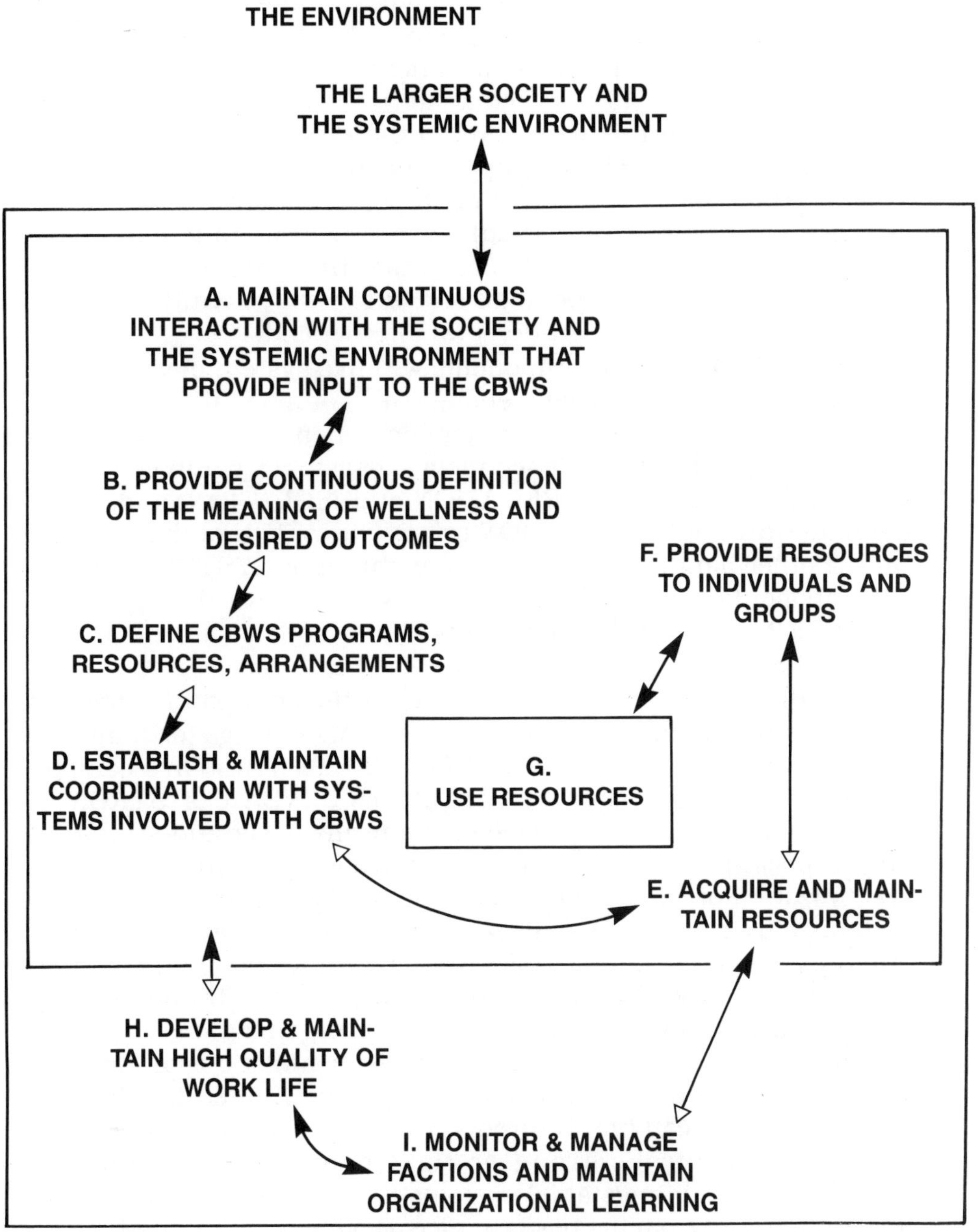

Each of the primary functions defined above has a set of sub-functions that are to be developed at a higher level of resolution. Those sub-functions then have their own sets of component functions.

STATIC RELATIONSHIPS are characteristics of HAS's that are rather closed. In discussing systems types in Chapter One, the rigidly controlled and the deterministic types are the ones that can be characterized as having static relationships. These are the least sensitive to changes in the environment. On the other hand, DYNAMIC RELATIONSHIPS are characteristics of open systems, the types we are concerned with here. In these systems the PROPERTIES and ATTRIBUTES of components do vary through time and so does their pattern of relationships, their structure. These changes potentially come about by changes in functions. It is through these dynamic relationships that the system moves from being a collection of independent and autonomous entities toward the systemic state of integration and interdependence.

INDEPENDENCE of components within a system means a lack of integration. It means that a change in a component or a subsystem does not affect changes in other components or subsystems. A tendency toward independence moves a system's components toward PROGRESSIVE SEGREGATION and ISOLATION, and eventually toward the DISSOLUTION or TERMINATION of the system. On the other hand, a progressive integration or SYSTEMIZATION of components of a system moves the system toward progressive INTERDEPENDENCE (of the components) and toward an INTEGRATED STATE.

Another observation we can make in the context of systemic relationships among the components of HAS's brings forth an important issue. The PATTERN that CONNECTS a system's components may be established by the HAS as a WEAK or STRONG/TIGHT COUPLING. On the face of the terms weak and strong, it might appear that weak coupling indicates weaker integration and systemization of components. This perception dominated human systems inquiry a couple of decades ago and still prevails in some practices. This perception was grounded in systems engineering and operation research notions of "hard systems" thinking. (See Note 3.) This early view of HAS's conceived organizations as rather closed, being the rigidly controlled or deterministic type. In this view, people/components in the system have limited freedom of choice. Hierarchically structured systems are managed topdown, by coercive control. Strong or tight coupling characterized STEADY (unchanging/stable) systems STATE and was seen to be the guarantee of systems performance. Business and industrial organizations, the military, public/administrative agencies, and public education are some examples. Disease control-focused health organizations, described earlier, are also of this kind.

In the course of the seventies, a more open "organismic" view of HAS's emerged (Note 4). From the early eighties on, what we call a SOFT SYSTEMS view has come to fore as the emerging perception of what HAS's are. This view was described in Chapter One in some detail. The purposive, heuristic, purpose-seeking types (also described in that chapter) have the characteristics of having—as we move from the purposive to purpose-seeking—increasingly more freedom of choice; being increasingly more open, more dynamic, complex, ready-to-change, pluralistic, and nondeterministic. The notions of control, coerciveness, and ownership by a few are replaced by the notions of motivation and commitment of—and ownership by—the many; by people in the system. These three notional characteristics enable HAS's to be much more flexible and dynamic (than the rigidly controlled and deterministic types), require less tight control and coupling, and extend more autonomy to the components and people in the system. (The "wellness-serving system," about which I speculated earlier, should have these characteristics.) These systems are not less integrated and not less systemic, just the opposite. They are more so by the shared intent, purpose, and commitment of people in the system. These characteristics are the guarantees of true integration; they provide the SYNERGIC QUALITY by which components take on the characteristics of the system and these are the reasons why people identify with the system. Furthermore, it is from these characteristics and qualities that the WHOLENESS of the system emerges.

There is an important implication of wholeness or the lack of it. Wholeness means that although we can think of a system as one which evolved from the synthesis/integration of its parts, once the system attains that synthesized quality of wholeness, it becomes indivisible. Division uncouples the system. The independent excellence of parts does not guarantee the excellence of the whole. The most profitable control system that guarantees the excellence of the parts does NOT exclude the bankruptcy of the whole. (See Note 6.) If a division occurs that in the long run affects the integration that makes the system work, then the adequacy or even the excellence of any given part is irrelevant to the survival of the system. The recurring problem of systems inquiry in human activity systems is the issue: How do we separate (mark as an entity) a particular viable system from the rest of the universe without committing an annihilating division? Our answer to this question was and is to be found in the coevolution of HAS's with their environment.

ACTIVITY # 27

Focus the functions/structure systems lens on the components of your selected Educational Activity System (EAS), their structure (their pattern of relationship), and their relationship to the functions you have earlier identified. Describe whatever you can see in your existing system by looking through this lens. Then, considering the functions you identified for your EAS as "should be," define components that can best carry out these functions, and select the structural arrangement that would be the most desirable. Introduce your findings into your notebook.

SUMMARY OF THE FUNCTIONS/STRUCTURE GENERAL MODEL

Human Activity Systems are created by people in response to their intent and shared purposes as well as the expectations and requirements that emerge from their environment. The purposes that are formulated from these two sources are the bases upon which functions are identified (that are appropriate to attain purposes) and components are selected that have the potential and have the attributes that qualify them to carry out the identified functions. Components are integrated into what becomes the HAS by establishing patterns of relations and defining interdependence among them. This emerging pattern is the STRUCTURE of the HAS. Components that serve a specific purpose are organized and integrated into subsystems. Through progressive integration of components and subsystems the HAS becomes ever more systemic, indivisible, and whole. To achieve true wholeness is a salient aim of HAS's.

The functions/structure model gives us a good image of what a HAS IS at a given moment. But it is far from being able to give us a complete picture of a HAS. It cannot tell us what the system DOES over time. This picture is developed in Chapter Four. This picture will focus on the dimension of TIME. Before we develop this picture in Chapter Four, we portray the functions/structure model of EAS's.

SECTION TWO:

YOUR FUNCTIONS/STRUCTURE MODEL

In SECTION ONE of this chapter, I presented a general functions/structure model of human activity systems. You are now asked to transform my general model into a functions/structure model of your selected educational activity system (EAS), by applying the general concepts and principles presented in the model in the context of your selected EAS. The purpose of this activity is NOT to learn certain systems terms, but to APPLY what you have learned in the preceding text in the real-life context of your selected system as YOU SEE IT. Only through such applications will those concepts/principles COME TO LIFE, as you make them your own. The first attempt to develop your model may be a brief one. You will require a more in-depth systems view as you work with the functions/structure lens in the next three sections. Introduce your description in your notebook.

SECTION THREE:

A FUNCTIONS/STRUCTURE MODEL OF EDUCATIONAL ACTIVITY SYSTEMS (EAS's)

In the section above, you worked with a set of concepts and principles—organized into a general functions/structure model—and transformed them into the context of your own system. Thus, you formulated a functions/structure model of a particular EAS of your choice. In this section, you will work with my formulation of a functions/structure characterization of educational activity systems (EAS's) and will use my characterization in order to develop a possibly revised and extended systems description of your own. My description is a generic description of the functions/structure model of EAS's, it was NOT developed in a specific functional context. It elaborates the systems concepts and principles you have worked with in the two previous sections and introduces some additional concepts and principles that are pertinent to EAS's. Your description—unlike mine—will be developed in the functional context of a specific EAS. As you work with the text that follows, make notes that will help you to revise/extend your characterization of your selected EAS in Section Four. Activities in this section will help you to apply some of the systems ideas in your selected context. Integrate the findings that emerge from your activity work into the description (in SECTION FOUR) of your selected system. A general functions/structure model of EAS's follows next.

A GENERAL FUNCTIONS/STRUCTURE MODEL OF EDUCATIONAL ACTIVITY SYSTEMS is developed in this section by: (1) defining (or creating) the IMAGE of an EAS, (2) formulating a SYSTEMS DEFINITION (purpose and systems specification), (3) identifying the FUNCTIONS that are carried out in order to attain the purpose, (4) designating the COMPONENTS that carry out functions, and (5) defining the STRUCTURE: the relational arrangements of components. These five are bound together in systemic relationship and interaction and jointly constitute the functions/structure model of EAS's.

As you work with the concepts and principles that portray a general functions/structure model of EAS's, ask the questions: How do the statements in the text apply to the specific EAS you have selected? How can you interpret my generic statements and transform them in order to reflect and explain the functions/structure characteristics of your selected system? Develop your description in a way that will be meaningful and useful to you and to others in your selected system.

DEFINING THE IMAGE OF EAS's

Guided by images, EAS's seek to fulfill their purposes. As Kenneth Boulding said (Note 7), "The image not only makes society, society continuously remakes the image." A new societal image has emerged in the course of the last four decades, affecting all aspects of our lives. Our educational system is an exception: its image is still grounded in the image of the industrial society of the 19th century. (See discussion on this in Chapter One and see Note 8.) The continued use of such an outdated image in our EAS's has opened up a developmental gap between education and the society and has created the current educational crisis. We are in search of a new image that can guide the transformation of education and lead us into the 21st century. There are two dynamics that can help us to create the image. One is the educational interpretation of the new societal image and the other is the development of an awareness of the unworkability of the current educational image, which is still based on industrial machine age thinking and practice.

The creation of an educational image cannot—and should not—be the prerogative of a chosen few. It is the collective responsibility of people and social groups in each and every community and of those who are in the EAS. This collective responsibility is carried out by exploring two sources for the creation of an image. One source is the society, the other people in the system. Viewing the society we consider: (1) the educational implications of emerged societal characteristics, the societal relevance of education, the learning content and the way we offer it, the relationship of education to the society, and—consequently—the designation of its societal functions; and (2) the educational expectations of the systemic environment and the community. The second source is people in the system and their expectations of: (1) what education should be about, (2) what contributions it should make, (3) how it should serve learners and work with other systems in the community, and (4) how it can express their values and ideas about the collective life of the educational activity system. In Section One of this chapter, I offered a speculative image of a "wellness system." Inasmuch as it was envisioned as a social service system, you might find that it might have similarity with EAS's. The image example that follows was created with the use of a framework. (I described this framework and its use recently, referenced in Note 9.) The image—presented below—has been adopted from the same source. The following image example has seven markers:

(1) Educational activity systems should be built around the learning experience level; arrangements should be made in the environment of the learner by which to enable the full realization of his/her potential as an individual and as a participating and productive member of the society.

(2) Integrate all arrangements for learning and human development into a community-based and community-wide comprehensive system that nurtures and promotes individual, social, and community development.

(3) The content of learning should be relevant to the emerged societal characteristics and should embrace all domains of the human existential experience, including the sociocultural, ethical, moral, physical/mental/spiritual wellness, economic, political, scientific/technological, and the aesthetic.

(4) A wide range of modes of learning: self-directed, other-directed, individually supported group learning, cooperative team

learning, learning facilitated by technology, and social and organizational learning.

(5) Resources and arrangements for lifelong and continuous learning and human development of all members of the community, with the aim of building a learning society.

(6) Large reservoir of resources, opportunities, and situations available in all systems and domains of the community to support learning and human development.

(7) Education should reflect as well as shape the society through coevolutionary interaction as a future-creating, innovative, and open system that is capable of continuous learning and development.

The seven markers represent my "wish image." I wish to design systems that would bring that image to life. Such an image could become the genesis of formulating the core definition of educational activity systems.

ACTIVITY # 28

You have two tasks. First, using the seven markers of the image introduced above, (re)construct an image of the EAS you selected. It is most likely that your image will be very different from what is described above. Then, in view of the image you described earlier, and considering the seven image markers above, revise—if you wish—that image, and describe your findings in your notebook.

A general assessment of existing educational activity systems leads me to make an attempt to construct a "prevailing image" of our currently operating EAS's. I will attempt to do this by using the seven markers in the example of my "wish image" and contrast it with the "generic image" of existing EAS's as I see it. In describing the image, I follow the numbering of the image markers in the example above. A speculative image of existing EAS's might include the following markers:

(1) Education is now organized around the instructional level: arrangements are made that enable teachers to present subject matter to students.

(2) The education we provide is separated from other social service and human development functions.

(3) Education focuses on the basics and preparation for citizenship and employment.

(4) Teacher-class interaction is the primary means of providing education.

(5) We now provide education to individuals during their "schooling years."

(6) Schools are autonomous agencies, separated from other social service and community systems.

(7) Schools try to make limited adjustments to cope with societal changes and operate as rather closed systems.

You might look at the seven items above and compare them with your characterization of the image of your selected EAS. Whatever image is defined and is constructed from exploring an existing system, it becomes the genesis for formulating the core definition of the system.

CORE DEFINITIONS OF EDUCATIONAL ACTIVITY SYSTEMS (EAS's)

A core definition has two components: (1) a STATEMENT OF PURPOSE(s) and (2) SYSTEMS SPECIFICATIONS that describe the characteristics that an educational activity system should have in order to attain its purpose(s). The core definition should be formulated in such detail that it can become the basis for defining the FUNCTIONS that the system should carry out in order to attend to the core definition.

PURPOSES OF EAS's

A statement of purposes of an EAS interprets the image in more detail. There are purposes of EAS's that are inherent in the fact that EAS's are human activity systems. These "generic purposes" were reviewed in SECTION ONE and they are examples of how an educational community might define such generic purposes of its EAS. Then, there are purposes that are specific to EAS's, those which address educational and human development societal functions. These two types are discussed in turn.

GENERIC PURPOSES discussed here interpret the generic purposes of HAS's discussed in Section One. (The four pursuits and the seven dimensions are synthesized here. These purposes include: (1) the acquisition of information and knowledge needed to develop increasingly more effective means to conduct the affairs of the EAS; (2) the acquisition of resources required for the support of the life and operations of the EAS (for its members individually and for the system collectively); (3) the articulation, establishment, and realization of the ethical and moral beliefs and responsibilities of the EAS (by its members individually and by the system collectively); (4) the nurturing of the physical/mental/spiritual well-being of members of the EAS and the collective of the system; (5) the exposition and realization of aesthetic qualities in the life of the EAS, and the attainment of the highest possible inner quality of life of individual members and collectively of the system; (6) the establishment of systemic governance and guidance that ensure social and economic justice within the EAS. (A characteristic of systemic governance is explained below.) The generic purposes introduced above are to be formulated and integrated into a system of interrelated and interdependent purposes (which is the first mark of systemic governance). Such formulation is also the first stage of formulating a core definition of an EAS. I must say that I have yet to see a statement of educational purposes that would address all the above (and possibly more) and have yet to see a statement of purposes which is formulated as a SYSTEM of PURPOSES.

SPECIFIC PURPOSES OF an EAS focus on what the EAS is doing for: (1) the larger society, (2) the systemic environment and the community, (3) other systems in its systemic environment, (4) its clients: learners in the community, (5) its stakeholders, (6) people who are in the system and who serve it, and, finally, (7) how it wants to see itself as a system. The examples which follow are adapted from my earlier work (Note 10). An educational activity system proposes to:

* Be a societal institution that has a collective global vision of society as a whole, and which makes a purposeful contribution toward human betterment.

* Provide programs, arrangements, and resources by which individuals and social groups in the community can attain their fullest potential, enrich their inner quality of life and the quality of their environment, and learn to direct their own lives and the lives of the systems to which they belong.

* Develop the community as a learning society; a society in which learning, fulfillment, and attaining high human qualities are collective aspirations to live by.

* Create a coordinated inter-organizational linkage of all social and human service systems in the community in order to offer integrated arrangements and resources for learning and human development; arrangements that are coherent, easy to use, and continuous.

* Involve all those in the community who have a "stake" in

education and human development in a participative mode in the life and guidance of the EAS.

* Ensure a high quality of working life to its members, encourage and reward cooperation among individuals and groups, and facilitate and reward personal and professional development.

* Become a self-directive and self-organizing system that can learn as an organization, be able to give directions to its continuing development through design, and manage itself by the widest possible participation of its clients and members.

The purposes that reflect the specific aspirations of the EAS are to be formulated in a system in order to understand and articulate their relationships and interdependence. The generic and specific purposes constitute the first major part of formulating a core definition of an educational activity system. Next is an opportunity for you to work with purposes.

ACTIVITY # 29

You have already formulated both generic and specific purposes for your specific EAS. Your task is now to revisit those and, in view of my statement of purposes, possibly reformulate your statement if you so choose. Enter your statements in your notebook.

SPECIFICATIONS OF AN EDUCATIONAL ACTIVITY SYSTEM

The second part of formulating a core definition of an EAS is to define the specifications (characteristics) of the EAS in line with the stated purposes. The cluster of questions below was adapted from the same source as the examples for purposes (Note 9), and includes the following:

* Who are the clients of the EAS? What educational and human development services are offered to them? What characteristics do these services have? Where, when, and how are these services provided?

* Who "owns" the EAS? How is ownership distributed? What rights and responsibilities do owners have?

* What is the EAS's responsibility to its clients, its members, its community, to other systems, and to the larger society? How are these responsibilities handled?

* How is the EAS related to the various levels of government and how are these responsibilities handled? What are the responsibilites of various levels of government to the system? How are those responsibilities handled?

* What is the relationship of the EAS to the community in general, to community organizations, to the private sector, and to other relevant systems?

* What are the environmental constraints that the EAS has to consider? How do these impact on the definition of the system? How do these potentially affect the life and functions of the EAS?

* What is the "world view" (an image of the world) that is collectively shared by members of the EAS and which guides the thinking and action of members individually and collectively?

The sets of questions above invite specific answers that you can develop as you work in the context of a specific system.

ACTIVITY # 30

Answer the specific questions above in view of the current status of your selected EAS. Enter the findings in your notebook.

FUNCTIONS OF EDUCATIONAL ACTIVITY SYSTEMS (EAS's)

An EAS is established in order to attain purposes. Purposes are attained by carrying out functions. Purposes and functions are the primary markers of an EAS and are the bases upon which to select the components of the EAS that have the capability to carry out the identified functions. The relational (systemic) arrangement of functions provides us with the first system model of an EAS. This model is built on several levels of resolution. At the lowest level of resolution are the primary functions of the EAS, arranged in a system of interacting functions. Each primary function has a set of sub-functions that portray a higher level of resolution. Each of these sub-functions has its own component functions arranged again as a system of component functions; representing—again—an even higher level of resolution. We can identify two kinds of functions; functions that are generic to all human activity systems, and those that are specific to EAS's. In the text below I discuss both kinds.

GENERIC FUNCTIONS OF EAS's

The exploration of generic functions of EAS's helps us now to realize how a systems view of EAS's develops and becomes gradually elaborated. We worked with certain generic systems functions in SECTION ONE. These were functions that are generic to all kinds of systems, such as interacting, integrating, providing input and output, accommodating, and adjusting. These functions operate through time; thus we shall discuss them in some detail in Chapter Four. Our exploration of generic purposes of human activity systems has become the source of identifying how these generic purposes are manifested in EAS's. From these we can define now another large set of functions. Questions that guide the identification of these second kinds of functions would address the six domains of generic purposes of EAS's described earlier. We might ask, what functions have to be carried out in order to:

* Acquire information and knowledge needed to develop increasingly more effective means to operate the EAS?
* Acquire resources required to support the life of the EAS?
* Establish and realize the ethical and moral beliefs and responsibilities of the EAS?
* Nurture the physical/mental/spiritual well-being of members of the EAS and the collective of the system?
* Realize aesthetic qualities of the EAS and qualities of the inner life of members of the EAS?
* Govern and guide the EAS so that we can ensure social and economic justice in the EAS and we can attain the purposes of the EAS with the broadest possible participation of people in the system.

ACTIVITY # 31

In the purpose section, you worked with an activity that explored the generic purposes of your selected EAS. Given findings of your work, and the questions stated above, select/identify functions that respond to the questions above. Enter your findings into your notebook.

SPECIFIC FUNCTIONS OF EAS's

Functions that are specific and unique to an EAS are derived from an understanding of the purposes that are specific to the EAS.

(Earlier, I presented an example of a set of functions that is specific to a "community-based wellness system," and in an activity you formulated a set of specific functions relevant to your selected EAS.) Given the purposes of EAS's, as I described in this chapter, I make an attempt here to identify purposes that EAS's might carry out that are specific to their educational responsibilities. These might include the following:

A. Maintain continuous and intensive interaction with the societal environment in order to explore the education implications of emerging characteristics of the society and interpret these implications for creating/re-creating the image of the EAS.

B. Define on a continuous basis the purpose of the EAS and the desired learning and human development outcomes.

C. Define EAS-relevant systems (in the community and the larger environment) and identify the resources, arrangements, and situations these systems can offer for learning and human development.

D. Establish and maintain linkage and interorganizational coordinated arrangements with systems identified as relevant and ensure the acquisition and use of their identified learning and human development resources, arrangements, and situations.

E. Provide easy and quick access to individuals, groups, and the community in general to programs, resources, and arrangements that provide for learning and human development.

F. Use educational and human development resources, arrangements, and situations, and monitor and guide their use to ensure changes/adjustments if indicated.

G. Develop and maintain programs and arrangements for ensuring a high quality of working life for those who are in the system.

H. Monitor, guide, and manage all functions described above to ensure continuous organizational learning as well as the continuous development and renewal of the EAS.

Figure 3.3 provides an image of the systemic arrangement of the primary functions of the EAS.

Each of the primary functions shown in Figure 3.3 has a set of subfunctions that is developed at a higher level of resolution. In turn, these subfunctions have their own component functions.

FIGURE 3.3 A MAP OF PRIMARY FUNCTIONS

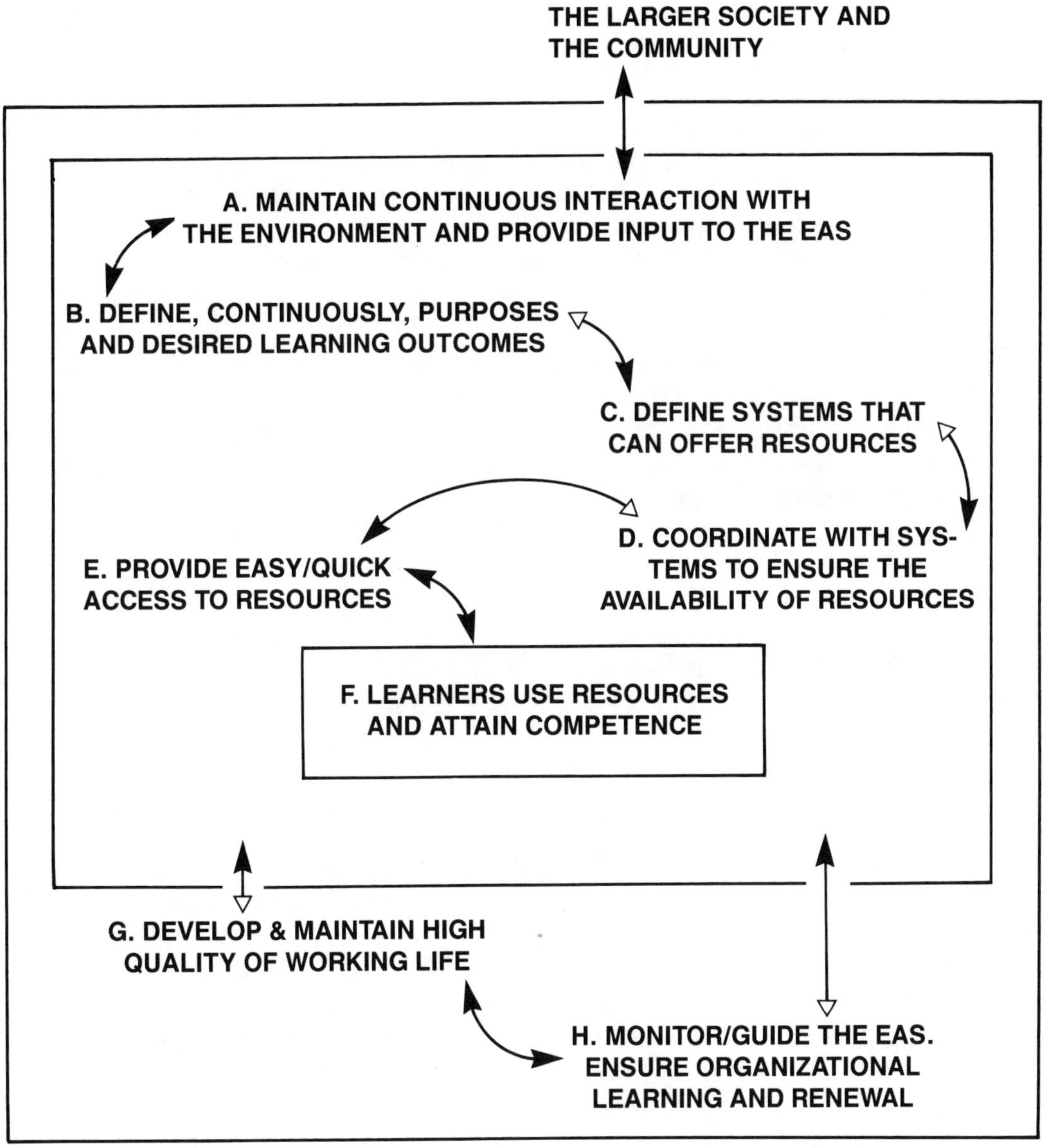

Note the CENTRAL position of learners in this map, according to the previously stated guiding principle of organizing the system around the learning experience level.

ACTIVITY # 32

You have already identified a set of specific functions for your selected EAS in an earlier activity. Your task now is to rethink your set in view of the functions I described above, and if you deem it useful, revise your set of functions. Introduce your findings in your notebook.

One way to test and demonstrate a systemic view and description of an EAS is to explore and explain the relationship and interdependence of IMAGE, PURPOSE, and FUNCTIONS. Up to this point we followed an unfolding approach. At this point a "foldback" approach will guide us in answering the following questions: Do the functions as stated attend to all the purposes we described? If not: What additional functions are to be identified? Do the purposes as stated reflect the image? If not: What purpose is missing? Does the image reflect the educational implications of emerged and emerging characteristics of the society, its educational expectations, and the aspirations, values/ideas of people in the EAS? These questions demonstrate well the applications of a systems view to education and the systemic quality of EAS's if viewed in the way described here.

COMPONENTS OF EDUCATIONAL ACTIVITY SYSTEMS

Components of an EAS are selected and employed on the basis of their potential and ability to carry out the functions of the EAS that are required to attain the purposes of the system. We can clearly and explicitly see the same systemic principle in operation which I explained above. In an unfolding sense: PURPOSES determine FUNCTIONS in which an EAS has to engage and FUNCTIONS determine the CAPABILITIES that COMPONENTS should have. Another significant application of the systems view is the arrangement of each of the identified major markers of an EAS (image, purpose, functions, components) in a systemic relationship. In Figure 3.2, I demonstrated the systemic arrangement of educational functions. COMPONENTS are connected in patterned relationships that form the EAS explicitly and visibly. We call this patterned relationship the STRUCTURE of the EAS. The structure is formulated by the relationships and connections of the components to each other and it comes to "life" by their interactions as they attend to the functions. It is relationships and interactions that fuse the components of an

EAS into a system. It is what emerges from these relationships and interactions that makes the EAS MORE than the SUM of its COMPONENTS.

Interactions among the components of an EAS can be rather static when the EAS is the highly controlled, deterministic type. These types of EAS's tend to be closed systems and are the least sensitive to environmental changes; in fact they are often protected from them. These types are controlled from the top down and organized in well-defined hierarchical levels as a coercive, tightly coupled kind of organization. In most EAS's, such structured top-down hierarchy is explicit. These systems are organized at such systems levels as GOVERNANCE, SCHOOL ADMINISTRATION, and INSTRUCTION. The learning experience level does NOT exist as an authentic system level on its own. (For a discussion of this issue see Note 11.) Public education systems in the USA are organized around the administrative level, which is the primary systems level. Policy guidance and resource input are received from the governance level (school board), based on which the school administration makes decisions and provides directives to the instructional level: defining and regulating programs, instructional outcomes, standards, materials, etc. The instructional level implements directives coming from the administration and provides instruction to students.

On the other hand, in the (very) few EAS's that are the more open, heuristic, and purpose-seeking type, the relationship and interaction among components are dynamic. The attributes of the components and the components themselves will change through time in response to changing functions and purposes that come about from the changes in the environment or changes in the perspectives, aspirations, and ideas of people in the EAS. In these systems the notions of top-down, tight control, and coercion and ownership by a few would be replaced by the notions of broadly distributed participative management, motivation (rather than control), collective commitment, and ownership by people in the system. These EAS's would extend more autonomy to their components and people in the system.

ACTIVITY # 33

In an earlier activity you already grappled with the application of the functions/structure lens. You now have two tasks. First, in view of the text above and the reading referred to in Note 12, portray the structure of your selected EAS as it exists now. Second, create the picture of the structure of your selected EAS the way you wish it would be. Enter your findings in your notebook.

In Figure 3.4, I map out a structure of my imaginary EAS. The presentation of the structure is based on the educational functions I identified in Figure 3.2. It is a functions-based structure. As you

FIGURE 3.4 A MAP OF STRUCTURAL ARRANGEMENTS

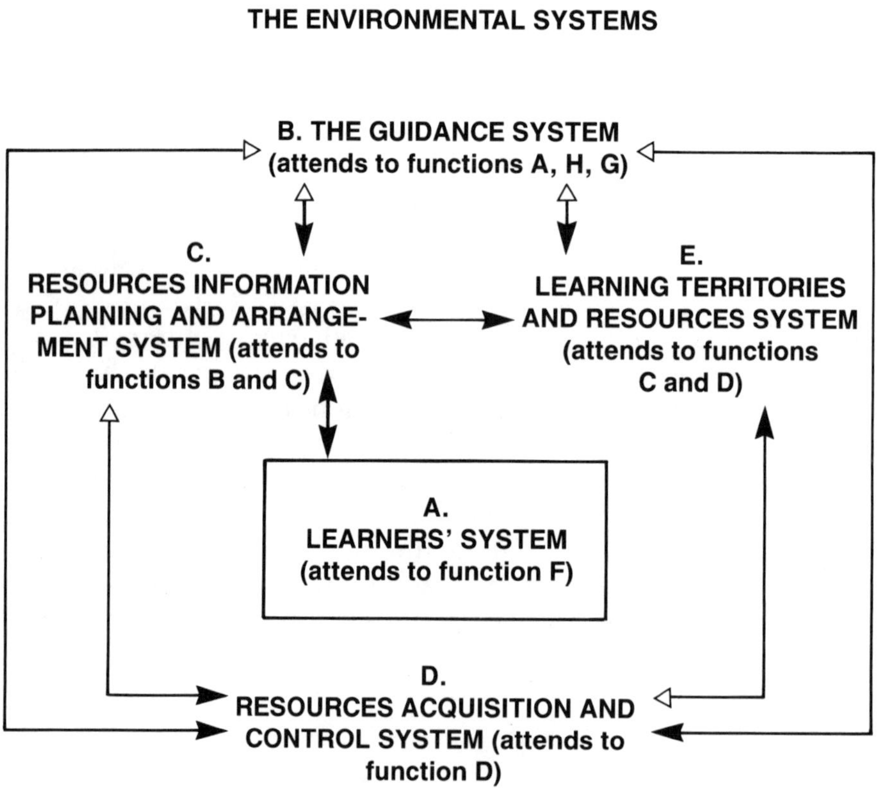

Functions A–H are listed on page 86.

can see from the map, this structural arrangement is very different from the current structure of EAS's. In its center is the learning experience system, and the whole EAS is built around it and responds to it.

SUMMARY OF THE FUNCTIONS/STRUCTURE MODEL OF EAS's

Educational Activity Systems are created by people in response to educational requirements of the society and the intent and shared expectations of people in the system. The image and the purposes are formulated from these two sources and are the bases upon which educational functions are identified and components selected that have the potential to carry out the functions. The systemic/interactive arrangement of the components constitutes the structure of the EAS. The functions/structure model gives us a good picture of what an EAS IS at a given moment of time but it does not show what it DOES through time. It remains for the process model to complete the development of the systems view of education.

SECTION FOUR:

THE RE-VISIONED FUNCTIONS/STRUCTURE MODEL OF YOUR EAS

In Section Two you developed the first representation of the functions/structure model of your selected EAS. Your task now is to re-vision/re-conceptualize that model based on the text presented in Section Three and the activities you developed while working in that section. The challenge is not just to elaborate the earlier version of your functions/structure model, but to step back from your description (in Section Two), consider my general functions/ structure model, and develop your revised description. The activities you completed in the course of working with Section Three have helped you to get some new insights that will assist you with your description. Questions surely have arisen as you worked with my text. Try to answer those on your own, based on your work in the larger context of the first three chapters. If questions are still left unanswered, it means that you have to go on in developing your systems view. In the next section we continue our journey toward capturing that view.

SECTION FIVE:

ASSESSMENT OF SELF, THE MODELLED SYSTEM, AND THE GENERAL MODEL

The purpose of working with the functions/structure model in the previous sections of this chapter was to foster the development of a ''still-picture or snapshot'' view of EAS's. In this closing section of the chapter, I introduce some perspectives that enable you to assess your progress and assess the adequacy and usefulness of the model itself.

SELF-REFLECTIVE ASSESSMENT

In the four sections above we jointly embarked on a journey to develop a functions/structure systems lens of EAS's, internalize it in our thinking, and bring it into life in our systems. It is appropriate now to reflect upon the question: Is there any disposition I may have that hinders me from acquiring the systems view? This is an important question to raise because the development of a systems view very often requires us to change our mind sets, and the way we view ourselves, our environments, and the systems in which we are involved. These dispositions, the old mindset, and the customary ways of viewing the world will make it difficult for us to acquire the systems view. They constitute a barrier. The recognition and understanding of such a barrier become important conditions for mastering the systems view. I will now speculate about some dispositions that create these barriers. As I describe these, think about your own disposition.

The most obvious disposition that hinders the development of a functions/structure systemic perspective is the celebration of the dominance and sanctity of structure. Usually people define an organization by displaying its organizational chart as lines drawn among boxes. The stability of the structure gives us a feeling of safety and permanence. This disposition reminds me of a statement made by the superintendent of a large school district: "My grandmother was a teacher and she said that when visiting her old school she found that its practices were the same as they were fifty years ago."

Another disposition is the tendency to stick to the hierarchical structuring of EAS's. This disposition makes it difficult for us to view a nonhierarchical, horizontally distributed structure (pictured in Figure 3.4) in which components are arranged in nonhierarchical fashion based on their function in the system. From a structure-focused and hierarchically inclined disposition there flows the comfort of: (1) reliance on decisions of higher authorities, (2) the protection of hierarchical boundaries and well-defined routines, (3) doing things our usual ways, in the context of our familiar surroundings, and (4) having clearly bounded responsibilities of the well-defined roles we carry out.

A typical disposition is to consider the whole as being the sum of invariable parts. According to this conception, the system can be identified by adding up its parts. This disposition has been the basis of the "tinkering with parts" approach of recent educational improvement efforts. We have hoped that improving the efficiency of certain problem-laden parts can mitigate the bankruptcy of the system. We have to overcome the disposition of dealing with single components. Considering a part out of the context of the total system, dealing with one thing at a time, isolating variables, and dividing up the system are some of the ways of violating the wholeness of the system. Acquiring a systems view of EAS's, on the other hand, enables us to handle all parts simultaneously, work with a great number of variables, and account for them not because of what they are in isolation, but because of what they are by their integration into the system: BECAUSE OF WHAT THEY DO JOINTLY.

You should reflect upon these dispositions and others that you might have and ask the questions: What can I do to overcome well-rehearsed dispositions that hinder my acquisition of a functions/structure based systems view? Probably, I should give up those comforts that protect me from change. I should be willing to open up myself to the new, to the unknown, and be willing to capture a vision of a functions-based educational activity system.

ACTIVITY # 34

This activity aims at helping you to clarify in your own mind if you indeed have some dispositions that hinder you from embracing the functions/structure systemic view we jointly developed in the previous four sections. It is not easy to do this. Go through your notes and find instances when in working with various systems notions you felt ill-at-ease about certain propositions I have made about the systems view. Such feelings might give you a clue about dispositions that are counter to the systems view. Enter your findings into your notebook.

THE ASSESSMENT OF THE MODEL OF YOUR EAS

In the preceding sections you worked with concepts and principles that constitute a general functions/structure systems model and transformed these into building a model of your selected EAS. Now you are asked to work with a set of questions that will probe the functions/structure systemic adequacy of your selected EAS. The questions below offer a summary assessment of your EAS from the perspective of a functions/structure systems view. Respond to each question by introducing your comments in your notebook.

1. In viewing the existing state of your selected EAS: What evidence do you have that there was a purpose-functions-component sequence followed in the conceptualization/organization of the system?
2. Are the purposes and functions of the system clearly stated? What evidence do you have that the functions are derived from the statement of purposes? Do they respond to all the purposes?
3. Are all identifiable functions purpose-serving? Which functions do not serve purposes? Are there some "missing" functions, the presence of which would enhance the attainment of purposes? What functions are missing?
4. Is there evidence of criteria for the function-based selection of components? Are alternatives considered in selecting components? Are there components that do not serve functions? Are there some "missing" components? (Meaning that not all functions are served by designated components.)

5. What kind of relationship exists between components? Static? Dynamic? Are the relationships hierarchical or rigidly defined? Is there any evidence of flexibility and change-readiness in the structure of the system?
6. Is there evidence of a tendency toward the segregation or integration and independence or interdependence of components?
7. What evidence exists that speaks for the wholeness of the system? Or the lack of it?

ACTIVITY # 35

Using the notes you have taken in exploring the questions above, develop a summary description of your assessment of the overall functions/structure adequacy of your EAS.

ASSESSING THE MODEL

In this closing part of the chapter you have an opportunity to make an assessment of the functions/structure systems model. The model can be tested by asking some questions, such as: Have you found that the system concepts and principles described and applied in this chapter: (1) Were useful to you in understanding and describing an EAS? (2) Have explanatory power in the context of an operating EAS? (3) Have helped you to gain new insights into the true nature of an EAS?

What other questions would you ask that would test the adequacy of the model? You are encouraged to explore questions of your own. Most significantly, tell: What have been truly important understandings/revelations/insights that you have gained by working with this chapter? Introduce your answers into your notebook.

You might use the findings you have generated in Section Five for the purpose of revisiting the description of your system (Section Four). Such revisiting could lead to a revision of the description of your EAS.

REFLECTIONS

We have reached another milestone in our journey to acquire a systems view. We have developed a functions/structure image of human activity systems and transformed that image in characterizing a functions/structure model of educational activity systems. We now continue our journey as we explore a process/behavioral model of human activity systems and apply it in the context of educational activity systems.

NOTES

(1) Russel Ackoff (1981) in: *Creating the Corporate Future*. New York: John Wiley, makes a distinction between growth and development and uses the four markers of the concept of development that ancient Greek philosophers identified.

(2) Bela H. Banathy (1988, No. 4). "The Design of Evolutionary Guidance Systems." *Systems Research*.

(3) Geoffrey Vickers (1983) in: *Human Systems Are Different*. London: Harper & Row, defined the maintenance of human relationships as the most significant function of human activity systems.

(4) A detailed differentiation between hard and soft systems thinking and practice is provided by Peter Checkland (1981) in: *Systems Thinking, Systems Practice*, John Wiley, New York.

(5) James Miller (1978) in: *Living Systems Theory*. New York: McGraw-Hill, introduces an organismic characterization of all living systems, including social systems.

(6) Stafford Beer (1976) in: *Platform for Change*. New York: John Wiley, develops the idea that the optimization of a component of a system does not prevent the bankruptcy of the system as a whole.

(7) The notion of image and its significance in social systems are developed in Kenneth E. Boulding's book: *The Image* (1956). The University of Michigan Press, Ann Arbor.

(8) For a detailed characterization of the outdatedness of the current image of education, see Chapter One in my book *Systems Design of Education* (1991). Educational Technology Publications, Englewood Cliffs, NJ.

(9) A possible image of an EAS was presented in Chapter Seven of the source quoted in (8).

(10) The purposes described in the text are adopted from the source quoted in (8).

(11) The primacy of systems levels is explored in Bela H. Banathy, "Instructional Systems Design." In Robert Gagné (Ed.), *Instructional Technology: Foundations* (1987). Lawrence Erlbaum Associates, Hillsdale, NJ.

(12) See the system of functions in Chapter Ten, quoted in (8) above.

CHAPTER FOUR

The Process Lens: The Motion-Picture Model

In this chapter, our journey toward the development of a systems view of educational activity systems reaches an important milestone as we jointly develop the third model: the process model of educational activity systems (EAS's). This chapter, like the previous chapters, leads us through five "spirals," presented in five sections. This type of exposition allows us to gain an increasingly broader and deeper understanding of the systems view as it applies to human and educational activity systems.

In SECTION ONE, from sets of general systems concepts and principles, I construct a process model that is generic to human activity systems. In SECTION TWO, you are asked to transform these concepts and principles into your selected EAS and to build a process model of educational activity of your own. In SECTION THREE, I use the process lens to develop a motion-picture or process model that is generic to educational activity systems. This model—unlike the one you developed in Section Two—does not stipulate any specific functional context. Furthermore, in this section, I expand the scope of the use of the process lens beyond that which I have done in Section One. In SECTION FOUR, your turn comes as you explore my generic characterization of EAS's, and using what you have constructed in Section Two, you will create a synthesis of your model and my generic model of EAS's. In SECTION FIVE, I present three lines of inquiry that probe into: (1) dispositions that might hinder the development of a systems view, (2) the adequacy of your EAS from the perspectives of the process model, and (3) the systems process model's adequacy to explain the ongoing life of human activity systems. Figure 4.1 depicts the five sections of this chapter.

You can see from the above description that your involvement in the program described above continues to guide you in your journey on the road to developing a systems view of educational activity systems. It is expected that as the result of working with the five sections and the activities, you will: (1) gain new insights

FIGURE 4.1 THE DEVELOPMENT OF A PROCESS VIEW OF EDUCATIONAL ACTIVITY SYSTEMS

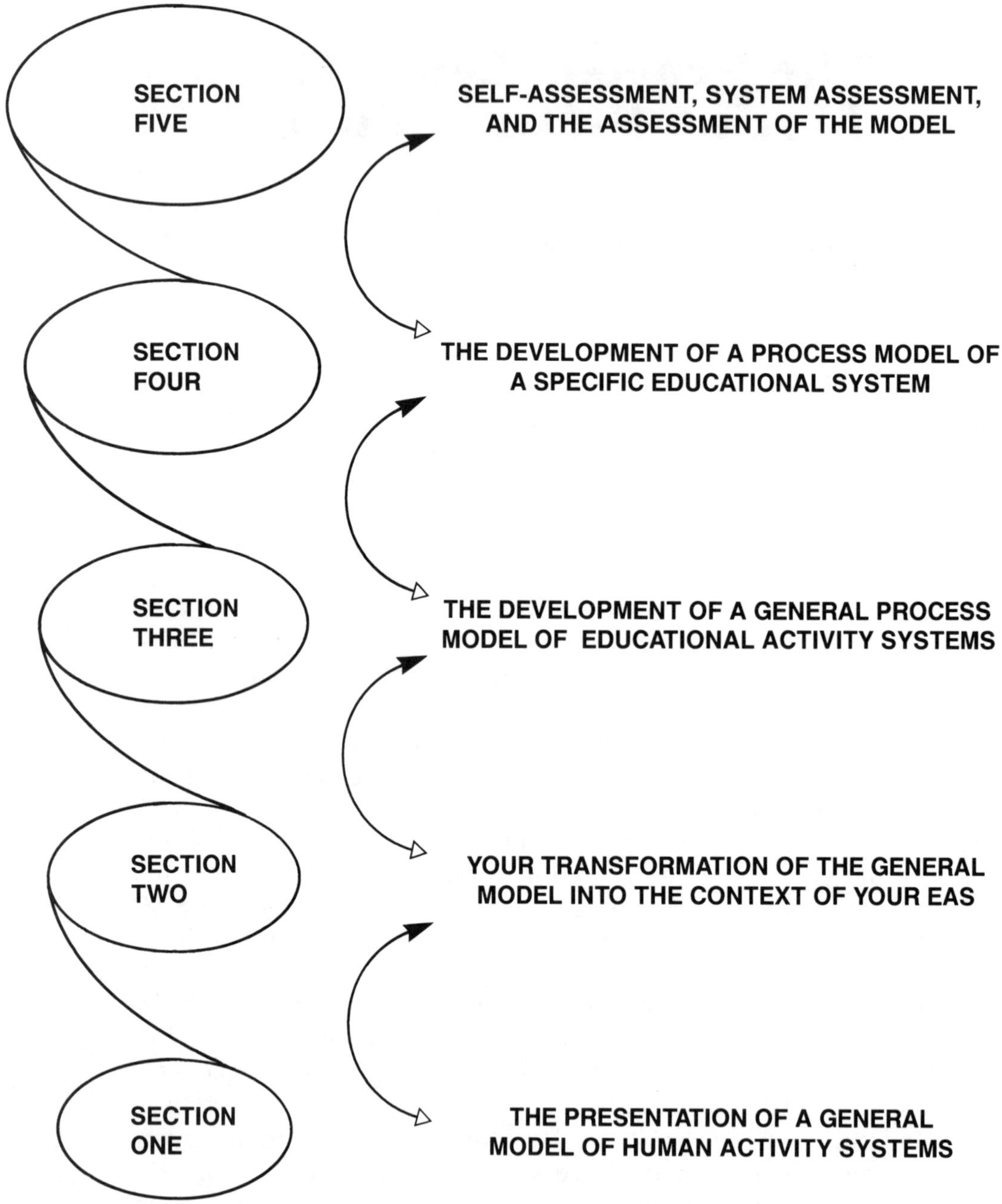

into the process characteristics of EAS's, and (2) apply the insights you gain in evaluating and reconceptualizing educational activity systems.

In advancing from one section to the other you will work with sets of concepts and principles that characterize systems processes and will apply those to your selected educational activity system in contexts that are meaningful and useful to you. The description of the process model is substantially longer than that of the earlier models. Therefore, as you read the text, make notes that will help you in making your transformation.

SECTION ONE:

A GENERAL PROCESS MODEL OF HUMAN ACTIVITY SYSTEMS

The systems-environment model introduced concepts and principles relevant to human and educational activity systems in their environmental CONTEXTS, and explained systems-environmental relationships. The still-picture or functions/structure model characterized the STATIC state of systems and showed what a system IS at a given moment in time. It did not show us HOW the system does whatever it is all about. Human and educational activity systems are not static, they are alive and cannot be fully understood from an examination of spatial models only. The two earlier models presented us the LANDSCAPE of systems life but not the DRAMA of life. They could not exhibit the ongoing, unfolding system behavior. To complete our understanding of systems, we have to examine their behavior through time and observe the changes that take place in their entities and in the behavior of these entities. Thus, in this section, I use the process lens and introduce a process view and model of HAS's, and add a temporal dimension to the already developed spatial and contextual dimensions.

Developing a process view of HAS's in general, and specifically of educational activity systems, will not be easy. As a rule, we are not used to thinking in process terms. As I already mentioned, we have a predisposition to think in terms of structures and input and output of HAS's. The inquiry is framed like this: given certain input (purpose, information, and resources), what output is produced? Between the input and output there is that "black box": the organization, the "structure" that is responsible for producing the output. Using only the structure lens, what happens between the input and output remains a mystery. We know what is produced, but we can only speculate about why. The process lens, process thinking, will open up the black box and will make it a transparent "glass box."

The still-picture displays an image at a given moment of existence. A motion-picture projects images through time, revealing movement, action, and behavior. The still-picture model has helped us to describe what the system IS. The motion-picture model reveals HOW the system operates. This section describes: (1) an overview of systems operations, (2) input processing, (3) transformation, (4) output processing, and (5) system guidance.

AN OVERVIEW OF SYSTEMS PROCESSES

From the systems-environment and the functions/structure models we have learned that the systems we are concerned with are rather open systems; they change and coevolve with their environment and are defined by both the environment and by people in the system. These systems turn inputs—coming from the environment—into specified outputs. And the system operates in a way to ensure this process and—if indicated—either: (1) makes adjustments and corrects for differences between the actual and desired output, or (2) changes the system itself. With this broad characterization in mind, we can say that the processes of the system must include those that process input, act upon the input, and transform it into the desired state, process the output, and guide, adjust, or change the system. An initial, low level of resolution, model of systems processes is shown in Figure 4.2. These operations are outlined as follows:

A. **INPUT PROCESSING** implies operations that provide for interaction between the system and its environment or suprasystem. It is through such interaction that input—information and resources—flows into the system as we search for and identify systems-relevant input, introduce the input into the system, and activate the system by it.

B. **TRANSFORMATION** implies operations that bring about conditions and activities by which the input is transformed into output, and the system is maintained/developed/changed.

FIGURE 4.2 AN INITIAL, LOW RESOLUTION VIEW OF THE PROCESS MODEL

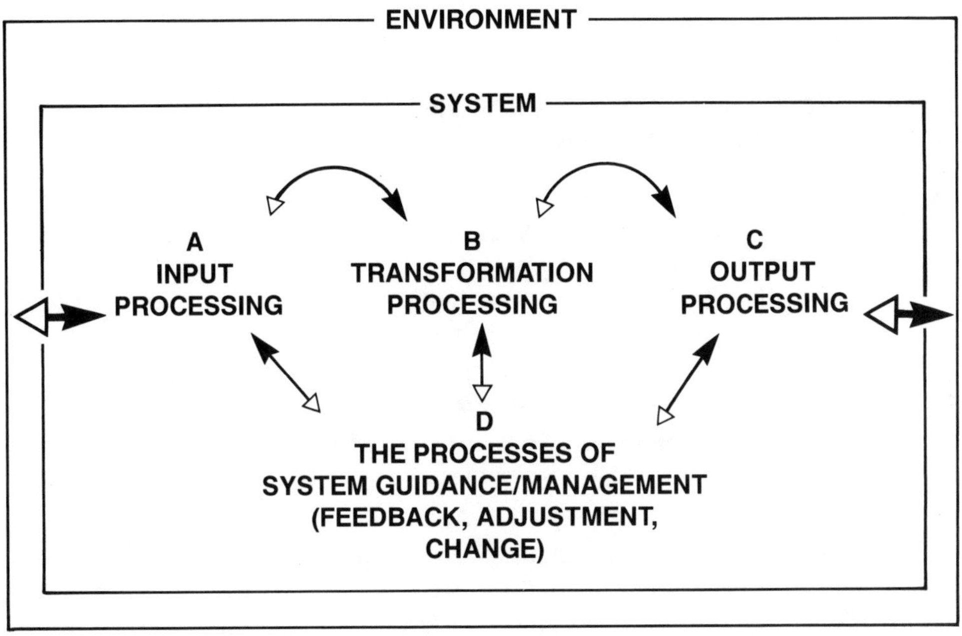

C. **OUTPUT PROCESSING** implies operations that bring about conditions and operations by which we provide for: (1) the identification and assessment of purpose(s)-relevant output, and (2) the dispatch of the output into the environment.

D. **SYSTEM GUIDANCE/MANAGEMENT (FEEDBACK, ADJUSTMENT, CHANGE)** provide for the management/guidance of the system. In addition to a range of guidance/management processes that match the characteristics of the particular systems type, this process involves: (1) the analysis and interpretation of information relevant to the assessment of all the system's processes and outcomes; (2) based on it—if indicated—the introduction of adjustments, and (3) if environmental or internal system requirements call for it, system change/system redesign.

The four systems processes depicted above are RECURRING within each of the process domains. For example: OUTPUT PROCESSING (1) receives input from transformation, (2) transforms the outcome of transformation production into an output state, (3) dispatches (puts out) the output, and (4) assesses the output process itself and introduces changes/adjustments if indicated. The four processes also recur at the subsystems level and in all components of the subsystems. (The four major process domains are explored and described in greater detail in the rest of this section.)

DESCRIPTORS FOR CATEGORIZING SYSTEMS PROCESSES

In considering and describing systems processes, the scope of consideration embraces a range of five conceptual levels that I have to make explicit before I discuss system concepts and principles relevant to the process behavior of systems, and construct from these concepts and principles a model of systems processes.

A. At the most general level we should consider systems processses that are descriptive of all living systems.

B. At the next level, we can designate systems processes that are generic to human activity systems.

C. Within the class of human activity systems we can differentiate based on considering various systems types (as discussed in Chapter One), such as types ranging from rigidly controlled to purpose-seeking.

D. Within the large class of human activity systems we can designate systems processes that describe specific categories of systems, such as educational systems.

E. Finally, at the next level, within the class of educational systems, we can consider a specific operational system of education in a specific functional context.

Within the scope described above—in this work—my task is to deal with levels A, B, C, and D. Your task is to focus on level E, which is a specific educational system of your choice. More specifically, (1) I have explored general systems concepts and principles and selected the most salient ones that pertain to human activity systems; (2) of the various types of human activity systems, I have focused on those concepts and principles that are relevant to heuristic and purpose-seeking system types; (3) given the selections from (1) and (2), I have, then, constructed from selected concepts and principles a general process model of educational activity systems. This model was already pictured in Figure 4.2.

THE INPUT PROCESSING

Human activity systems are created by their environment and are co-created with people in the system in order to bring about an expected/desired outcome/output. The environment contributes information on its expectations as well as providing information and resources required to produce the outcomes. The expectations and system-relevant information are introduced into HAS's as input, by input processing. There are four distinct and significant components of input processing. These are:

* INTERACTION (process) between the system and its environment or suprasystem.

* IDENTIFICATION (process) by which the relevance of the input (to the system) is established.

* INTRODUCTION of system-relevant input for transformation processing, bringing about the ACTIVATION of the system.

* GUIDANCE/MANAGEMENT (feedback/adjustment) of the above processes.

The mode of interaction between a human activity system and its environment is COMMUNICATION. Expectations, requirements, constraints, and the availability of resources have to be communicated. Communication SIGNALS, relevant to these, are constantly coming from the environment. As the system interacts with its environment, it receives, decodes, and registers these signals. Signals are registered and screened for their relevance to the system. The POTENTIAL INPUT ENTITIES, which these signals represent, are identified, and their values (to the system) are qualified, and if possible, quantified. Not all potential input becomes actual input. Only input of value to the system is entered into the system, and it is through this process that the system is activated. Furthermore, not all signals represent clear messages. Some signals are more like noises that often create problems in the course of the input process.

The input processes described above can now be organized into a motion-picture model of systems processes. Figure 4.3 presents an image of this model. It should be noted that within the four subsystems of the input system model, the four "general" systems processes: input, transformation, output, and guidance/management (feedback/adjustment) are all operative.

Guidance/Management in the input system and in its subsystems includes the overseeing of all the processes/operations and the introduction of adjustment/change.

FIGURE 4.3 A MODEL OF INPUT PROCESSING

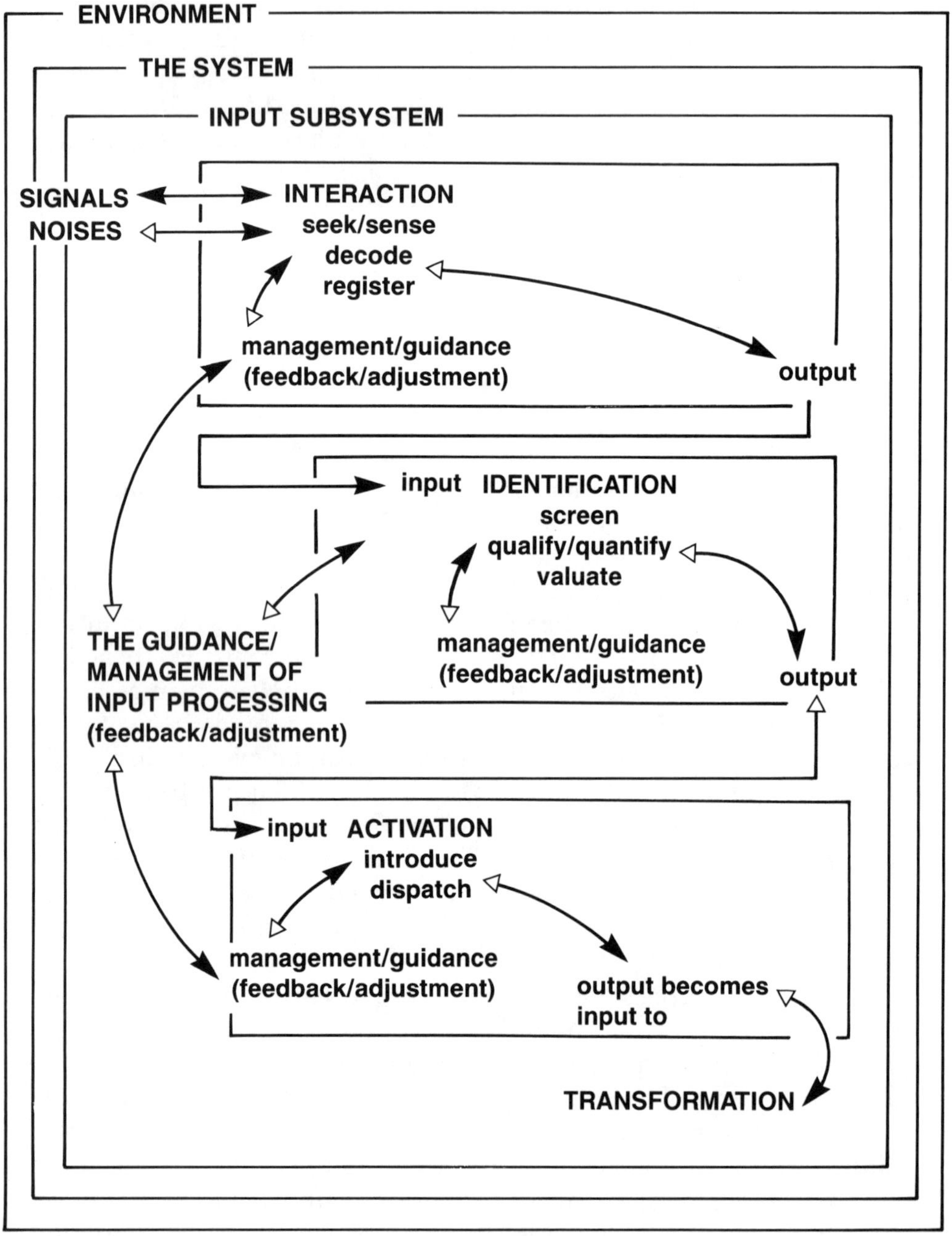

INTERACTION OPERATIONS

Interaction embraces the first set of input operations. These operations enable the HAS to seek/sense, receive, decode, verify, and register potential INPUT ENTITIES that come from the environment. Such entities include: (1) the SUBJECT of the system, which is the KEY SYSTEMS ENTITY (such as people in a wellness system), (2) SIGNALS that communicate information of various kinds (as discussed in Chapter Two), and (3) required RESOURCES that are coming from the environment. The subjects and resources are always accompanied by communication; thus from here on in the text communication SIGNALS or INPUT ENTITIES represent these three major kinds of input. Signals that are clear are decoded and become input to identification. Others may be less distinctive, weak, or noise-like, thus the message is less clear. Garbled signals are treated by the system as disturbance. If the signal is not clear, the system will activate processes by which to increase its ability to seek/sense, receive, and decode signals, or it will ask the source of the signal to improve the clarity or strength of the signal (the transmission mode) of the message. Thus, interaction also implies that the system continuously verifies with the source of the signal (in the environment) through feedback what has been sensed, perceived, and registered. Interaction processes input entities that appear to be targeted for introduction into the system. A model showing the interaction operations is pictured in Figure 4.4. We see again the recurring use of the four major systems processes.

It is important to make a clear distinction between "seek" and "sense" as the first interaction operations. Seeking means an active and even aggressive search for systems-relevant information and resources in the environment as well as environment-relevant information and contributions (by the system). It is through such information that coevolution and co-action with the environment can be maintained. Sensing implies "hearing" messages (about information/resources) communicated to the system by the environment.

IDENTIFICATION OPERATIONS

The signals and entities received by the interaction operations become input for identification. The purpose of identification is to interpret the incoming input from the point of view of the system; namely, to identify and select those signals and entities that are relevant to the purpose and operation of the system. The identifica-

FIGURE 4.4 THE MODEL OF INTERACTION

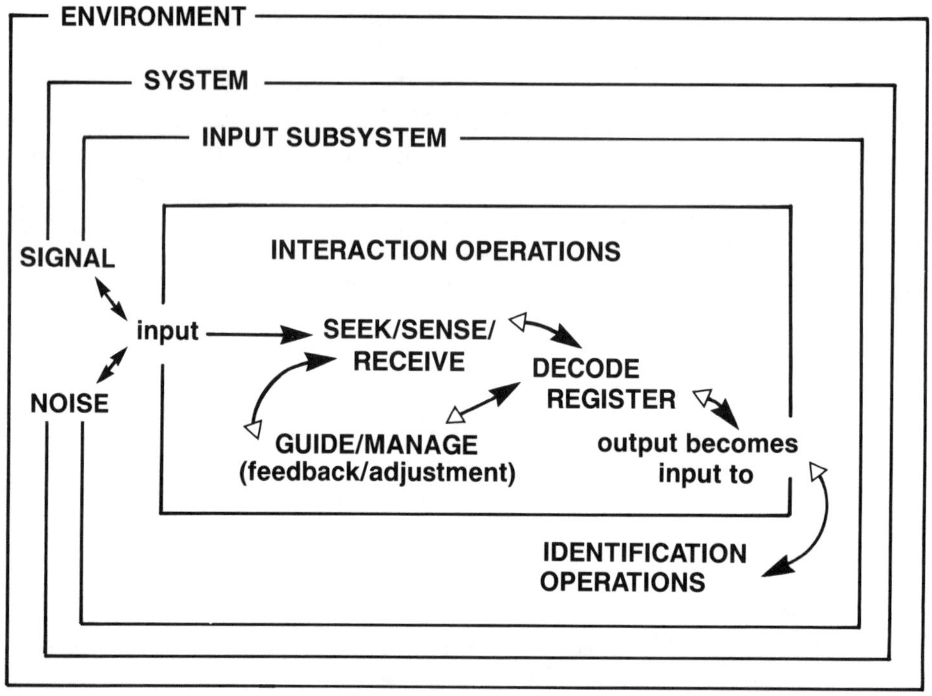

tion process is basically an ASSESSMENT-based SCREENING and SELECTION. This process ensures that only such input that is RELEVANT to the system will be allowed to enter the system. This process will reject (absorb) those input entities that are judged to be irrelevant (to the system) so that they will not disturb the system.

Those who are involved in this process need to have information from which to determine what IS system relevant. They have to have in their possession not only information on input requirements but also a detailed model of the system. Furthermore, they need to have communication access to all parts of the system, so that they can verify their judgment. Discharging the responsibility of screening and selection is most critical. In some HAS's, this task is viewed as one of "protecting" the system from environmental influences. This protection often goes to such extent that input will be screened out even though it might be of utmost importance to the system; particularly if such input would signal a need for change in the system. Protecting the system from input that is system-relevant, but one which would "rock the boat," does not do any service to the system. Such protection is counterproductive. It could lead to the isolation of the system from its environment. The system might become irrelevant to the environment, leading to its eventual termination.

Through the assessment/screening/selection operations of the identification process, we designate systems-relevant input that is now identified for its value to the system. Depending on the nature of the input and the means of assessment available, a judgment of value (to the system) can be qualitative and quantitative. For example, information input that represents systems-relevant environmental changes is QUALITATIVELY valued. Given two such inputs we ask the question: Which is more important to the system? And Why? Resource inputs, such as financing, are QUANTIFIABLE. The outcome of the identification process is a designation of systems-relevant input. The correctness and adequacy of the identification operation is ascertained by feedback/adjustment. Our criterion for judging the adequacy of the input (and the identification process) is the prevailing model of the particular HAS. This model defines the required state and properties of the input as well as those of the system. It is this model to which we compare the outcome of identification in order to introduce adjustments in the identification process. Figure 4.5 depicts an image of this process.

THE PROCESS OF INTRODUCTION/ACTIVATION

The last process of input is comprised of two operations: the introduction of the selected input entities into the transformation process and—by this—the activation of transformation. The introduction and activation operations will deliver the specific input needed at the specified place and time. These two operations are subject to two kinds of feedback:

* The feedback/adjustment of the introduction operation will determine if all input entities required by the system are available for delivery and if they have the needed characteristics.

* Feedback from the system on what is to be introduced will verify that the input is appropriate for entry into the system (by which the system becomes activated). Or—if not—the feedback (from the system) asks for adjustment in the input. Figure 4.6 pictures the model of introduction/activation.

FIGURE 4.5 A MODEL OF THE IDENTIFICATION PROCESS

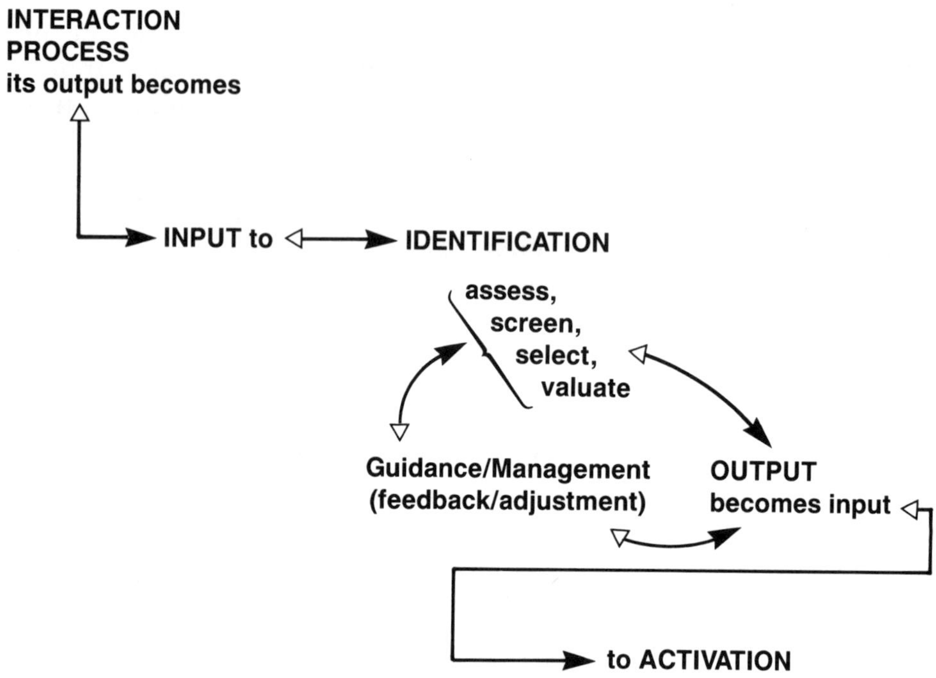

THE GUIDANCE/MANAGEMENT OF INPUT PROCESSES

Interaction, identification, introduction/activation are the three subsystems of the Input Process. They are integrated and synthesized by a GUIDANCE PROCESS that embraces all three sub-processes. The processes involved in guidance are similar to the guidance of the entire system, but the scope of guidance is limited to overseeing the input. Guidance links up, coordinates, guides, and monitors the three (sub)processes in order to ensure information flow and the appropriate—and internally consistent—use of the system's "map." It is this map (such as the three systems models discussed here) that enables people who operate the processes to make judgments about the relevance, timeliness, accuracy, and adequacy of such inputs as the subject (the key systems entity), information, and resources.

FIGURE 4.6 A MODEL OF INTRODUCTION/ACTIVATION

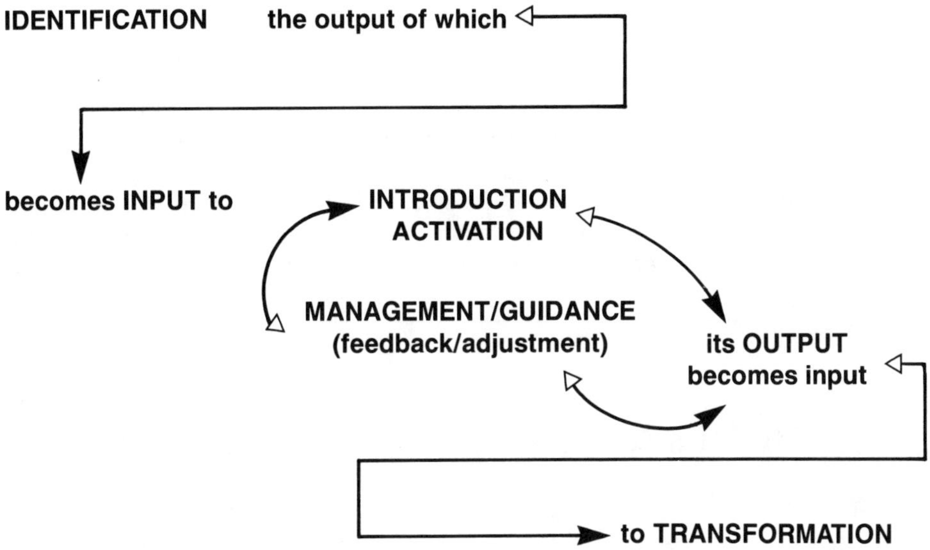

SUMMARY OF THE INPUT PROCESS

The inquiry of how systems work at their input range has resulted in the description of four major "generic" input processes: interaction, identification, introduction/activation, and input guidance/management. These processes are organized in a system that constitutes an interacting and interdependent whole. In our discussion of the processes of input in this chapter, and in earlier chapters, we understood that the outcome of input is the introduction into the transformation process of the system such input entities as:

* The KEY SYSTEMS ENTITY, which becomes the SUBJECT of the system, such as in a wellness system where the people wish to promote their physical/mental/spiritual health.

* INFORMATION about THE SYSTEMIC (and GENERAL) ENVIRONMENT.

* EXPECTATIONS/ASPIRATIONS that are formed both outside and inside the system.

* INFORMATION/KNOWLEDGE and other RESOURCES THAT ARE NEEDED to accomplish the transformation.

* CONSTRAINTS under which the system is to operate.
* INFORMATION generated by FEEDBACK from the system.

ACTIVITY # 36

Review the description of the input model, study your notes, and develop a description of the input processing of your selected system. (It is my hunch that you will have difficulty at times in describing your system in the terms introduced in the text. A lack of conscious and purposeful attention to the process of input is a main reason for inadequate systems performance in education.) Once you develop the description of your transformation, you might speculate about the input process of your imaginary "wished for" system. Introduce your findings in your notebook.

THE TRANSFORMATION PROCESS

The four major systems processes are input processing, transformation, output processing, and guidance (feedback/adjustment). Given initial conditions that are created by the input process—BY WHICH THE SYSTEM IS ACTIVATED—it is transformation which brings about the desired outcome or output. Transformation has three major interacting and interdependent process domains: transformation production, transformation facilitation, and transformation guidance/management. These three major transformation processes are defined in the text below.

TRANSFORMATION PRODUCTION is the primary transformation process (and the key process) of any HAS. Through this process the subject(s) of the system and other system components that are required to carry out the work of the system are engaged in integrated systemic operations and use resources in order to accomplish the purposed transformation.

TRANSFORMATION FACILITATION serves the primary transformation process, the production of transformation. It also aims to energize/motivate all components participating in the transformation so that they can make continuous and effective contribution to the transformation process.

TRANSFORMATION GUIDANCE/MANAGEMENT serves the two processes described above. Its purpose is to ensure that all components, resources, and information that are required for the work of the system are available at the time and place needed. It monitors the transformation process, analyzes information obtained, and introduces adjustments and changes if indicated.

Figure 4.7 pictures the first model of transformation, depicted at a low resolution level.

FIGURE 4.7 A GENERAL MODEL OF TRANSFORMATION

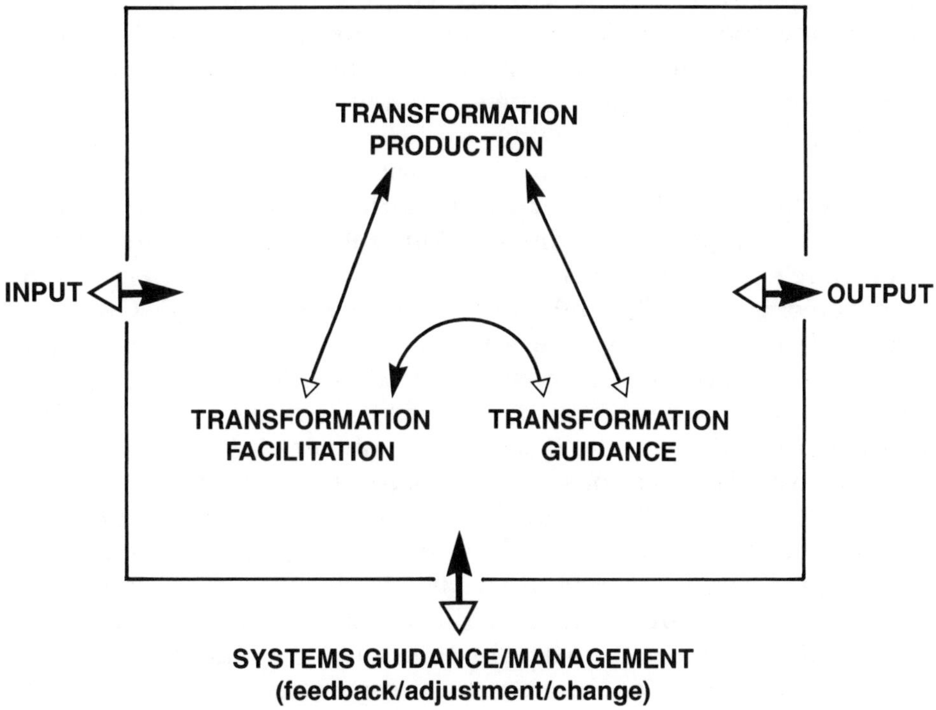

TRANSFORMATION PRODUCTION

Transformation production is composed of operations that aim at the transformation of the subject of the human activity system from the input state to the desired output state. For example, in a community-based wellness system the subjects are people in the community, and the transformation process aims at the attainment, reestablishment, and improvement of their physical, mental, spiritual wellness. As noted earlier, the outcome model described all the aimed-for characteristics of the subject of the system. (The wellness characteristics of people of the community.) There are two kinds of transformation processes operating in

HAS's. One is generic to all types of HAS's. The other type is specific to the purpose of the system. The specific types are those in which the subject of the system and all other components of the system engage in order to attain the desired outcome state of the subject and the system. We call these: SPECIFIC TRANSFORMATION PRODUCTION PROCESSES. (These will be considered as we discuss the specific transformation production processes of educational activity systems.)

The transformation processes that are generic to all HAS's are the SYSTEMIZATION/INTEGRATION PROCESSES that aim to make components of the system ever more "systemlike" and integrated, and produce or bring about a state of "wholeness." As the input activates the system, the system is set in motion by its purposes, around which it develops and in response to which the system gradually becomes a unified whole. In this process even the purposes are becoming ever more clarified and specified. During systemization, patterns of interaction among components become ever more specified (in terms of the system), weaving them into an integrated whole. Through such PROGRESSIVE INTEGRATION AND SYSTEMIZATION, the subject of the system and systems components take upon themselves increasingly more characteristics of the total system. In so doing they become ever more involved in the work and life of the system. The process just described here is a purposeful process of *self-organization* that is distributed in all parts of the system. This requires that all those involved in the system have a clear image of it. They need to understand their role in it, and their relationship to others in the system. Such an image is created by the development of the kinds of systems models described in this work. In order for this self-organization systemization to work, each component of the system has to have "imprinted" in it the total image of the system. Morgan defines this as holographic self-organization. (See Note 1.)

The two kinds of processes, the transformation of the subject of the system (transformation production) and the systemization/integration process, are simultaneous and integrated.

TRANSFORMATION FACILITATION

Human activity systems are ongoing. They exhibit behavior that transforms input into specified output. In order to be able to do this: (1) all those involved in the system must MAINTAIN BEHAVIOR that will result in the intended outcome and—at the same time—(2) all of them have to be ENERGIZED/MOTIVATED to participate in and make their contribution to the transformation process. Operations related to energizing/motivating people in the system jointly constitute TRANSFORMATION FACILITATION.

Only those systems components will be energized that develop and maintain behavior appropriate to the attainment of the purposes of the system. As we already have seen in describing the functions/structure model, the stipulation of being appropriate to purposes and functions was kept in mind in selecting the components of the system. The capability of components/resources in carrying out the needed transformation operations is carefully assessed (initially) and measured continuously. Energizing and motivation charge up system components and provide them with the energy and motivation needed to participate in and make their contribution to transformation. Without energizing/motivating we cannot reasonably expect that system components will make their contribution effectively and appropriately. On the other hand, only such behavior should be energized that will serve the system's purposes and functions. Thus, through energizing and motivation, system components are maintained in a state that enables/empowers them to carry out purpose- and functions-serving transformation operations. But how do we get information on the appropriateness of the behavior of components? Operations that guide the transformation processes, discussed next, provide us with answers to this question.

TRANSFORMATION GUIDANCE/MANAGEMENT

Transformation GUIDANCE/MANAGEMENT is embedded in and informs systems guidance/management. While systems guidance is concerned with the guidance of the entire system, transformation guidance is concerned with overseeing Transformation Production and Transformation Facilitation, and linkage with the Input and Output Processes. Furthermore, while systems guidance is concerned with both the (total) system and the environment, transformation guidance focuses on its own domain. The overriding concern of this guidance is whether: (1) transformation production satisfies systems requirements (the designated outcome) and (2) the transformation process is adequatly facilitated. Information is collected on these two concerns and is acted upon by transformation guidance.

Transformation guidance faces two major tasks. FIRST, it is to ensure that components of the transformation processes perform in a way that guarantees the eventual attainment of systems purposes. Thus, at any point—and at certain designated intermediate points—performance measures are taken relevant to the system and the subject of the system and compared with their relevant performance models. If there is a difference between the IS and SHOULD BE, adjustments are introduced to correct for deficiencies. Monitoring, measuring performance, analyzing it, and adjusting constitute the PERFORMANCE-EFFECTIVENESS dimension of transformation guidance.

SECOND, transformation guidance is to ensure that the desired outcome of transformation will be achieved within cost constraints. This is the COST-EFFECTIVENESS dimension of transformation guidance. Within the two dimensions—mentioned above—there is usually a conflict: cost and effectiveness are usually in opposition. Transformation guidance has to exercise judgment and seek a balance between these two dimensions. A judgment of such a balance is a major factor in deciding whether adjustments should be made. Adjustments aim at the improvement of transformation. The implementation of adjustment is complex. It includes such options as: (1) replacing an existing function or component or interaction patterns with another one; (2) providing for additional functions, components, and interactions; (3) altering or increasing capabilities, functions, and interactions; (4) engaging already available capabilities (components) still unused or potentially-existing functions and interaction patterns not yet activated; (5) increasing arrangements for facilitating (energizing/motivating) transformation; and/or (6) considering and instituting changes in outcome expectations, effectiveness criteria, cost, etc.

Transformation guidance, a subsystem of the transformation system, oversees the operations of transformation production and facilitation. Jointly, these three subsystems are directly involved in transforming input into the desired outcome. Figure 4.8 provides a summary image of transformation.

Before we move on to the next major systems process, the output process, an activity will help you to transform this segment.

FIGURE 4.8 A MODEL OF TRANSFORMATION

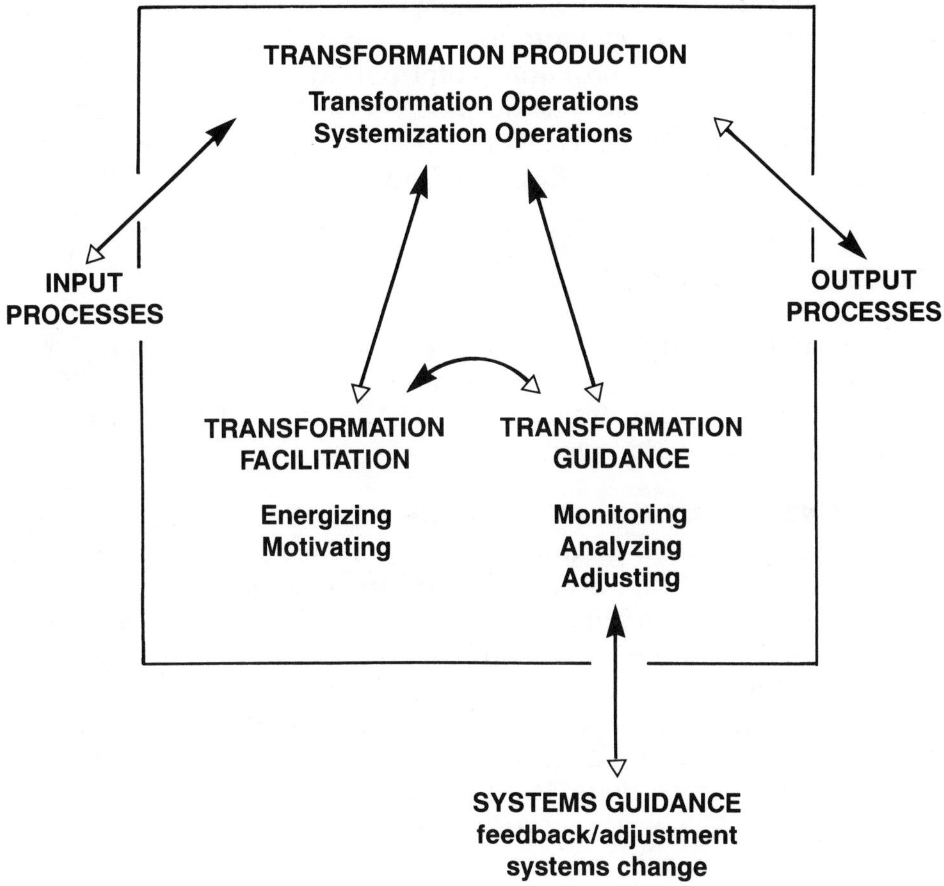

ACTIVITY # 37

You are asked to make notes as you work with this text. Review the text again and study the notes you have taken and transform my general transformation process model of human activity systems into a transformation model of your specific educational system. By so doing you will make an assessment of the systemic adequacy of your selected system. You might also speculate about the transformation behavior of your "imaginary," "wished for" system. Enter your findings into your notebook.

OUTPUT PROCESSING

Output processing is concerned with: the identification and assessment of systems-relevant output, dispatching this output into the environment, and providing information to systems guidance on the state of the input. The output process has three component processes: DISPATCH OF OUTPUT, OUTPUT PROCESS FACILITATION, and OUTPUT PROCESS GUIDANCE/MANAGEMENT.

DISPATCH OF OUTPUT

Dispatching output involves three operations: (1) Output Identification and Assessment, (2) Dispatch of Purpose-Relevant Output, and (3) Providing Information on the State of the Output to Systems Guidance/Management.

IDENTIFICATION AND ASSESSMENT. Upon the completion of transformation production—as we introduce the outcome of this production to the output process—the task of the system is to determine if the intended output meets stated expectations. There are three options. (1) A HAS produces output that IS relevant to the purpose of the system. (2) It may produce output that may NOT be relevant to the purpose of the system. Then, (3) it may produce output that is relevant but is NOT ADEQUATE, because it does not match stated expectations. But how do we know this? How can we determine RELEVANCE and ADEQUACY?

We need to identify and assess the relevance and adequacy of the intended output. This can be done only if there is some MODEL that represents the desired and EXPECTED STATE of the OUTPUT. Given such a model, we can compare the output to its model and determine the degree of correspondence. We call this the OUTPUT MODEL of the system. This model is constructed on the basis of the purpose of the system, based on which relevant (to the purpose) criteria (and criteria measures) can be developed and exhibited as the model of the output. The adequacy of the model and the sensitivity of the measures are of primary concern, because we cannot detect output dimensions/characteristics that have not been specified, that have not been qualified or quantified and defined as standards of our expectations. By a process of comparison of the intended output and the actual input, it becomes possible to determine whether or not the output is RELEVANT and ADEQUATE (enough) to be dispatched.

DISPATCHING. If the comparison between the intended output and the output model shows that the intended output is both relevant (to the purpose) and adequate (as measured by the criteria assessment), the intended output becomes actual output and is dispatched to the designated environmental system(s). This dispatching involves two operations: (1) Communication (with the environment) that accompanies the output. The communication "labels" or describes the various output entities in terms of the output model. (2) The acquisition of confirmation (feedback) from the appropriate environmental system as to the adequacy of the output.

PORTRAYING FINDINGS. This process involves a detailed portrayal of: (1) the findings of the assessment of the intended output, (2) the state of the output, and (3) feedback received from the environment on the adequacy of the output. Information generated on these three items is developed for use by systems guidance.

OUTPUT PROCESS FACILITATION

Output process facilitation is similar to the facilitation of the transformation process. Thus, I review this process only briefly here. The genesis of facilitation is a concern to maintain behavior which is required (and is appropriate) to carry out the process of dispatching the output. Facilitation is accomplished by energizing and motivating all components that engage in the output process. Only those components of the output processing are energized that contribute effectively to the process. (For details consult the section on facilitating transformation.)

OUTPUT PROCESS GUIDANCE/MANAGEMENT

This output process component is, again, similar to that of transformation guidance. It involves: (1) monitoring all output processes and components, (2) assessing the adequacy of the process, and (3) introducing adjustments if indicated. In addition, (4) findings on accomplishing the output process are communicated to systems guidance. Figure 4.9 pictures the output process.

FIGURE 4.9 A MODEL OF THE OUTPUT PROCESS

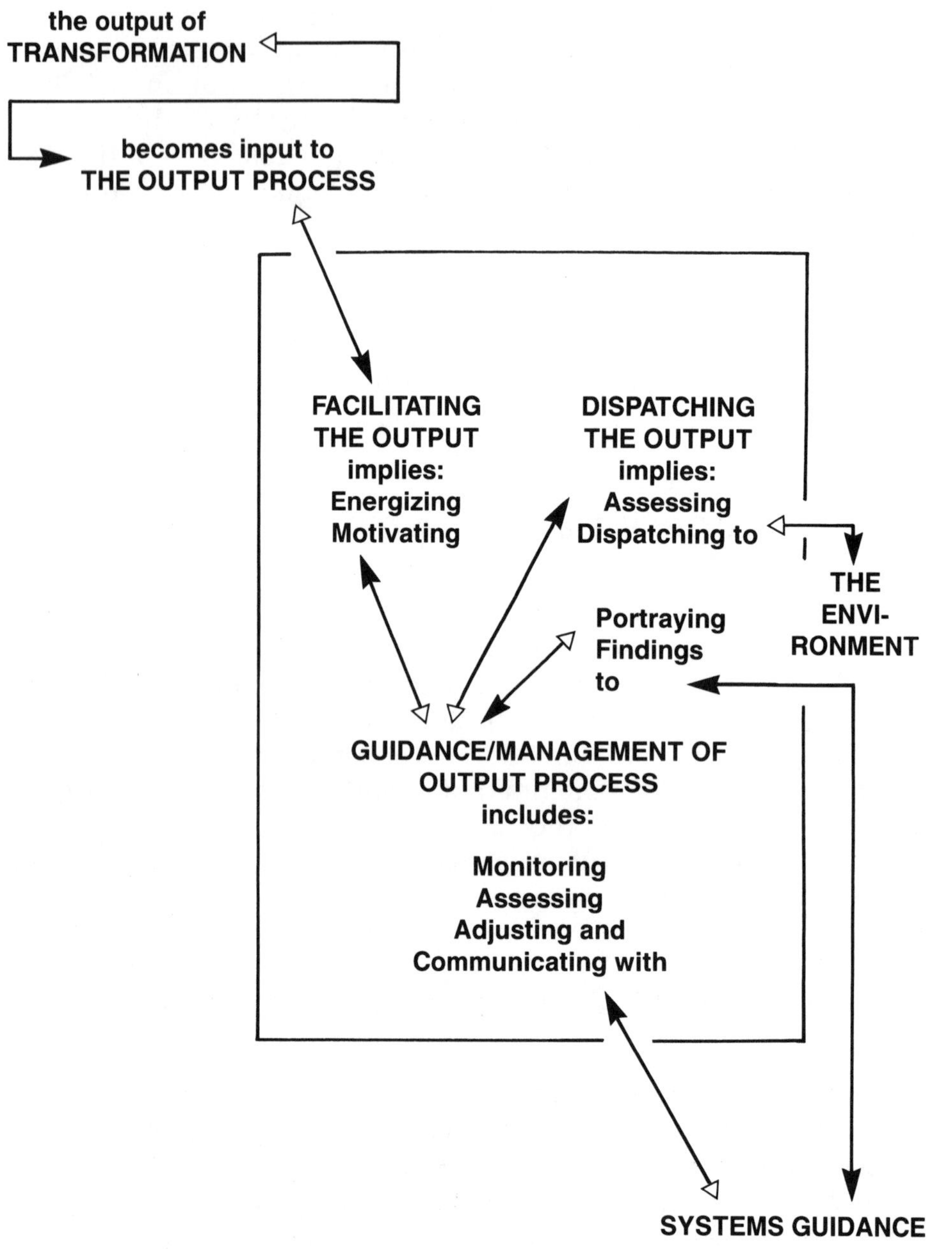

ACTIVITY # 38

In working with the above section, you have been asked to make notes that will assist you in transforming my description of the output process of human activity systems. Review the text again and the notes you have taken, and describe how the output is processed in your selected system. While so doing, you will be able to make an assessment of the systemic adequacy of handling the output in your system. If you wish, you can, then, speculate about your "wish" system and describe its output processing the way you would like it to be. Enter your findings in your notebook.

SYSTEMS GUIDANCE/MANAGEMENT (FEEDBACK/ADJUSTMENT/CHANGE)

We have now arrived, in the course of our journey toward developing a systems view, at the last major process of human activity systems: the process of guidance/management and feedback/adjustment, and systems change. This process comprises the fourth process domain, as it follows the sequence of Input–Transformation–Output. A most significant difference between human enterprises that operate as systems and those that do not is that systems are adjusted based on information gained from feedback and are changed if feedback (information) from the system or the environment indicates that the system should be not only adjusted but also changed by redesigning it. Systems guidance and management processes are of two kinds: (1) those that permeate all aspects of systems processes/operations and (2) those that are activated primarily based on information coming from the output process and from the environment. In the text that follows, I first describe this latter kind.

FEEDBACK/ADJUSTMENT

FEEDBACK from the system and/or the environment triggers ADJUSTMENT in some processes or invites CHANGE that involves the entire system. The reason for discussing adjustment first is that much of this process flows directly from the output process, and it determines whether there is a need to introduce adjustments in the system.

As we have already discussed in earlier chapters (primarily in Chapter Two), human activity systems operate on two types of feedback: negative and positive. Negative feedback tells us that we should consider some adjustments in certain aspects/processes of the system. Positive feedback, on the other hand, indicates that adjustments will not suffice any longer—we had better look at the whole system and contemplate and bring about changes in it by the redesign of the system. The processes of feedback/adjustment are based on evidence collected, that is relevant to the adequacy of the output and to the adequacy of the functioning of the system. Feedback/adjustment involves:

* Collecting evidence of the adequacy of the output and systems operations.
* Analyzing and interpreting this evidence.
* Constructing a model of adjustment.
* Stipulating the consequences of adjustment.
* Introducing adjustment in the system.

Figure 4.10 pictures the relationships of the five operations identified above and their relationships to the system.

COLLECTING EVIDENCE. Adjustments in systems behavior and/or the product of the system are based on the analysis and interpretation of evidence we collect as to the adequacy of the output and the effectiveness of systems processes/operations that produce the output. Obviously, these two kinds of evidence are interrelated. But, in collecting them separately (on adequacy and effectiveness), we can shift our attention from one to the other. There are several sources to use in collecting evidence on output adequacy.

FIRST, a part of output operations was to apply the output model against the intended output in order to make a judgment if the (intended) output demonstrated the characteristics and capabilities and performance expectations projected by the output model. If it did, then it was dispatched as a worthwhile product. If not, then, obviously, adjustments were called for. In the type of human activity systems we are interested in here, we apply the model to the key entity, individuals and groups, who are the subjects of the system. In addition to applying the output model, we also seek evidence from them (the subjects) and ask for an assessment of their readiness, and their judgment of their attainment of what they want to become when they leave the system. For example, in a wellness system, it is primarily the judgment of those who are involved in the wellness program that reveals the adequacy and

FIGURE 4.10 A SYSTEMIC PICTURE OF ADJUSTMENT OPERATIONS

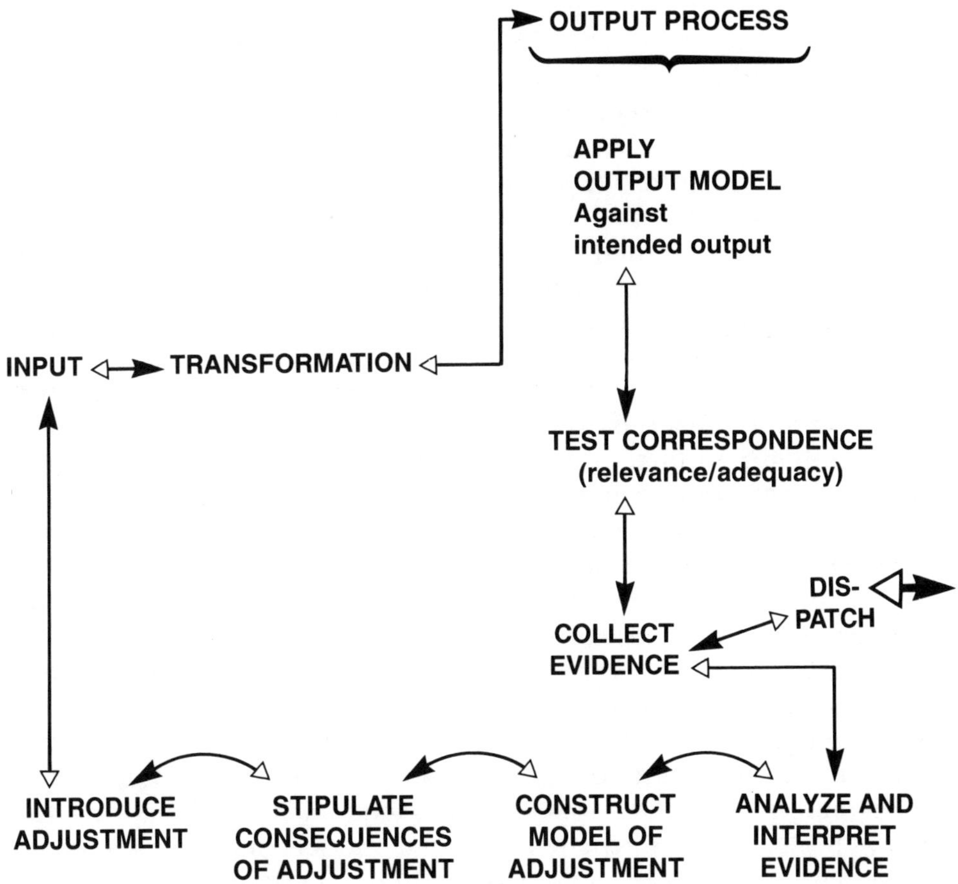

relevance of the system. Findings generated from this two-pronged assessment of outcomes are the main source of evidence that is communicated by feedback to Guidance/Management.

SECOND, we reach beyond the output process and augment the findings—generated by the assessment of the output—by assessments we have made during the various operations of the transformation and input processes. These assessments give us insight into the life and performance history of the subjects of the system as well as the adequacy and effectiveness of the systems processes/operations. The assessment accumulated during input and transformation—while the subject was introduced into the system and was transformed into the output state—is often more useful than testing it only at the output stage. It is through such continuing assessment that we can open up the "black box." Unless we use assessment constantly from input through output, we cannot make adjustments at the most effective and most appropriate times. If we leave it to the end, we shall have "rejects" for sure.

The THIRD source is systems in the environment to which we dispatch the output. These systems pass judgment on the adequacy of the output. This judgment is made from the point of view of the targeted system(s). It is for this reason that we have to make sure that the "model of output" is known to—and is approved by—the receiving system. If there is a discrepancy between the assessment of the target system (in the environment) and the system that produced the output, adjustment is in order. An analysis and interpretation of the discrepancy information will indicate the kind and size of adjustment(s) to be made. In case the output model is judged (by the target systems in the environment) to be inadequate or less than relevant, we are faced with a major issue of adjustment, possibly even total systems change.

As hinted above, we are to collect evidence relevant to the adequacy and effectiveness of systems processes/operations. This evidence is collected in regard to all systems processes and operations from the initial systems-environment interaction of the input process, through other component processes of input, transformation, and output, as well as those of feedback/adjustment. Evidence is collected on the process/operations adequacies by comparing the actual performance to the performance models of processes/operations. This assessment is guided by such questions as:

* What aspects (processes/operations, components, attributes of components, performance models, attributes of models) are lacking that prevent the attainment of desired outcomes (outcome characteristics)?

* What aspects (see above) are deficient and thus contribute less than their desired share in bringing about the desired outcomes (outcome characteristics)?

* What aspects (see above) bring about outcomes that are not relevant to outcome expectations? Or serve something other than the stated purpose(s) of the system?

* "Are we getting our money's worth?" and: Can we improve the economy of the system?

These are very broad questions. But they help us to understand the scope of the inquiry we are to apply in collecting evidence and the task we face as we shred-out these broad questions and generate specific inquiries.

ANALYZING AND INTERPRETING EVIDENCE. The evidence accumulated from the various sources relevant to the adequacy of the output and the performance of the system is now analyzed to determine the nature, the size, and the intensity of the discrepancy between the actual and desired output and the actual and desired systems processes/operations of the performance of the systems components. The outcome of the analysis should then be interpreted. The main thrust of this interpretation should be to answer the question: What do findings of the analysis of the various kinds of evidence mean as to the kind of adjustment(s) we should entertain? Analysis has shown us the difference between the IS and the SHOULD. Interpretation (of the analysis) will probe into the source and implications of this difference (or discrepancy). Interpretation must answer such questions as: What went wrong? Where, how, and why? Answers to these questions provide the basis for constructing "Models of Adjustment," stipulating their consequences, and introducing the adjustments.

CONSTRUCTING THE MODEL OF ADJUSTMENT. Once we interpret the meaning of the analysis from the point of view of the system, what that means to the system, we can propose certain measures. If introduced into the system as adjustments, they are expected to correct for the difference between the IS and SHOULD. The organized description of the relational arrangement of these measures constitutes the model of adjustment. The interpretation of the evidence reveals the weakness of the system; it tells us what caused the less-than-desirable outcome. We now want to use this valuable information to construct the model of adjustment. The specifics of the model of adjustment will correspond to specific points of system failures and inadequacies. They are to be "mapped into"—or superimposed on—the systems map. According to the nature of systems failures, adjustments will be proposed in such aspects as: processes/operations, in functions and their relational arrangements, in components and their distribution (or structure), in performance models, and systems maps. The failure can be of high or low intensity. The intensity of the adjustment is to match the level of the intensity of the system error. The key consideration in selecting adjustment measures and designing the model of adjustment is the consideration of ALTERNATIVES. We are to weigh and TEST a range of adjustment alternatives and select the alternative(s) most appropriate to ensuring the attainment of the desired outcomes. This "testing" is the next component process.

STIPULATING CONSEQUENCES. We test adjustment (model) alternatives by stipulating the consequences of introducing the various alternatives. To stipulate consequences is to assess such aspects as: (1) the power of the alternative to bring about the desired adjustment; (2) ease vs. difficulty of implementing the alternative; (3) possible long-range effects; (4) compatibility with the subject(s) of the system and other systems processes/operations, and components in the adjustment environment; (5) possibility of serious systemic disruption caused by the introduction of the adjustment; (6) constraints/limitations within which the alternative would be implemented; and (7) cost and time factors. These and possibly some other relevant factors must be considered in assessing the advantage(s) and disadvantage(s) inherent in introducing the planned adjustment.

INTRODUCING ADJUSTMENTS. Once adjustment alternatives have been tested and one particular alternative has been selected and a decision made for its introduction, we need to determine the appropriate time and circumstance for its introduction. Questions we face include the following: What is the best time to introduce it? What preparations may be required? How much time do we need for preparations? Is there a need for training? We might find that it is best to treat the adjustment as tentative, until we are certain of the attainment of desired effects. The way in which we introduce adjustment is significant. It should be introduced by clear and unambiguous communication with all those affected by it. There should be a two-way communication by those who design the adjustment and those who implement it. This communication should continue until the desired outcome of the adjustment is clearly demonstrated. Furthermore, the proven adjustment should be introduced into the "map" or "model" of the system.

SYSTEMS CHANGE

The processes of adjustment—discussed in the section above—are driven by negative feedback. Negative feedback tells us that the outcome does not match stated expectations as defined in the outcome model. It tells us that some component, some process or operation, or some interaction in the system does not do its job well. Thus, we need to find out what it is IN the system that is not doing things well, so that we can correct or change that particular part, process, or interaction. This finding out and doing the correction(s) is what I described as making adjustments. It means that we adjust something in the system so that we can reduce or eliminate "deviations" from the outcome model. Thus, negative feedback signals the need for deviation reduction.

But what happens if it IS the *outcome model* that does not meet expectations? The outcome model represents the total effort of the system. So, if the outcome model is not working anymore, then it means that the system is not working for us anymore. The SYSTEM has to change. Now we are not in the business of reducing deviation, we need to INCREASE it. It is here that positive feedback comes in. Let us return to the example of the wellness system. A couple of decades ago we nourished ourselves with a dozen eggs a week and consumed big juicy steaks; key elements in our ideal nourishment "model." Then, we found out that this model was wrong. We changed it and changed our whole system of nourishment.

Who makes judgments about the correctness/adequacy of outcome models in human activity systems? As we already discussed, such judgments are made by people in the systemic environment and those in the system; all who have an interest, have a "stake in" the system, who are affected by it, and who are in it. Thus, in HAS's we are involved in an intensive dialogue among many partners about: (1) agreeing upon new and different expectations, (2) creating a new "image of the system," (3) formulating a new "outcome model," and (4) designing a new system that has the organizational capacity and human capability to make the image come to life and meet new expectations. Going back to our example of a wellness system, a couple of decades ago (and even today) the systems model of health services was defined as providing for "disease control." In the course of—at least—the last decade, this model has been rejected and a new model has emerged. This model aims at "promoting and maintaining overall (physical/mental/spiritual) wellness." Recently, there has been an increased interest in designing systems that can implement new models of "wellness." (For reference on a detailed discussion of systems design see Note 2.)

The difference between the two major modes of systems processes—adjustment in the system and changing the system—can be restated as follows. Negative-feedback-driven adjustment CONFIRMS the outcome model of the system, saying that the model is all right. Positive-feedback calls for NOVELTY, saying that we need a new outcome model and, therefore, a new system. (See Note 3.)

GUIDANCE/MANAGEMENT

As a closing discussion of the PROCESS MODEL of Human Activity Systems, I return to the issue of guidance/management in HAS's. I briefly review the characteristics of HAS's that have emerged in the course of the last decade or so, and then I explore their implications for the guidance/management of those systems.

In Chapter One, I briefly discussed the major societal transformation that has brought us from the industrial to the post-industrial age. I noted that some of our HAS's are still rooted in the thinking and practices of the industrial/machine age.

EMERGED CHARACTERISTICS. In the text below, I contrast systems characteristics of the two eras in order to highlight distinctions between the two. (The examples are adapted as indicated in Note 4.) Contrasting characteristics include the following:

* Today, the amount, the variety, and the availability of knowledge—as well as its absolute growth—are significantly higher than in the industrial era. In order to cope with such knowledge explosion, HAS's have to effect a marked increase in (a) specialization and diversification AND (b) integration and generalization.

* Complexity has greatly increased. The more discrete the component systems in the systemic environment, the greater the complexity of the HAS, requiring an increase in the amount and kind of information that has to be processed by the HAS in order to meet environmental expectations and enhance systemic effectiveness.

* Today, both the level of external and internal turbulence and their absolute growth have become significantly greater than in the previous era. Such increase has placed a premium on organizational flexibility, the ability to learn as an organization, and to engage in continuous organizational design/redesign.

* An increase in the rate of change is another characteristic of the current era. This increases the pressure on HAS's to process information rapidly, distribute it to a larger number of groups, and transform it into organizational knowledge.

An understanding of the nature of systems change (discussed earlier) and the emerged societal characteristics exemplified above may guide us in exploring their implications for the guidance/management of the types of HAS's we are concerned with here. Examples of implications are introduced next. Human activity systems that serve the society and are served by it should be able to:

* Interact with their constantly changing and multiple envi-

ronments, and coordinate with other systems in their systemic environment.

* Deal creatively with constant change, uncertainty, and ambiguity, and maintain their viability by coevolving with their environment by changing and transforming themselves and by effecting changes in their environment.

* Involve all those concerned, interested in, having a stake in, and contributing to the life of the system. Enlist their participation and guidance in order to make the system ever more relevant to their service.

* Become organizational learning systems and differentiate between situations, when maintaining the system by adjustment/correction is appropriate and changing and (re-) designing are called for (Note 5).

* Respond to the continuing increase in the amount and kind of information/knowledge to work with, by: (a) increasing BOTH specialization and diversification, and integration and generalization, and (b) increasing ability to handle information more rapidly, distributing it to a larger number of people, and transforming it into organizational knowledge.

The examples above indicate systems behavior that is related primarily to systems-environment co-action. It is your turn now to work with this last systems process.

ACTIVITY # 39

In working with the text on Systems Guidance and Management (feedback, adjustment, systems change), you have been asked to make notes that will help you to model your system. Review those notes and the text above and describe the feedback, adjustment, and systems change behavior of your selected system. Sometimes you will have to make inferences. The processes I described are often not implemented and are hidden in our educational systems. If you like, you can also speculate about your "wish" system of education and describe how you would like it to behave. Enter your findings into your notebook.

SUMMARY OF THE PROCESS/BEHAVIORAL GENERAL MODEL

Human Activity Systems are created by people in response to their intent and shared purpose as well as to the expectations that emerge from the environment of the system in which the system is created. In Chapters Two and Three, we developed a systems view of systems-environment interaction and relationship and portrayed a functions/structure description of HAS's and EAS's. In these chapters we laid out the "landscape" of HAS's and EAS's but not the "drama" that goes on through time in these systems. In the first section of this chapter, therefore, I have used the process lens and introduced a process view—a general process model—of HAS's. In SECTIONS TWO and THREE, we continue the development of this process view and apply it to the characterization of educational activity systems.

SECTION TWO:

THE PROCESS MODEL OF YOUR SELECTED SYSTEM

In Section One of this chapter, I developed a general process model of human activity systems. You are now asked to transform my general model into a "motion-picture" model, use the process lens, and apply the generic concepts and principles—presented in the model—to your selected educational activity system. The purpose of this activity is beyond reinforcing your understanding of certain systems concepts and principles—to help you to apply the concepts and principles you have studied in Section One in the real-life context (of your selected EAS) as YOU SEE IT. These concepts and principles will come to life and become your own only through such application. Do not be concerned if your first description is not yet complete. It will be more developed and functional as you "redevelop" it as you work with the next sections of the chapter. So, now you can proceed with writing the "process story" or making the motion picture image of your EAS. Use my text, the comments you made as you worked with the text, and the activities you completed in constructing the story. Introduce the description of your model in your notebook.

SECTION THREE:

A GENERAL PROCESS MODEL OF EDUCATIONAL ACTIVITY SYSTEMS (EAS's)

In Section Two, you worked with a set of systems concepts and principles—organized into a process model of HAS's—and you transformed those into the context of your own selected system. Thus, you created a process/behavioral model of a PARTICULAR EAS. In this section, you will work with my formulation of a process/behavioral characterization of EAS's and you will use my characterization in order to redevelop—possibly revise and extend—your process description. As you have seen, my description was not developed in the context of a specific EAS. Yours is. As you work with the text that follows, make notes that will help you to rewrite the "process story" of your selected EAS. Activities in this section will help you to apply the systems process ideas in your selected context. In Section Four, you will integrate the findings that emerge from your activity work into the process description of your selected system. A description of a general process model of EAS's follows next.

The systems-environmental model introduced concepts and principles relevant to human and educational activity systems in their environmental context and explained systems-environmental relationships. The still picture model—or functions/structure model—characterized the static state of systems and showed what a system IS at a given moment of time. It did not show HOW the system does whatever it is about. But human and educational activity systems are not static, they are alive and cannot be fully understood from an examination of spatial models only. The two previous models have shown us the LANDSCAPE of the life of educational activity systems but NOT the DRAMA of the systems' life. They could not reveal the ongoing and unfolding behavior of EAS's. To complete our systems view, we have to examine and characterize their behavior, HOW they operate through time, and observe the changes that take place in their entities and in the behavior of those entities. In this section, I use the process lens I developed in Section One, and—through the lens—look at educational activity systems and introduce a process view and model of

EAS's. Thus, I add the temporal dimension to the spatial and contextual dimensions already developed.

People who are working with, who are in, or who have an interest in EAS's—as a rule—are not used to thinking in process terms. Most of us in the educational community have a predisposition to think and focus on the structure and components of the system. We focus on the input and output of the system and use what is called input-output models. Our inquiry is framed like this: given a certain input (goals, information, resources, facilities), what output is produced? Most frequently we stipulate the adequacy of an EAS by saying: we invest this much money per student, and that is what the test scores show. That's it. Between the input and output there is that BLACK BOX: the educational organization, its components, their structure, and the people who are responsible for producing the output. Using only the structural lens, what happens between the input and the output remains a mystery. We probably know what has been produced, but we can only speculate as to why. That is where the process lens comes in. It helps us to open up the black box, make it transparent, and transform it into a "glass box."

The still-picture displays an image of an EAS at a given moment of its existence. The motion picture model projects images through time, revealing movement, action, and behavior. It unfolds and reveals the life of the system. In this section, I describe the GENERAL process behavior of EAS's. I accomplish this in five parts. First, I present an overview of systems processes of EAS's. Then, I describe the three major flow-through processes: the input, the transformation, and the output processes. Finally, I characterize the feedback/adjustment/change and guidance/management processes that enfold the three other processes.

AN OVERVIEW OF SYSTEMS PROCESSES IN EAS's

An Educational Activity System—as a human activity system—is an open societal system. It changes and coevolves with its societal environment and is defined collectively by its systemic environment and by the people who inhabit the EAS. EAS's serve the society by engaging individuals—by processes of INPUT—and providing them—in the course of the TRANSFORMATION process—with arrangements, opportunities, resources, and guidance by which they can attain the desired and specified outcome (OUTPUT), such as: knowledge, understanding, skills, values, dispositions, and attitudes. An EAS operates in a way to ensure that the processes mentioned here will be carried out. If there is a discrepancy between what is desired and what has been attained as learning and development, we shall make corrections through the processes of FEEDBACK and ADJUSTMENT and reduce/eliminate the discrepancy. If there is a discrepancy between what the system does—as a whole—and what it should do, the whole system might be changed/redesigned. GUIDANCE and MANAGEMENT integrate the processes defined above. An initial definition of these processes is provided next at a low level of resolution. They are pictured in Figure 4.11.

FIGURE 4.11 A LOW RESOLUTION VIEW OF THE PROCESS MODEL

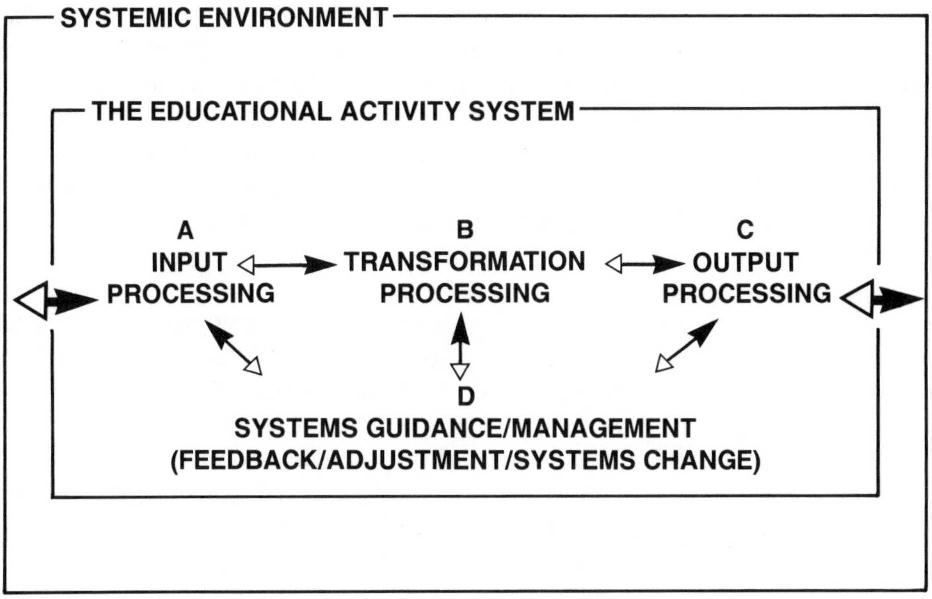

A. INPUT implies processes that provide for interaction between the EAS and its systemic environment: the community. It is through such interaction that designated input: learners, people who carry out the processes, information, resources, etc., enter into the system as we search, identify, engage systems-relevant input, and activate the system by it.

B. TRANSFORMATION in EAS's implies processes that bring about conditions and provide for operations and activities by which the learner attains mastery of knowledge, understanding, skills, dispositions, values, and attitudes as proposed by the learner and those who assist him/her. Transformation also provides for conditions that enhance the carrying out of the transformation processes, operations, and activities.

C. OUTPUT PROCESSING provides for conditions, operations, and activities by which we provide for: (1) the identification of mastery attained by the learner, the learner's introduction to the next phase of learning or to the environment; and (2) the assessment of the adequacy of outcome as well as the adequacy of processes/arrangements/components that generated the outcome.

D. SYSTEMS GUIDANCE/MANAGEMENT is aided by the PROCESSES OF FEEDBACK/ADJUSTMENT/CHANGE and provides—in general—for the coordination and integration of the three processes identified above. It involves the analysis and interpretation of information that comes from output assessment as to the adequacy of the attainment of the learners' mastery and the adequacy of systems' processes/arrangement/components. Based on the assessment, it guides the design and introduction of adjustments if called for. If the environment or internal systems requirements call for it, it guides and manages the change or redesign of the whole system.

The four systems processes described above are recurring within each process domain, within their sub-domains, within their operations, suboperations, and activities. They are "holographic." They are generic to EAS's (and to all human activity systems). What these processes actually focus on—what they actually do—is specific to the particular system, to its purposes and characteristics. What follows is the modelling of the processes and subprocesses of the four major systems processes of EAS's at increasingly higher levels of resolution.

INPUT PROCESSING IN EAS's

Educational Activity Systems are created (and re-created) jointly by people in their systemic environments (the community) and by the people who are in the system, in order to provide for arrangements, conditions, opportunities, resources, and situations by which individuals and groups can master desired learning and develop to their full potential. The environment and people in the system provide information on desired/expected learning outcomes; they provide resources/facilities and systems-relevant information and knowledge. All these constitute the INPUT, which is handled by INPUT PROCESSING. The KEY INPUT ENTITY (for whom the system is created) is THE LEARNER. There are four distinct input processes:

* INTERACTION processes that create a working relationship between the EAS and its environment or suprasystem.

* IDENTIFICATION (process) by which the relevance of the input to the EAS is assessed and is established.

* INTRODUCTION of systems-relevant input for transformation, bringing about the ACTIVATION of the system.

* GUIDANCE/MANAGEMENT aided by the processes of feedback/adjustment oversees the input process.

The processes described above are arranged in relationship to each other in Figure 4.12, picturing the input model of EAS's.

INTERACTION establishes a working relationship between an educational activity system and its systemic environment by COMMUNICATION. Educational expectations, requirements, constraints, and the availability of resources are communicated and negotiated. Communication SIGNALS—relevant to these—are constantly coming from the environment. As the EAS interacts with its environment, it receives, decodes, and registers these signals. Signals are registered and screened for their relevance to the system. The POTENTIAL INPUT ENTITIES, which these signals represent, are IDENTIFIED and their values (to the system) are qualified, and, if possible, quantified. Not all potential input entities become actual input. Only input of value to the EAS is ACTIVATED and entered for transformation. Furthermore, not all signals represent clear messages. Some signals are more like noises that often create problems in the course of input processing. The subprocesses of input are characterized next.

THE INTERACTION PROCESS OF EAS's

The process of interaction embraces the first set of input operations. These operations enable the educational activity system (EAS) to establish a working relationship with its environment. It is the front-end and KEY INTELLIGENCE-GATHERING process (of the EAS), carried out by a series of subprocesses that: SEEK, SENSE, RECEIVE, DECODE, VERIFY, AND REGISTER INPUT ENTITIES that come from the environment. Input entities of EAS's

FIGURE 4.12 A MODEL OF INPUT PROCESSING IN EAS's

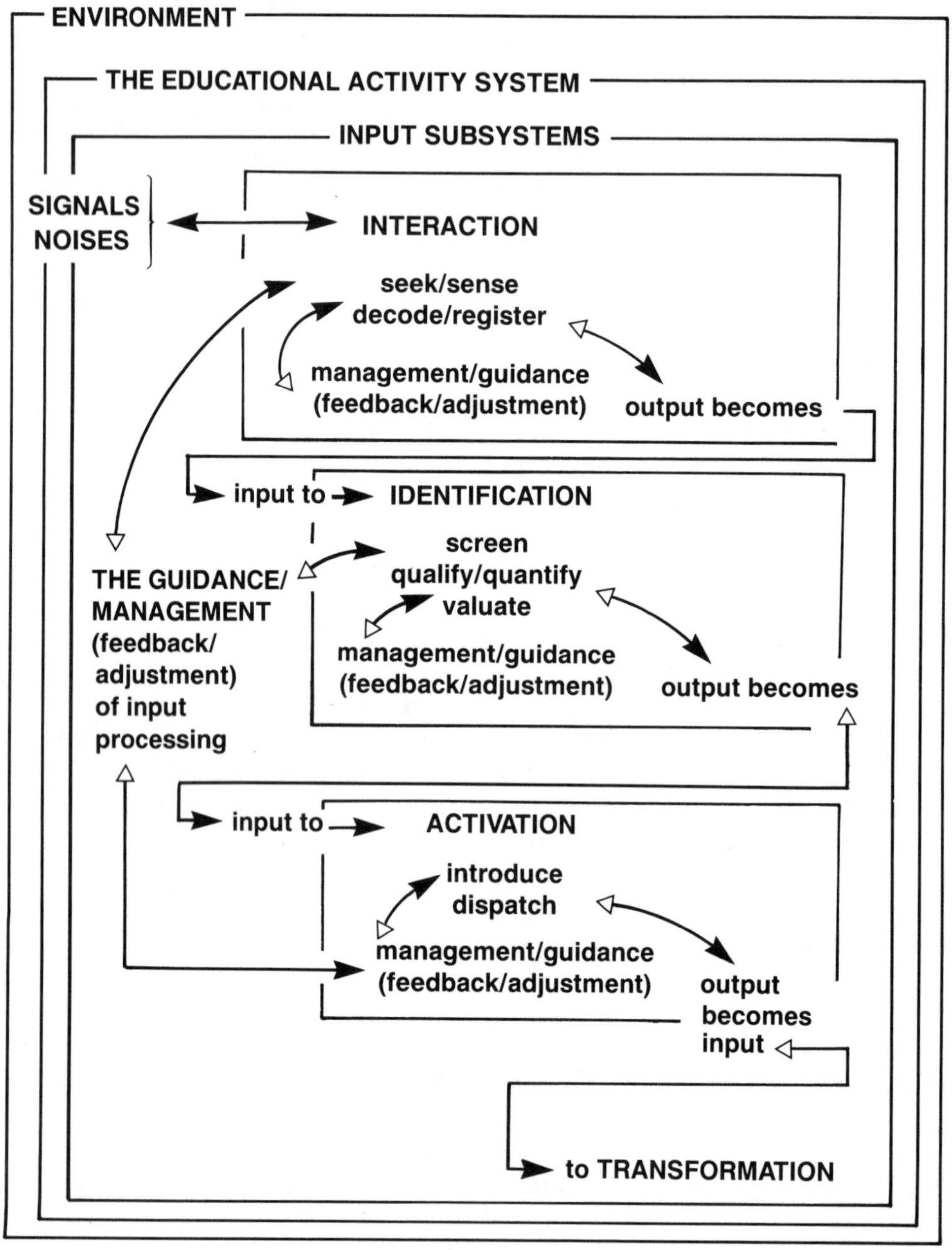

Guidance/Management integrates and oversees the three input processes and their subsystems, makes an assessment of their adequacies, and introduces adjustment and change, if indicated.

include: (1) the LEARNER, who is the SUBJECT and the KEY INPUT ENTITY of the system; (2) COMMUNICATION SIGNALS that bring into the system a variety of information (discussed in Chapter Two) and systems-relevant knowledge; (3) RESOURCES of many kinds (people, financing, facilities, materials) that are required for the life and operation of the EAS. Let us take now a systems view perspective on the three input entities identified here, and ask some questions.

Viewing education as a human activity system at this very point when we are considering what should be the input we process, we are faced with some crucial questions in terms of the three kinds of input entities introduced above. We have already discussed the issue of key entity (the learner) in Chapter Three, when we asked the question: Around whom do we build the system? A systems view helped us to recognize that in existing EAS's the system IS built around the teacher. So we face here a wrenching predicament and troubling anomaly. On the one hand we say (officially) that the key input entity is the learner. On the other hand the system lens helps us to recognize that today we do NOT build the system around the learner. I know we have many excuses, such as: our educational tradition, cost factors, the classroom focused preparation of educational professionals, no R&D support/models/money to do otherwise, and a host of other reasons. But here, as we use the (systems) process perspective, we have to be consistent. If the learner is the key entity then the whole systems process—input and transformation included—has to be arranged around the learner.

ACTIVITY # 40

As your next activity, examine the systems you selected by asking the question: Who is the key entity in your system? What evidence do you have that enables you to answer this question? Take notes so that you can enter your comments in your description in the next section.

Next I take up the issue of RESOURCES that we consider relevant for entry into our EAS's. In the current classroom-based and instruction-focused EAS we have a very narrow scope of what resources are relevant and needed. As we already discussed in Chapter Two, if we draw the boundaries around systems of learning and human development so that they include the whole community as a territory for learning, we immediately broaden and expand the scope of the potential learning resource base. In a sense, the community becomes the classroom and we create unlimited "learning resources for unlimited learning." The current EAS can be characterized as "instructional resources limited" for "limited learning." In the instructional/classroom focused system, resources are usually delivered/requisitioned routinely. On the other hand, in a "learning resources unlimited" system, the input process has to become a very aggressive search as we have to map out potential learning resource territories and identify and ensure the availability of resources. In this case we shall have a very different profile of the input process.

Another input entity issue is the consideration of information/knowledge we enter as input into the EAS. We first confronted this issue in Chapter Two, as we used the systems-environment lens. There we noted the tendency to keep our existing EAS's rather closed and limit the scope of information that we consider in the course of systems-environment interaction. But, as we open up the EAS to the rich information/knowledge source that the exploration of societal characteristics and their educational implications would bring into the system, we have significantly changed the nature of the input and the process by which we bring the input into the system. And if we open up the system to the resources of the community, we again change significantly the scope and nature of information we shall process.

ACTIVITY # 41

In view of the description of resources above, examine in your selected system the scope and nature of the resource and information/knowledge input and the process by which the input is handled. Enter your findings into your notebook.

Each and every input entity is accompanied by communication that labels/defines/describes them. Thus, from here on—in the text—the various INPUT ENTITIES will be handled as SIGNALS. Signals that are received are checked and verified with their source of origin. Signals that are clear and unambiguous are decoded in "language" that is used and understood by people in the EAS. They are registered/recorded/stored (as input received) and are dispatched to the next input process: IDENTIFICATION. Signals are always coming into an open system—such as an EAS—that are less distinctive, ambiguous, weak, or noiselike. A lack of clarity may be related to our inability to receive the signal. Or, it may indicate that we should increase our capacity to seek/sense/receive/decode in order to improve our potential to handle input. We might also go to the source of the signal and ask the source to improve the clarity or strength of the transmission of the message. In either case, interaction is always two-way. It implies not only receiving, but also verifying with the source—through feedback—what has been sensed, received, decoded, and registered. The interaction operations described above are shown in Figure 4.13 as an image of the model of INTERACTION.

It is important in working with EAS's to understand the distinction between SEEK and SENSE. Seeking means an active and

FIGURE 4.13 A SYSTEMS MODEL OF INTERACTION

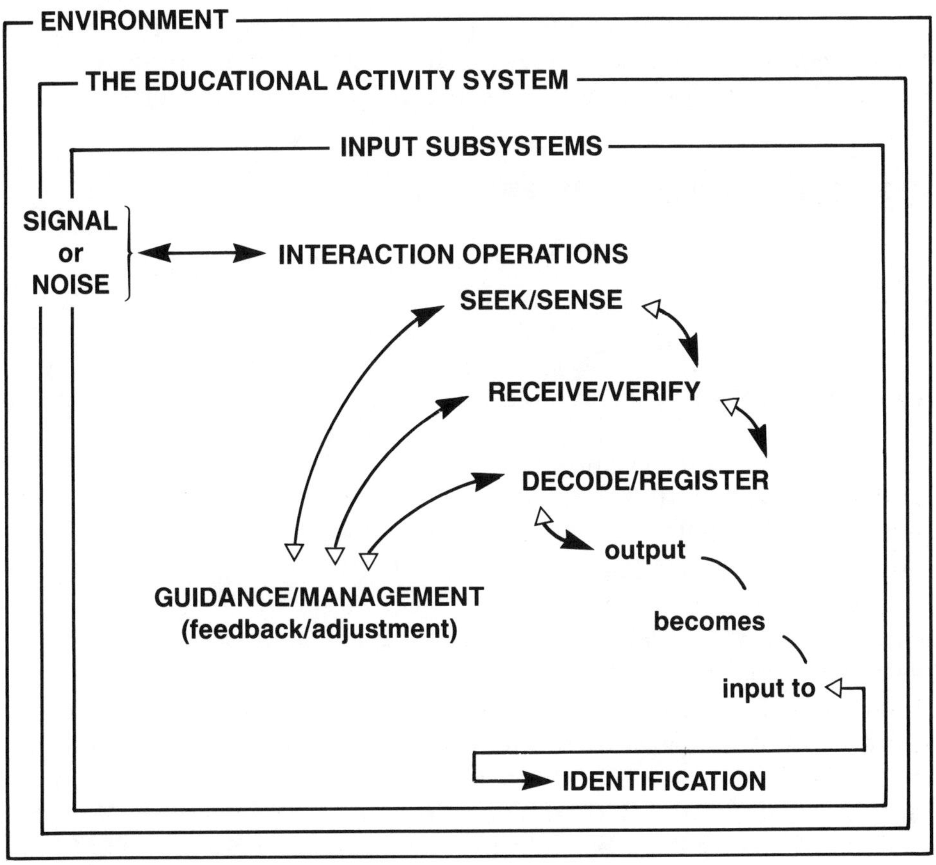

Note that the four systems processes: input, transformation, output, guidance/management/feedback/adjustment again recur at this system level; and are recurring within each of the component operations of interaction.

even aggressive search for systems-relevant information/knowledge and resources in the environment. Sensing implies listening to and considering signals that are coming in, that are offered by various sources in the environment, and are communicated to the system. A major oversight of recent educational improvement efforts has been focusing on sensing, rather than actively/aggressively searching for system-relevant input. An active search is true INTELLIGENCE GATHERING. It would, for example, recognize the massive societal changes that have taken place in the course of the last few decades. It would face up to the new realities that have emerged. It would attempt to understand the educational implications of those new realities. Seeking/searching would bring in such critical information rather than waiting for somebody else to do it. It is only through such active seeking that EAS's can expect to be able to coevolve with their environment and become socially responsible to their clients: the learner (the primary client); to people in the system; to the community and the larger society.

IDENTIFICATION OPERATIONS

The signals and entities that have progressed through interaction operations now enter into the next component process of input, and become subject to identification. The purpose of identification is INTELLIGENCE ANALYSIS, the interpretation of input from the point of its relevance and usefulness to the educational activity system. We identify and select those input entities that are relevant to the stated educational purposes and to the operations of the EAS. The identification process is basically an ASSESSMENT-based SCREENING and SELECTION. This process ensures that only such input that is relevant to the EAS will be allowed to enter into the system. This process will reject (absorb) those input entities that are judged to be irrelevant to the EAS, so that they will not disturb the system.

Those in the EAS who are involved in this process need to have some basis upon which they can determine what IS systems-relevant.They must have in their possession not only information on input requirements but also a detailed model of the DESIGN of the EAS. This design is elaborated in terms of the EAS's societal functions, the core ideas and core values that are collectively shared and articulated, the mission, purposes, specifications, and systems functions that are to be carried out to attain the purposes. (Examples of core values/ideas are referenced in Note 6.) Furthermore, those who are involved in interaction need to have constantly ongoing communication with people who are responsible for the various functions/operations of the system, so that they can verify relevancy. Assuming responsibility for identification and for screening for selection is most critical. Today, in many EAS's this task is often basically flawed for two reasons. One is the use of an outdated DESIGN. The model that represents the design of our current EAS's is some hundred years old. It is hopelessly outdated. Unless we change this design and bring it in line with the design of the post-industrial information society, education will become increasingly irrelevant. The other flaw is a tendency to "protect" the EAS from environmental messages that call for a change of the EAS. These messages are often interpreted by the "protectors" of EAS's as "dangerous disturbances." This protection has gone today to such an extent that some input is screened out—selected out—even though it is of utmost importance to the EAS. This is particularly the case when such a signal indicates a need for basic change OF the system itself and not only change IN the system. Protecting the EAS from input which is relevant to it, one which would "rock the boat," does not do any service to the EAS. Such protection is counterproductive. It will isolate the EAS from "reality," from information/knowledge that is of crucial importance to it. This isolation may lead to a separation of the system from its environment. If it continues to go on, the EAS might become increasingly irrelevant to the society, possibly leading to its termination.

Through the assessment/screening/selection operations of the identification process we designate input as being relevant (or not being relevant) to the EAS. We also establish the value of the input to the EAS. Depending on the nature of the input and the means that are available to assess its value to the EAS, a judgment can be made which could be qualitative or quantitative. For example, information that conveys the educational implications of changed societal characteristics can be qualified in terms of relevance to help us determine what should be learned and how, and how we can best guide learning. (For examples of educational implications of emerged societal characteristics see Note 7.) On the other hand, financial resources required (by the EAS) are obviously quantifiable. The outcome of the identification process is a designation of systems-relevant input. The criterion for judging relevance and adequacy of the input is the prevailing model of the design of the EAS. This model helps us to define the required state, properties, and characteristics of the desired input. It helps us to determine to what extent the state, properties, and characteristics of the input match those of the EAS. It is this model to which we compare the outcome (output) of identification in order to: (1) verify or introduce adjustments in the identification process and its component operations, and (2) verify the adequacy of input or identify what input is NOT coming in that should be available to the EAS. But it should be understood that this model is always subject to change if, for example, the educational implications of emerged societal characteristics call for a change in the design of the EAS. Figure 4.14 depicts the image of the model of identification. It is through guidance/management that we ensure the appropriate use of the "model" of the system as well as verify the appropriateness of the model itself.

FIGURE 4.14 A MODEL OF THE IDENTIFICATION PROCESS

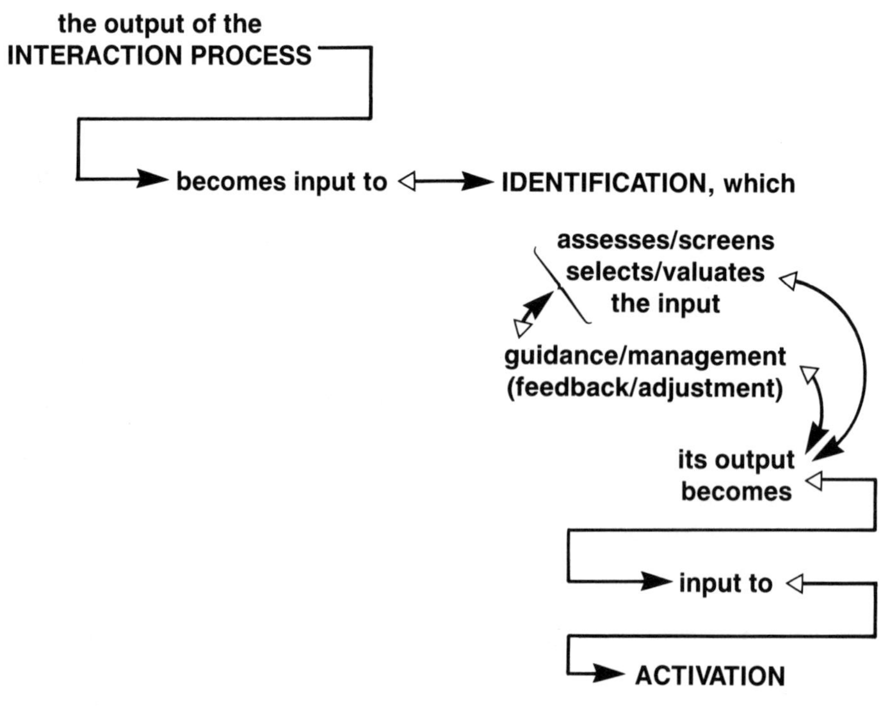

THE PROCESS OF INTRODUCTION/ACTIVATION

The last process in the input sequence of EAS's is comprised of two operations: the INTRODUCTION of the processed input for transformation and—by this—the ACTIVATION of the transformation process. These operations deliver the specific input needed at the specified place and time. The process of introduction/activation is subject to two kinds of feedback and feedback-based adjustment:

Feedback/adjustment will determine if all input entities that are required for the activations of the EAS are indeed available and if they have the needed characteristics. This determination is made based on the model of the system that specifies what is required, desired, or needed, and when and where.

Once introduced for transformation, feedback from transformation guidance/management will verify adequacy, or it will challenge the adequacy of the input provided. If this is the case, it calls for adjustment. This second type is a very dynamic process. It does not rely only on the model of the system but also on the reasoned judgment of those who receive the output of the introduction/activation process. Figure 4.15 depicts the model of introduction/activation.

FIGURE 4.15 A MODEL OF INTRODUCTION/ACTIVATION

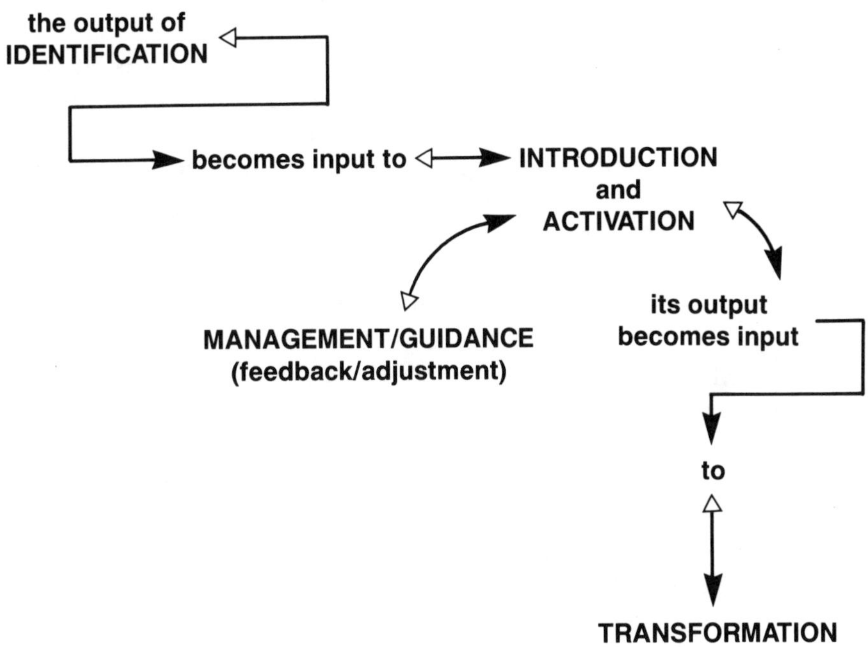

Interaction, Identification, and Introduction/Activation are the three sequential subsystems of processing input in EAS's. They are coordinated, integrated, and managed by a GUIDANCE process that embraces the three subsystems of INTELLIGENCE GATHERING/ANALYSIS/VERIFICATION. The GENERIC characteristics of guidance/management are similar to those of the guidance/management of the entire system, but their scope is limited to the input process. In its SPECIFICS, GUIDANCE/MANAGEMENT ensures: (1) the purposefulness of the interaction with the environment, particularly the agressiveness of the search process, (2) a smooth input flow through the three processes into transformation, (3) internal consistency in the operations of the three processes, (4) appropriate use of the system model (by which the relevance/adequacy/accuracy/timeliness of the input is determined), (5) the appropriateness of the system model we use, (6) recording/documentation/storing/distributing input, (7) interaction with the transformation process, (8) interaction and integration with the guidance/management of the EAS, (9) adjustment/change if indicated, and (10) continuous organizational learning and capacity and capability development. Figure 4.16 pictures guidance/management.

SUMMARY OF THE INPUT PROCESS

The inquiry of how educational activity systems work—or rather should work—at their "input range" has resulted in the description of four major processes that are "generic" to all HAS's and are generic to the various EAS's. These processes—interaction, identification, activation, and guidance—are organized as the front-end intelligence gathering and analysis processes of the EAS and comprise a system of interdependent, interacting, and integrated whole. The input entities that this front-end system is processing in EAS's are now reviewed as follows:

* The LEARNER, who is the key systems entity, who becomes the key subject of the EAS, and around whom we should build the EAS.
* INFORMATION/KNOWLEDGE about the characteristics of the societal environment and the implications of these characteristics to education.
* EXPECTATIONS/ASPIRATIONS/MISSION/PURPOSE, SPECIFICATIONS, and SYSTEMS FUNCTIONS that are formed JOINTLY by people in the community and the EAS.
* INFORMATION/KNOWLEDGE, PEOPLE, MATERIAL/FINANCIAL RESOURCES, and FACILITIES that are needed to accomplish transformation.
* CONSTRAINTS, under which the system is to operate.
* INFORMATION generated by FEEDBACK from the ENVI-

FIGURE 4.16 THE MODEL OF INPUT GUIDANCE/MANAGEMENT

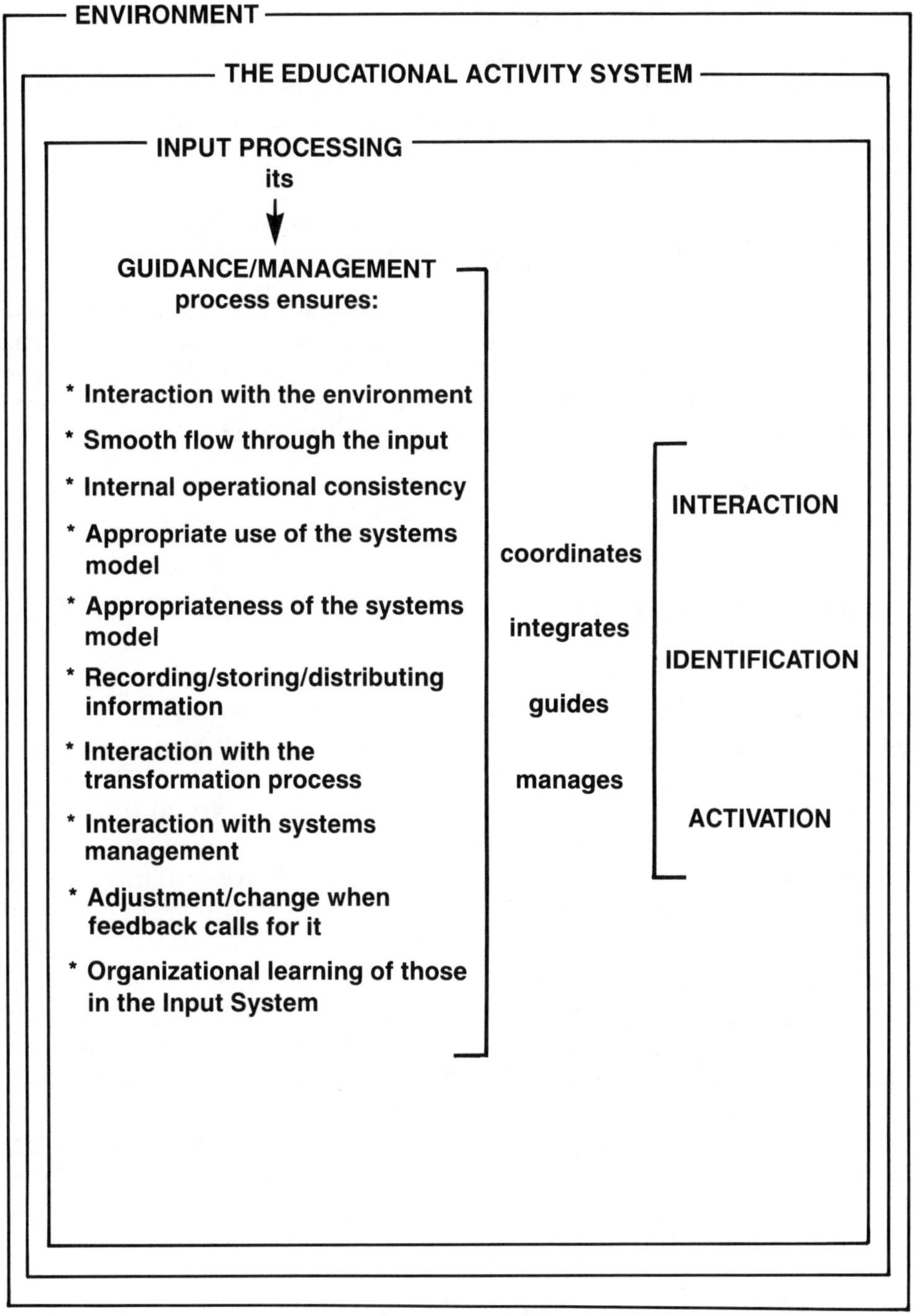

RONMENT (as to the adequacy of the output of the system) and FEEDBACK from the SYSTEM ITSELF (see later under systems guidance/management).

In reviewing the complexity and the dynamics of the input processes we should be impressed by their significance and criticality to the life and operations of EAS's. It is my assessment that these processes are the ones that are the least understood and manifested in education today.

ACTIVITY # 42

You have been asked to make notes as you worked with the text above. Use your notes, my description, and your earlier description/formulation of the input model of your selected EAS and synthesize the three sources. If you developed two descriptions (a description of the selected system as it IS, and a description of what that EAS SHOULD be), enter both synthesized descriptions in your notebook.

THE TRANSFORMATION PROCESS IN EAS's

The four major systems processes in educational activity systems—information processing, transformation, output processing, and guidance/management (aided by feedback/adjustment)—bring the system to life and mark its progress through time. Given the initial conditions created by the input process by which the EAS is activated, it becomes the TASK of the transformation process to bring about the desired outcomes: (1) the learner's mastery of knowledge and understanding, skills and dispositions, values and beliefs; and (2) the development of the learner's full mental, physical, spiritual, and social potential. There is no more important task than this and there can be no more noble undertaking by people than working with the learner to attain these outcomes. Transformation has three major interdependent, interacting, and integrated processes that comprise the transformation (sub)system of the educational activity system. These are: transformation production, transformation facilitation, and transformation guidance/management. These are defined next, and are pictured in Figure 4.17, and discussed in the text below.

TRANSFORMATION PRODUCTION in EAS's is the primary transformation process. In fact it is the primary and most salient process of the entire EAS. This process is what an EAS is about. In the course of this process, the key systems entity, the LEARNER, all others who assist the learner, and all the specific means/resources by which learning experiences are mediated, engage in integrated systemic operations and use appropriate resources/facilities/arrangements in order to accomplish the goal of transformation. This goal is the TRANSFORMATION OF THE LEARNER into a state where the learner attains the desired mastery of learning and develops his/her full potential.

TRANSFORMATION FACILITATION serves, enables, and empowers the primary transformation process: the transformation of the learner. It aims at energizing and motivating the learner and all those who work with the learner in the "learning experience venture," so that they can collectively make continuous and effective contributions to the attainment of desired outcomes.

TRANSFORMATION GUIDANCE/MANAGEMENT serves the two transformation processes described above. The purpose of this process is to ensure that all components, resources, and information/knowledge that are required for the main work of the EAS—the transformation of the learner—are available at the time and place needed with the appropriate capabilities, capacities, and attributes. Guidance/management oversees and leads the transformation operations, monitors, and analyzes them, based on which, changes are designed and introduced if indicated. Figure 4.17 pictures the first model of transformation. It presents an image of the three transformation processes and the relationship of transformation to the input processes.

TRANSFORMATION PRODUCTION

The key process of transformation is the transformation of the KEY ENTITY OF THE SYSTEM, THE LEARNER, from an input state to a state where the desired outcomes are achieved: learning mastered and the learner's potential fully developed. Viewing this process from the prevailing "schooling" perspective, we might say that this process involves helping individuals finish high school or attain a degree or degrees. From a systemic viewpoint this represents a VERY LIMITED perspective. A systems view leads us to see the wholeness of people, in the scope of their entire life, and in the context of unlimited opportunities/resources/situations that are available for learning and human development. In this view, learn-

4.17 A SYSTEMS MODEL OF TRANSFORMATION

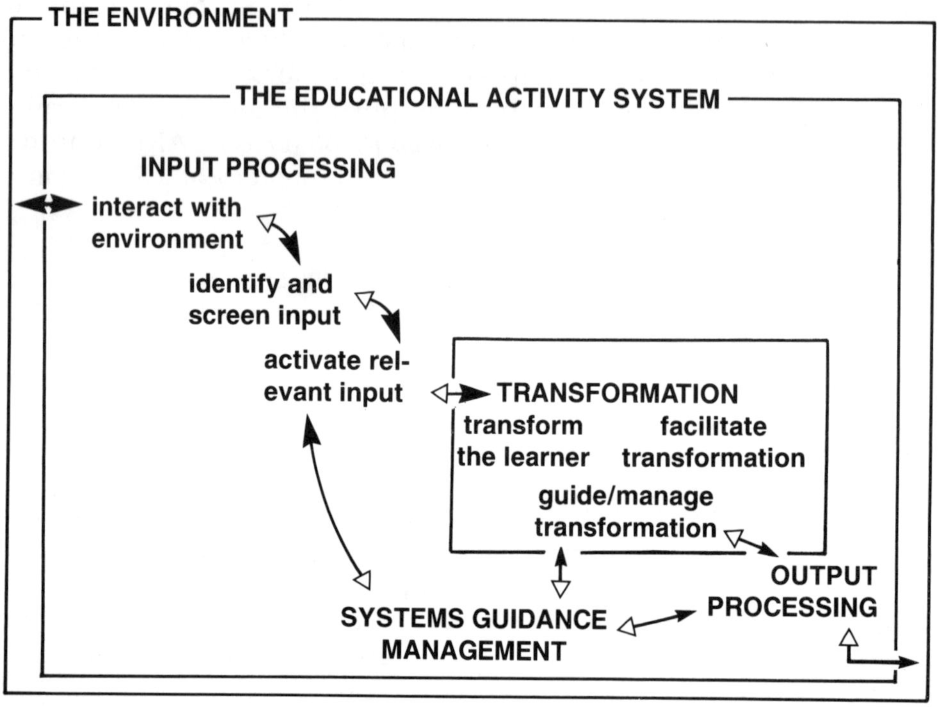

ing NEVER ends. We are projecting—again—the concept of "learning resources unlimited" for "unlimited learning." The transformation of the learner is comprised of two component processes. The first process includes operations that are SPECIFIC to EAS's. The second is identified—in SECTION ONE of this chapter—as a process that is GENERIC to all HAS's. We call this the SYSTEMIZATION/INTEGRATION process of transformation. These two are discussed below.

THE TRANSFORMATION OF THE LEARNER is a process that is specific to the EAS. This process has a set of operations that can be defined, based on: the statement of purposes of the specific EAS, its systems specification (which among other aspects specifies the client(s) of the EAS), and the system of functions that responds to the purposes and specifications. All these are formulated in the structural model AND through the input process. Given these, and a learner who is served by the system, the specific-to-the-system (and now also to the learner) operations include the following:

* Operations by which longer range learning goals and shorter range learning objectives are negotiated, are agreed upon, and formulated within such learning domains as knowledge, understanding, skills, values, dispositions, and attitudes.

* Operations by which—given learning goals and objectives in the various domains of learning—we identify learning tasks that have to be attended to in order to achieve the goals/objectives of the learner.

* Operations by which we select and organize streams of content that are appropriate to represent the identified learning tasks.

* Operations by which resources, arrangements, opportunities, situations, means and methods, learning support technologies, and learning territories are selected, organized, and made available to the learner, and which have the power to mediate the content through specifically designed learning experiences.

* Operations by which means and methods are selected and organized that are appropriate to the assessment of learning goals and objectives achieved.

* Operations by which all the above is guided and managed by the learner and those who support and provide for the experiences.

The operations above are in stark contrast with those that are carried out in the classroom-based and instruction-focused schooling practices. The text referred to in Note 8 provides a contrasting presentation of the instructional versus learning experience focused education.

ACTIVITY # 43

In view of the above text and the referenced material, examine your selected system and characterize the operations by which it provides for education. Enter your findings in your notebook.

SYSTEMIZATION/INTEGRATION. Operations of this process are carried out in order to make all aspects/components of this process of the EAS ever more systems-like and integrated, and to bring about a state of "wholeness." As an educational activity system is activated by the input process, it is set in motion by its purposes in response to which it organizes the components and initiates the processes that bring about the transformation of the learner. The functions of these components and the processes by which the components carry out these functions are becoming ever more clarified, specified, and integrated: they become ever more

SYSTEMS-LIKE. This is not accidental. It is a major SYSTEM'S PURPOSE that is generic to all HAS's and it is—and should be—a major purpose of an EAS. The process by which this purpose is achieved is: PROGRESSIVE INTEGRATION AND SYSTEMIZATION, that serves the transformation process.

The process of SYSTEMIZATION/INTEGRATION is one of SELF-ORGANIZATION that is distributed in all parts of the system. This requires that all those who are in the system have a clear image of what the EAS is about, what their role is in it, what their relationship is to all others in the system, and how they can become ever more involved in the work and life of the system. The very basis of integration and systemization is a COLLECTIVELY FORMULATED VISION of the societal functions of education and a vision of how OUR system will carry out such functions (how the vision is manifested in our EAS). A vision that is SHARED by all people who are in the system and who are related to it. It is NOT top-down driven. It is not even something to "buy-into." It is something we believe in and to which we commit ourselves. It is generated by the process of a "vision-quest" in which all participate and to which all contribute. It is a living and unfolding process that is shaped throughout the life of the system. Such a vision is the GENESIS of the formulation of the kinds of systems models we are developing here. (An example of a "visioning" is referenced in Note 9.)

The two generic processes of transformation production in EAS's—the transformation of the learner and systemization/integration—do operate simultaneously and they are integrated.

TRANSFORMATION FACILITATION

Educational activity systems are living, working, purpose-seeking, and fulfilling. To live and work and seek and pursue purposes, all those who are in the EAS need to be MOTIVATED and ENERGIZED, so that they can maintain behavior by which they can make contributions individually and collectively to the intended outcome: the transformation of the learner. Motivation and energizing are interdependent and interacting; their synergy brings about the facilitation of transformation.

MOTIVATION plays an important role in human activity systems. And in EAS's it plays a CRUCIAL role. In many HAS's—primarily in the private sector—transformation involves the production of goods and services. Even in the public sector the focus of transformation in most HAS's is on providing occasional services to the public. In EAS's, transformation is singularly unique. It involves the transformation of peoples' lives—through learning and human development—that goes on for years and years. Many believe that it should go on throughout one's life. Thus, motivation plays a uniquely important role in EAS's. But what kind of motivation do we speak of here that fits the notion of uniqueness?

We make a distinction between motivation that is **EXTRINSIC** and that is **INTRINSIC**. The source of the EXTRINSIC motivation of people in HAS's is an expectation of keeping a job, advancing or getting a promotion, being well paid, keeping the boss happy, gaining some recognition, or being praised for a job well done. This kind of motivation works in coercive systems in which compliance is expected, where the vision is espoused from the top down, expecting people to "buy-into" it or at least accept it. I suspect that in many EAS's this type of motivation is very much prevalent and is deemed to be adequate, e.g., "The problem is that we don't pay teachers enough." The situs of extrinsic motivation is the individual. Because of what it is expected to produce, it does put people in the HAS in competition (for promotion, recognition, etc). The force of external motivation is at best moderate and seldom moves people to do their utmost. In most HAS's, efforts/processes/programs by which to generate motivation are designed in view of the kind of expectations mentioned above.

INTRINSIC motivation comes from within. It is a driving force that is grounded in a collectively developed and shared vision, in a total commitment to that vision, in shared core values and core ideas, and in individual and collective mastery. It enables us to make optimum contributions to the transformation of the learner, in the practice of teamwork and cooperation with the learner and with others who work with him/her, and in the belief—the conviction—that nurturing the transformation of the learner is the noblest of all human ventures. Its situs is both the collective and the individual. A major difference between intrinsic and extrinsic motivation is that while the individual sources of intrinsic motivation can stand on their own and may engender motivation (e.g., more pay, or promotion, or recognition), for intrinsic motivation the various sources described above constitute an interacting and integrated SYSTEM (of motivation). A HAS that does not include the idea of intrinsic purposefulness and motivation falls back upon a mechanistic model. The fundamental task of HAS's that aspire to generate intrinsic motivation is to DESIGN FOR its development and for its continuing nurturing and enrichment. This is a crucial design task. But such a design cannot be created by others for an EAS. If we expect shared vision, total commitment, collective mastery, and collective/cooperative behavior, such can be generated ONLY by involving ALL people in the system, in its design, and in its implementation. No small task!

ENERGIZING. Considering ENERGIZING we are faced with two issues: WHO—or what system component—should be energized? and HOW should we energize? People—most importantly the learner—and entities (groups of people and other components) who participate in the transformation of the learner need to be maintained in a state or condition that enables them to contribute to the transformation process. This enabling is accomplished by energizing. Questions we might ask here include the following:

* Does the individual/group/component possess characteristics and capabilities that enable/ensure contribution to the transformation process?

* Does the individual/group/component actually make the contribution that is appropriate and needed for the attainment of the transformation of the learner?

If the answer to the questions above is YES, then we ask:

* Is the individual/group/component adequately energized to make the contribution?

As we have already seen in developing the functions/structure model, the stipulation of the appropriate contribution to the purpose/functions was kept in mind as components were selected. But that stipulation was *a priori*. Now the system comes to life through the transformation process, and the capabilities and the actions of all who participate in the transformation of the learner have to be carefully and continuously assessed, and at the same time they have to be continuously energized so that they are empowered to make their contributions.

The issue of HOW to energize depends on the issue of: What kind of motivation are we after? If we are satisfied with EXTRINSIC motivation, then we energize by meeting the conditions (of extrinsic motivation) as discussed above. Inasmuch as we have not looked at EAS's from a systems perspective until now, we have been satisfied with maintaining the conditions necessary to generate such extrinsic motivation. But once we begin to understand education from a systems perspective, once we focus on the learning experience level and define the learner as our key client, nothing short of developing and engendering INTRINSIC motivation will suffice. Thus, we shall engage in a process that enables us to attain: shared vision and total commitment to it, shared core values and ideas, individual and collective competence, and capability to act and participate in the transformation of the learner process through cooperation as a collective involvement of all people in the system.

ACTIVITY # 44

In view of the above description of TRANSFORMATION FACILITATION, explore the situation in your selected system and describe how the transformation of the learner is facilitated in it. Describe your findings in your notebook.

TRANSFORMATION GUIDANCE/MANAGEMENT

Transformation guidance/management is embedded in the guidance/management of the entire system and it provides on-going information to it. It oversees the processes involved in the transformation of the learner, and links up and coordinates with both the input and output processes. The primary concern of transformation guidance/management is: (1) whether the transformation of the learner is accomplished as anticipated and expected and (2) whether the transformation process is adequately facilitated. Information is collected continuously on the accomplishment of these two processes in order to introduce adjustments/changes if so indicated. Transformation guidance faces two major tasks.

First, it is to ensure that all those involved in the transformation of the learner perform in a way that guarantees the eventual attainment of the purpose of transformation. This task is accomplished by involving the learner and others who make arrangements for learning and by providing resources for learning in the assessment of learning tasks completed, as well as making assessment of the effectiveness of those who work with the learner as to their contribution to the transformation of the learner. If there is a difference between the IS and SHOULD, adjustments are introduced. Monitoring, measuring, and assessing performance, analyzing it, and making adjustments constitute the PERFORMANCE EFFECTIVENESS dimension of the transformation guidance/ management process.

Second, guidance/management of the transformation process makes an assessment about whether the transformation of the learner is accomplished within cost-constraints. This is the COST-EFFECTIVENESS dimension of transformation guidance. Within the two dimensions introduced here there is often conflict: cost and effectiveness are usually in opposition. An increase in effectiveness often calls for more resources. Transformation guidance seeks to attain a balance between these two.

The implementation of judgments made by transformation guidance takes the form of considering a variety of options, such as: (1) replacing an existing function or component involved in the transformation of the learner process or changing existing interaction patterns; (2) introducing additional functions, components, and interactions by which to facilitate the transformation of the learner; (3) altering/modifying/increasing the capabilities of those involved in the transformation of the learner; (4) engaging already available—but not yet activated—capabilities, resources, and opportunities that will facilitate learning; (5) increasing arrangements for facilitating (energizing/motivating) the transformation of the learning process; and (6) considering adjustments/changes in our expectations of what learning is to be achieved.

Transformation guidance/management, a subsystem of the transformation system, oversees the processes and operations of the transformation of the learning process and the process of its facilitation. Jointly these three constitute the very core process of an educational activity system.

ACTIVITY # 45

In this activity, focus on the guidance/management process of your selected EAS. Describe how it operates in overseeing the transformation process. If you wish, you can speculate about how it should operate. Introduce your findings in your notebook.

OUTPUT PROCESSING

Processing the output of EAS's involves such processes as: (1) the IDENTIFICATION AND ASSESSMENT of output that is relevant to the model of the expected outcome; (2) the introduction or DISPATCHING of the output (the learner and other output entities) to the environment, to other stages of the EAS, or to other EAS's;

FIGURE 4.18 A MODEL OF THE OUTPUT PROCESS

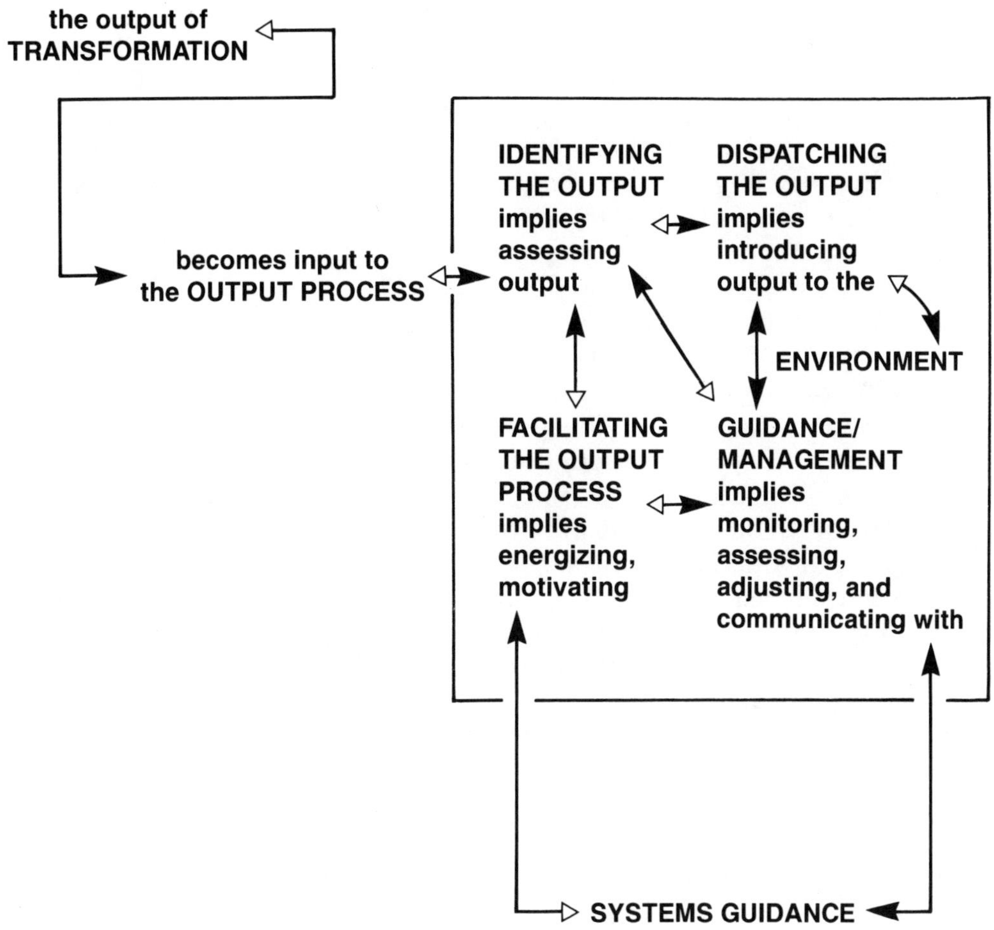

(3) FACILITATING the output process; and (4) providing GUIDANCE to and MANAGING the process. This model is shown in Figure 4.18.

IDENTIFYING AND ASSESSING THE OUTPUT

Upon completion of the transformation of the learner, the EAS enters into the next major systems process: the OUTPUT process. The identification and assessment of the output has as many dimensions as purposes that we identified for the EAS. (1) The primary dimension is the introduction of the learner who has gone through the transformation process—and information about the transformation process—for output processing. In the context of this dimension we are to determine and describe the achievement of the learner in terms of the knowledge, understanding, skills, dispositions, values, and attitudes attained and developed. (2) Other outcome dimensions reflect other stated systems purposes, such as: (a) the kind of relationship that should be maintained with the environment (e.g., coevolution), (b) the nature of the relationship with the community and (c) with other systems, (d) stated purposes for the quality of the working environment, (e) the development of organizational capacity and professional competence, (f) the nature of motivational characteristics to be developed, (g) continuous organizational learning, and some others.

The outcome model of the EAS is comprised of the outcome dimensions that reflect the purposes of the EAS, such as those mentioned above. The model describes the expected achievement in terms of the dimensions (purposes). The questions that drive the identification/assessment process include the following: (1) Is the outcome attained relevant to the outcome model? (2) Does it match the characteristics of the expected outcome state as described in the outcome model? (3) Have we produced outcome that is NOT relevant to the purpose(s), but may be (or may not be) of value?

Findings of the identification/assessment process are documented and communicated to those involved in dispatching the output and to the guidance/management of the output process. We should remind ourselves that identification and assessment are processes that happen continuously in the course of the transformation process and they aid an ongoing "formative" evaluation. In the course of the output process, however, assessment is "summative."

DISPATCHING THE OUTPUT

If the comparison between the intended output and the output model shows that the output matches the characteristics of the model, the intended output becomes candidate to actual input, and it is introduced or dispatched to the environment or sequential phases of the EAS or to other EAS's. Dispatching involves three communication operations: (1) communication with the environment that, for example, describes (labels) the output state characteristics of the learner, (2) the acquisition of information (feedback) from the environment or system that has received the output (pertaining to the adequacy of the output), and (3) sharing information on (1) and (2) with output process guidance/management.

OUTPUT PROCESS FACILITATION

This process is similar to the transformation facilitation. The concern of this process (briefly) is facilitating, motivating, and energizing behavior that enhances the output process. Only those components are energized that make appropriate contribution to the output process and to the attainment of the purposes of the EAS. Of special concern here is motivating the learner to continue a quest for continuing learning and development.

OUTPUT PROCESS GUIDANCE/MANAGEMENT

This process is similar to the guidance/management processes of input and transformation. It involves: (1) the monitoring of all output process components, (2) assessing the effectiveness/adequacy of the way the processes are carried out, (3) introducing adjustments if needed, and (4) communicating the findings—generated in the course of the output process—to systems guidance/management.

ACTIVITY # 46

You are asked now to review this text's characterization of the output process and use its propositions in describing and analyzing the output process of your selected system. You might also speculate about the difference between the existing output processing of your system and output processing that you believe SHOULD be developed in your system. Describe your findings in your notebook.

SYSTEMS GUIDANCE/MANAGEMENT (FEEDBACK/ADJUSTMENT/CHANGE)

In the course of our journey toward the development of a systems process view of education, we have arrived at the fourth and last major process domain of educational activity systems: the process of systems guidance/management and feedback/adjustment/change. Guidance/management permeates all process domains. Adjustment and change operate based on feedback-information that comes from the guidance/management of the input/transformation/output processes and from the environment. In the text below, first I discuss adjustment, then systems change, and finally, systems guidance/management.

ADJUSTMENT

As we already discussed earlier (primarily in Chapter Two), EAS's make adjustments based on information coming from NEGATIVE feedback. They stipulate and introduce (whole) system change based on information coming from POSITIVE feedback. Negative feedback driven adjustment involves five operations:

* collecting evidence on the adequacy of competence attained by learners, other output entities, and systems operation;
* analyzing and interpreting the evidence collected;
* constructing a model of adjustment;
* stipulating the consequences of adjustments;
* introducing adjustments.

Figure 4.19 pictures the relationship of the five operations identified above and their relationship to other process domains of the EAS.

COLLECT EVIDENCE. The processes of an EAS are manifested in the behavior of the system. Thus, if we wish to make an assessment of how well an EAS carries out its defined processes—and by so doing to what extent the EAS attains its purposes—we need to collect evidence by observing and assessing systems behavior and the outcomes resulting from such behavior. The assessment of evidence and its interpretation will be the bases for constructing and introducing adjustments. There are several sources we can examine to collect evidence.

The first source is findings derived by the application of the OUTPUT MODEL. As we already discussed, this model has as many dimensions—and criteria attached to those dimensions—as the purposes the EAS defined for itself. For example, the model that portrays learning to be attained; and other models that characterize: interaction with the environment, coordination with other systems that are relevant to learning and human development, the development of organizational capacity and staff capability, the

FIGURE 4.19 A SYSTEMIC PICTURE OF ADJUSTMENT

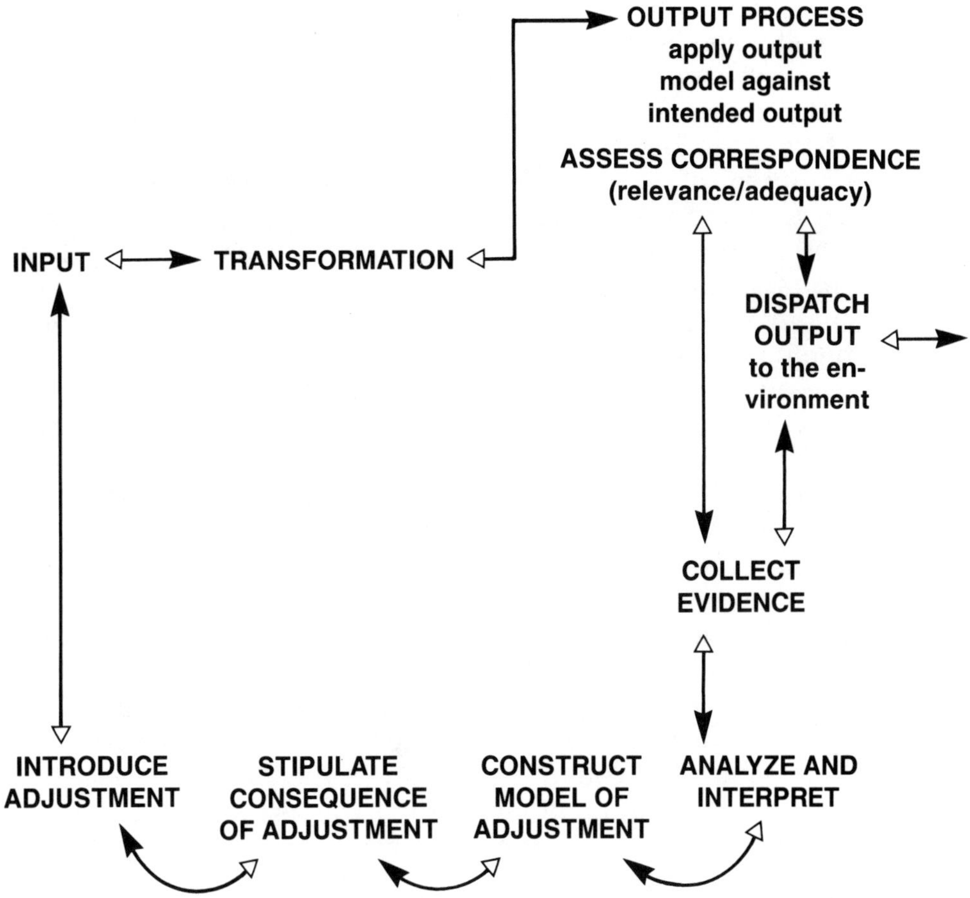

quality of the work environment, the model of motivation, continuous organizational learning, etc. In collecting evidence on learning attained, we use the model of learning outcomes as well as seeking evidence from learners as to their assessment of learning mastered, their judgment of readiness attained, and what they wanted to attain at this point. The same two-pronged approach could be used in collecting evidence in terms of all the other purposes. The evidence collected will be recorded (become part of the system's memory) and is communicated to the next phase of the adjustment process as well as to systems guidance/management.

Our second source of evidence is assessment information we have collected cumulatively in the course of the input and transformation processes. This assessment information gives us insight into the life and work of the EAS. This ongoing/continuous information collection is often more useful and more revealing than information collected in the course of the output process. It opens up the BLACK BOX of the EAS and helps us to find out what adjustments have been accomplished with what results. It is such ongoing assessment of the effectiveness of systems processes that enables us to make adjustments at the most appropriate time and place and reduce the risk of having "rejects"—as we have them today in large numbers in our EAS's—at the output stage. Our EAS's today still base their assessment on "input-output models." The ongoing assessment described here should also monitor those processes and their outcomes that are related to the other purposes of the EAS, such as those I mentioned above. In addition to being a source of evidence, the process described here provides us with a documentation of the "performance history" of our educational systems.

The third source of evidence is the systems in the environment into which learners and other outcome entities are dispatched. Information on reaction of the environment to the received output is collected in the course of the output process and communicated to systems guidance/management. Such information is a significant source of evidence. It is a salient responsibility of systems guidance/management to convey the "output model" to the systems that receive the output and to have their concurrence of the appropriateness of the model. Much of the discussion today is focused on the concern that systems that receive the output of education have about the inadequacy of and the lack of preparation of those who enter their systems. If there is discrepancy between output produced (by EAS's) and output desired or needed, adjustment and possibly even a systems change might be in order.

Some of the comprehensive inquiries that drive the collection of evidences include the following:

* What aspects of the EAS (such as processes/operations, components, attributes of components, and performance models and attributes of models) are not in evidence, the lack of which prevent the attainment of desired outcomes? (What is missing from the EAS?)

* What aspects of the EAS (see above) are deficient and thus contribute less than their share in bringing about desired outcomes and outcome characteristics? (What does not work well?)

* What aspects of the EAS (see above) bring about outcomes that are not relevant to the various dimensions of the outcome model or serve something other than the stated purpose(s)? (What is redundant?) But, if any one of these provides unexpected value, what should be done about it? How should it be used?

* Are we getting a good educational return on our investment? Are there ways that we can improve the economy of the system?

These are broad and "generic" inquiries, but they might help us to understand and appreciate the scope of the process of collecting evidence. The above comprehensive inquiries have to be shredded out into seeking specific evidence relevant to specific processes/operations/components/conditions of the EAS.

ANALYZE AND INTERPRET EVIDENCE. The evidence we have collected is now analyzed and interpreted for action to be taken. The analysis determines the nature, the scope, and the intensity of the discrepancy as revealed by the evidence. Interpretation, then, determines the significance of the findings of the analysis and makes judgments about priorities of adjustments to be implemented.

CONSTRUCT MODELS OF ADJUSTMENT. The interpretation of the evidence revealed weaknesses in the EAS. It told us what might have caused less-than-desired behavior and less-than-desired educational and other performance outcomes. Now we shall use this valuable information to construct models of adjustments. The specifics of the model (of adjustment) will correspond to the specifics of processes/operations/components that have brought about these failures and inadequacies. The size, the scope, and the intensity of the adjustment has to match that of the discrepancy. In constructing adjustment models, we should always create alternatives and select—for application—the alternative that is most likely to ensure the attainment of desired learning outcomes, the one that brings about appropriate process/component performance (such as organizational learning), or create the desired systems condition (such as a high quality working environment).

STIPULATE CONSEQUENCES. Alternatives of adjustment models are tested by making judgments on such aspects as : (1) the power of the alternative to bring about the desired adjustment; (2) the ease or difficulty of implementing the alternative; (3) possible short- and long-range effects; (4) compatibility with the learner, with others in the system, with the targeted processes, operations, conditions, and the adjustment environment; (5) possible disruptions; (6) possible side-effects, such as constraints caused by the alternative; and (7) time and cost factors. These aspects will help us to judge the advantage vs. disadvantage inherent in the planned adjustment. A key consideration is the need to involve the learner—if the learner is affected by the adjustment—in stipulating consequences, as well as all others in the system who would be affected by the adjustment.

INTRODUCING ADJUSTMENT. Once a particular adjustment alternative is selected, a decision has to be made about when and under what circumstances it should be introduced. Questions we consider include: What is the best time for its introduction? What preparations are required? What has to be learned by those who work with the adjustment? How do we involve all those affected by the adjustment in answering these—and possibly other—questions? It is wise to introduce adjustments on a tentative basis so that we can see how they work before we implement adjustments.

ACTIVITY # 47

Take a look at the system you have selected and explore ways that adjustments are made. Compare those ways (of adjustment) to the process of adjustment suggested in this text. Give some examples. Describe your findings in your notebook.

SYSTEMS CHANGE

As we have discussed above, the process of adjustment is driven by **NEGATIVE** feedback. It confirms the viability/appropriateness of the (model of) the educational activity system and its educational outcome model. It tells us DO NOT DEVIATE from the model. The system is OK as it is defined, but something IN it is not OK. It brings to our attention if we DO deviate from it; it tells us if there is a discrepancy between the actual system behavior and the model of the behavior, the actual educational outcome and the model of the outcome; so that we can correct (by adjustment) the educational outcome, the particular process, the particular component, the particular arrangement that is responsible for the deviation. Negative feedback tells us that something is wrong IN the system, again IN the system, and that something has to be done about it, something has to be adjusted IN it.

POSITIVE feedback tells us that the SYSTEM IS the ONE which has to be changed. It signals a judgment about the whole EAS, about its model, about its design, about its educational outcome model. In this case we are NOT in the business of reducing deviation but increasing it. Make the SYSTEM different: change it. But who makes the judgment? And, what tells us to change? As we have already discussed in Chapter Two, the two main sources (of positive feedback) are: the environment (and systems in the environment) and those who are in the system. Let me explore these two sources and their relevance to the change of an EAS.

IF an educational activity system has a healthy interactive (coevolutionary) relationship with the environment; IF it will continuously listen to it and try to understand it; IF it constantly explores emerging societal changes and grasps ongoing societal transformations; and IF it understands the educational implications of these changes and transformations, and senses and defines emerging educational requirements and human development aspirations, THEN it will be able to shape its coevolution with the society, and will be able to accommodate society's educational and human development requirements. The four "IF's" should be understood to be a system of interdependent and integrated processes with associated capabilities, the presence of which is necessary for systems change to happen. But the presence of those IF's is not sufficient yet for change to happen. Only if there IS a willingness (of people in the system) to change, and only if another systemic set of characteristics—internal to the system—is also present shall we have met the condition of sufficiency. These internal-to-the-system characteristics are described next.

IF the educational activity system has the kind of characteristics that I described earlier, namely, that its primary driving force is intrinsic motivation; IF it is guided by the shared vision and shared values and core ideas of all people in the system; IF its social climate is built on cooperation; IF it is a learning organization; IF it develops and maintains a high quality of the working environment; and IF people in the system develop mastery of competencies required for their involvement: THEN—and only then—will it be able to RENEW itself continuously and CHANGE itself whenever such change appears to be desirable either from within or by changes/transformations in the environment. The characteristics described here constitute the second system of conditions that are necessary for systems change.

IF the conditions—described above—are operating, THEN intensive and continuous communication between the "evolutionary partners," namely, people in the system and in the environment, will enable them to: (1) agree upon new and different societal functions that education should address, (2) new and different learning outcomes and human development goals, (3) articulate shared core values and core ideas, (4) create shared vision, (5) formulate a new image of systems of education and human development, (6) design, develop, and institutionalize the change of the system.

It should be noted that the single conceptual power that enables the synthesis of the two sets of conditions and characteristics described above IS systems thinking. It is the power of that thinking that integrates the two sets into a system of conditions and characteristics. The systems thinking—and the systems view of education—we are developing as we are working with the chapters of this book and completing the activities, will bring about a major shift in our thinking about the desired state and characteristics of EAS's. We shall clearly understand the difference between the two critical processes of the life and work of educational activity systems: adjustments within the system and changing the system itself. If there ever was a time when such an understanding is called for and if there ever was a situation when a major systems change—the transformation of education—was the order of the day, THE TIME IS NOW. And the present "crisis" state of education has created the SITUATION in which we have no other choice but to propose and engage in a total systems change, the redesign of EAS's.

ACTIVITY # 48

Review the nature and characteristics of systems change described above. In view of these, explore the EAS you have selected and describe: (1) if there is evidence of coordination and coevolution between the EAS and its environment, (2) if there is an understanding of the concept of total systems change, and (3) if there is a willingness to engage in the redesign of the system. Enter your findings in your notebook.

SUMMARY OF PROCESS MODEL

In concluding our work with the development of a process model of EAS's, we return to a discussion on the guidance/management process of EAS's. As stipulated earlier, the process of (negative feedback driven) adjustment is a major process component of systems guidance/management. Another process component is the process of systems change introduced above, which is guided by positive feedback. (1) The balancing of these two, (2) the overseeing of all systems operations that implement purpose serving functions, (3) the ensuring of the availability of resources needed by the EAS, (4) coordinating the guidance/management processes of the four major systems processes, and (5) facilitating the work of the entire system, comprise the complex system of guidance/ management.

In Section One of this chapter we reviewed some of the recently emerged characteristics of HAS's. These mark characteristics that EAS's should acquire IF they aspire to be viable in our contemporary society. Accordingly, educational activity systems that serve the society and are served by it should be able to:

* Develop an intensive and continuous interaction with our constantly changing and transforming society, and establish coordination with societal systems that are relevant to learning and human development.

* Live and deal creatively with constant change, uncertainty, and ambiguity, and maintain their viability by both: coevolving with their societal environment by changing and transforming themselves AND effect changes in their environment by their outcomes.

* Involve in the life and change of the system all those who are concerned with, have an interest and stake in, contributing to the life and development of the system. Enlist—on a continuing basis—their participation and guidance in order to make the EAS ever more relevant to their service.

The three capability-generating processes described above are ALL pertinent to enabling EAS's to CHANGE themselves and, thus, make contributions that serve and shape the society. The next two organizational capacities enhance the overall functioning of the EAS and increase its capacity to become an ever more viable system. These include the ability to:

* Become learning organizations that: (1) continuously empower themselves BY LEARNING so that they can SEEK and FULFILL PURPOSES and (2)—in terms of their guidance/management

functions—learn to differentiate between situations when maintaining the system by adjustments is called for and situations when changing and redesigning the system are appropriate.

* Respond to the continuing increase in the amount and kind of information and knowledge they are to work with, by increasing their organizational capacity and people capability to: (1) specialize and diversify AND integrate and generalize, and (2) handle information more rapidly, distribute it to a much larger group of people (than currently happens in EAS's), and transform it into organizational knowledge.

An understanding of what is implied in taking a systems view of guidance/management in EAS's leads us to state that IF we conceive and design EAS's that have the characteristics described here, we shall make a major shift from our current "HIGH VOLUME PRODUCTION" EAS's to "HIGH VALUE PRODUCTION" EAS's. This distinction between "high value" vs. "high volume" is made in the context of the economy and it is related to education in the resource identified in Note 10.

ACTIVITY # 49

In the preceding activity, you reflected upon the adjustment issue in your selected system. Now you focus on an assessment of the organizational capacity, the competence and willingness of people in your system to engage in the change of their system. Most likely, you will find that while adjustment is something for which we have "standard operational procedures," unfortunately, approaches and procedures for redesigning EAS's are not readily available today to the educational community.

The next section calls for a synthesis of my modeling of the processes of EAS's with your description of the process model of your selected system.

SECTION FOUR

THE RE-VISIONED PROCESS MODEL OF YOUR EAS

In Section Two of this chapter you developed the first representation of the process model of your selected EAS. Your task is now to work with that model, my description of the process model of education you have just reviewed, and the activities you have completed in Section Three; and mold them into a re-visioned, reconceptualized description of your process model. With this work done, you are completing the "modelling" of your EAS. But the journey toward developing a systems view of education is not yet complete. In Section Five you will make another assessment, this time an assessment related to the process behavior of EAS's.

SECTION FIVE:

ASSESSMENT OF SELF, THE MODELLED SYSTEM, AND THE GENERAL MODEL

The purpose of working with the previous sections of this chapter was to help you to develop a "motion-picture" image or a process model of your selected EAS. In this section you shall examine your own dispositions—possible biases—relevant to process thinking. You will make an overall assessment of the process adequacy of your selected EAS, and will contemplate the adequacy of the general process model of EAS's.

SELF-REFLECTIVE ASSESSMENT

In the course of working with the four sections of this chapter, we jointly embarked on a journey to develop a process/behavior view of EAS's. We have used a process lens to look at EAS's and understand concepts and principles relevant to process behavior and—by applying those—bring them to life in our EAS's. There were times in our modelling when it was rather easy to grasp and apply these concepts and principles, but—I am sure—at times it was not so easy. So the question: Are there some dispositions that might prevent us—or make it difficult—to work with the process perspective? This is an important question. Only if we do recognize a disposition or assumption that hinders the development of a (process) systems view can we "liberate" ourselves from the old mindset and our customary ways of viewing the world of education. Only then can we free ourselves to grasp the systems view and apply systems thinking.

You have to make a judgment for yourself if—in the course of working with the earlier sections—you felt at any time "surprised" or faced propositions that you questioned, or found ideas that were against your prevailing assumptions. Here, I can only point to some that I—as well as others with whom I have worked—have found to be against our customary way of seeing. First, and foremost, the whole notion of "process thinking" and saying that process is more important than structure goes against our old way of thinking. It seems to be counterintuitive. Another is the idea of the dynamics of multiple and simultaneous processes that keep everything moving and changing. As a rule, we like stability, cherish equilibrium and certainty. Then, there is the confusion about "positive feedback." Its meaning in current use is that basically things are "OK." Now we understand that positive feedback calls for changing the whole system, it may call for a new system. We also might have some difficulty with the "noncoercive" notion of management, the ideas of intrinsic motivation, shared vision, shared values and beliefs, and organizational learning. The idea of purpose-seeking might also be strange, as well as the notion to go out into the environment and aggressively explore the educational implications of societal changes and transformations. We might still have a problem with the dynamics of coevolution. Furthermore, we have nothing now that even vaguely resembles the complexity of the input process developed here. The notions of involving the learner in making judgments about learning attained—and its desirability (from the learner's point of view)—are other novelties. I'll stop here and let you work on this issue.

ACTIVITY # 50

You should reflect upon the above dispositions and surprises and others that you might have run into. First, go through your writings, the activities you completed, and my description of the process model, and clarify in your own mind if you indeed might have some dispositions that hinder you from acquiring a process view of EAS's. Note those that you discover. Then, ask the questions: Why do I have these dispositions and what can I do to overcome them? Enter your findings in your notebook.

ASSESSMENT OF YOUR EAS FROM A PROCESS POINT OF VIEW

A set of questions is introduced below that might guide you in developing a summative assessment of your selected EAS from a systems process perspective. As you work with the questions, introduce your comments in your notebook.

1. Is there a system of processes in evidence (in your EAS) that is designated to create a working relationship with the environment by having a set of dedicated interaction operations? What are those?
2. What is being done to explore the societal and the systemic environments? Who does it, how often, and for what result?
3. Are there dedicated identification/activation processes operating in your EAS? What are they? How are they handled?
4. Figure 4.16 displays the tasks of input guidance management. How are these tasks handled in your EAS?
5. Looking at the transformation production process, is it organized around the teacher or around the learner? What are the component operations of this process in your EAS?
6. What evidence do you have that there are processes (in your EAS) dedicated to systemization/integration?
7. Is there evidence of a collectively formulated vision of your EAS? What is it?
8. What can you say about the nature of motivation in your EAS?
9. What are manifestations of energizing in your EAS?
10. What transformation guidance/management operations are working in your EAS?
11. Is there an "output model" in your EAS? Describe its characteristics.

12. How is the output identified and assessed? What output operations are in evidence? How is output dispatched to the environment or to other EAS's? Is the learner actively involved in any of the output operations? In what way?

13. Describe existing processes of adjustment and compare them to those in Section Three.

14. Has there been any evidence of (whole) systems change in your EAS? What was it?

15. Review the description of systems guidance/management in the text of Section Three and compare it with the management operations characteristics in your system. What is your finding?

In conclusion, make a descriptive/summative judgment about the systems process adequacy of your EAS. How far or how close is it from being a viable EAS in terms of the systems concepts and systems principles that we have developed by the use of the process lens? What would you do to transform your EAS into a state that would match the process model we jointly developed here?

ASSESSING THE MODEL

It is time now to make an overall assessment of the utility and value of the systems process model and its related systems view developed in this chapter. You can make such an overall and broad assessment by asking the kinds of questions I raise next:

In what way did you find that the systems concepts and principles—introduced in this chapter—and the process model as a whole:

* Were useful in understanding and describing your selected EAS as a system?

* Have an explanatory power—and what kind—in the context of an operating EAS?

* Helped you to gain new insights into the true nature of an EAS? Name some of those insights.

What other questions would you ask that would test the adequacy and power of the model? Explore those additional questions. Introduce your answers in your notebook.

You might use the findings you have developed in this section for the purpose of revisiting your description of your process model and possibly revising it.

REFLECTIONS

We have reached the end of the first part of our journey as we jointly developed a systems view of educational activity systems in the preceding four chapters. In the course of the journey, we have applied the systems concepts and principles introduced in the text and created three systems models that portray and represent educational activity systems. In so doing, we have integrated those in our own thinking and have moved toward systems practice by using the insights we have gained: (1) in my case to make a general assessment of EAS's, and (2) in your case to assess a specific EAS.

People who begin to work with the three models often ask: Which model is the true representation of education as a system? Or which one is more important than the others? The systems-environment model? The functions/structure model? The process/behavioral model? I am sure for you these are by now bogus questions. No single model or even a combination of two is sufficient (even though necessary) in portraying human activity systems. Each presents certain characteristics, but not all the characteristics, of a system. The systems-environment model maps the system space and its context. It portrays systems-environment relationships and interactions and tells us why the system exists. The still-picture—or the functions/structure model—depicts what the system is in a given moment of time, what it is about, what it consists of, and how it is structured. The process/behavioral—or motion-picture—model reveals how the system does (what it does) and how it works and lives through time. ONLY IF CONSIDERED JOINTLY DO THESE MODELS TELL US THE REAL STORY OF A SYSTEM. ONLY TOGETHER DO THEY REVEAL THE TRUE NATURE OF SYSTEMS. Therefore, in order to develop a systems view, we should integrate the three models into our thinking as "mapped into each other." Only then are we able to analyze educational enterprises, design and develop educational organizations, and manage change in a systemic way. In the closing chapter, we continue the journey by "activating our systems view" and exploring the use of the three models in all domains of educational inquiry.

NOTES

(1) The "holographic" organizational principle is described by G. Morgan in his: *Images of Organizations* (1986). Sage Publications, Beverly Hills.

(2) A description of systems design is provided in B. H. Banathy: *Systems Design of Education* (1991). Educational Technology Publications, Englewood Cliffs, NJ.

(3) The concepts of "novelty" and "confirmation" are developed by Erich Jantsch in: *The Self-Organizing Universe* (1980). Pergamon Press, London.

(4) Emerged characteristics of the Post-Industrial Information Society are adapted from Chapter Four of source (2) above.

(5) The concept and the process of "organizational learning" are elaborated by C. Argyris's book: *Reasoning, Learning, and Action* (1982). Jossey-Bass Publishers, San Francisco.

(6) For emerged societal characteristics see Daniel Bell's book: *The Coming of Post-Industrial Society* (1976). Basic Books, New York; and Peter Drucker's *The New Realities* (1989), Harper and Row, New York.

(7) For examples of core values and core ideas see Chapter Seven in reference (2).

(8) For a contrasting description of instructional vs. learning focused education see Chapter Five in source (2).

(9) The notion of "visioning" in organizations is explained by P. Senge in: *The Fifth Discipline* (1990). Doubleday, New York. Examples of envisioning education are provided in Chapter Three of source (2).

(10) The concepts of "high-volume" vs. "high-value" production are developed by R. Reich, in: *The Work of Nations* (1991). Knopf, New York.

CHAPTER FIVE

The Activation of the Systems View

The process of working with the three systems models, transforming them, and applying them in the context of educational activity systems has provided the conditions for developing the systems view. You should now be able to think of yourself, the environment you live in, the entities that surround you, and those you are part of in a NEW WAY: THE SYSTEMS WAY. You have learned to look at and understand education from a systems point of view. You have even begun to activate the systems view as you analyzed an EAS of your choice. In this closing chapter I discuss a variety of ways that we might apply systems thinking and the systems view in the context of EAS's.

The activation of the systems view and the application of systemic thinking mean engaging in operations that will enable us to: (1) analyze existing systems in order to bring about an improved state and systems behavior, or change the system, (2) design new systems, (3) develop and institutionalize the designed systems, (4) guide and manage systems and manage change. In each of the four domains of disciplined inquiry—conducted in the educational arena—the three models we have worked with do apply. Their use—as we shall see shortly—has introduced a new concept in systems inquiry: THE SYSTEMS MODELS APPROACH. This approach is very different from certain conventional systems approaches that apply sequentially structured procedural steps. These are usually offered without an explanation of how they had been developed, how a particular scheme emanates from systems concepts and principles, or how they reflect a systems view. Thus, these schemes do not appear to be much more than prescriptions or recipes. The users of these systems approaches are often oblivious to the systems concepts and principles we have worked with in the preceding chapters.

On the other hand, the SYSTEMS MODELS APPROACH employs systems strategies, and always keeps in view the systems concepts and principles in which the strategies are rooted. The systems models approach is the activation of the systems view that emerges in our thinking as we internalize systems concepts, principles, and models. In this chapter, I introduce the use of the systems models approach in the various domains of disciplined inquiry in the context of educational activity systems.

THE EMERGENCE OF SYSTEMS THINKING IN EDUCATION

In the course of the last couple of decades—studying and working with social systems—we have developed an increasing realization of the inquiry power of systems theory and the insights we can gain from the systemic worldview of systems philosophy. In so doing, we have liberated ourselves from the constraints and limitations of the perspectives of the analytically-oriented and reductionist inquiry mode of the traditional disciplines. Systems inquiry enables us to orchestrate the findings of various scientific disciplines within the framework of systems thinking and guides us in developing and applying systems approaches, models, and methods to the analysis, design, development, and management of human activity systems. Education is such a system.

Enlightened by the concepts and principles of the general theory of systems, and—more recently—those of the general theory of dynamic systems as applied to human activity systems, we now understand the true nature of education as a social/societal system that operates in ever changing and dynamic environments and interacts with a variety of other social systems. The material in this book demonstrates the use of systems thinking and the application of the systems view in the context of education. Systems thinking in education and the application of the systems view enable us to explore, understand, and describe:

* the characteristics of EMBEDDEDNESS, as education is nested in the community and in the larger society;

* education as a COMPLEX SOCIAL SYSTEM, operating at various interconnected levels with interdependent and interacting components;

* the PURPOSES and BOUNDARIES of education as these emerge from a coevolution with the environment which defines the societal functions of education;

* the ongoing RELATIONSHIPS, INTERACTIONS, and INFORMATION/ ENERGY EXCHANGES between an educational activity system and its environment;

* the dynamics of INTERDEPENDENCE and PATTERNS OF CONNECTEDNESS among the functions and components of the educational activity system;

* the characteristics of WHOLENESS (the whole organizes the parts) and—as a result of this organization—the properties that EMERGE at various systems levels as the result of this systemic organization, integration, and synthesis; and

* SYSTEMS BEHAVIOR and CHANGE through time in the system, in its purposes, functions, and components.

A systems view of education generates insights into "ways of knowing and reasoning" that enable us to set forth and pursue a COMPREHENSIVE SYSTEM OF DISCIPLINED INQUIRY in education. This system has four internally consistent, complementary, and interacting domains of inquiry. These domains are: (1) THE DESCRIPTION AND ANALYSIS of educational activity systems (EAS's); (2) SYSTEMS DESIGN of EAS's; (3) SYSTEMS DEVELOPMENT and INSTITUTIONALIZATION; and (4) SYSTEMS GUIDANCE and MANAGEMENT. I describe these four domains of inquiry in this concluding chapter, but first I project an image that portrays the four domains and their connectedness (Figure 5.1).

The internal consistency among the four domains of the comprehensive inquiry is ensured by a set of organizing perspectives that guide thinking about BOTH the system and its relationship with the environment and other systems, AND the way that systems approaches and methods—relevant to the four domains—are applied in working with EAS's. These perspectives represent core values, guiding ideas and images that people in the system and in the systemic environment define and share. The arrows in the figure show that the domains are integrated into a system of inquiry by the shared organizing perspectives and their relationships and interdependence. Inquiry can start at any of the four domains and involve—potentially—all the other domains.

SYSTEMS APPROACHES TO CHARACTERIZING/DESCRIBING/ANALYZING EDUCTIONAL ACTIVITY SYSTEMS

Educational Activity Systems are complex societal systems, embedded in the community and the larger society, serving both. They are composed of complex subsystems of their own. Those who work in these systems should understand how their embedding community and the society affect their systems and how their

FIGURE 5.1 AN INTEGRATED SYSTEM OF DISCIPLINED INQUIRY IN EDUCATION

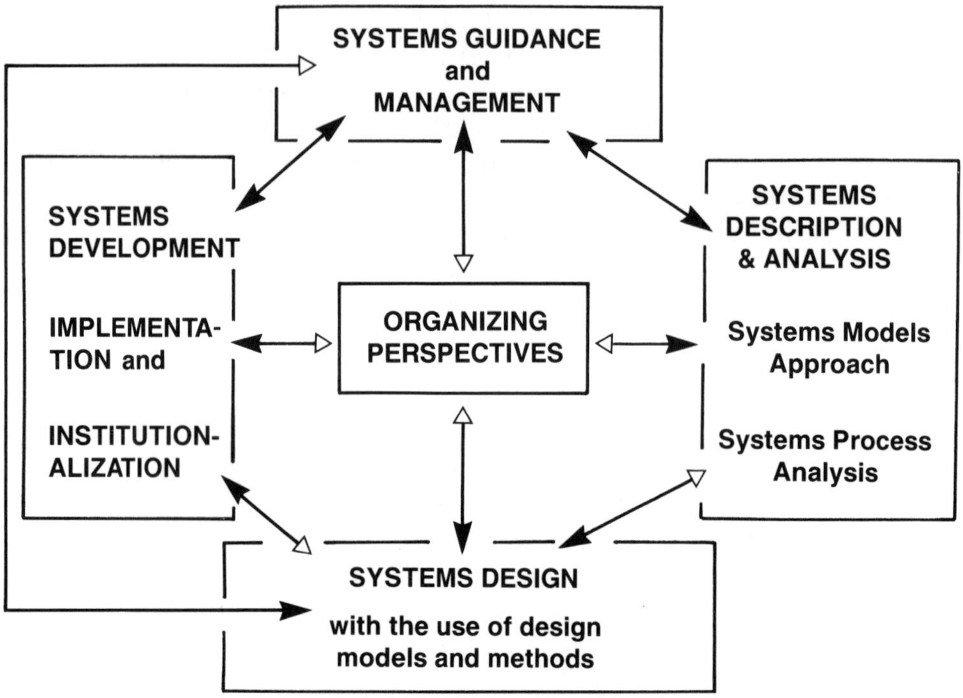

systems affect their community and the larger society. They should also learn to use approaches and methods by which they can assess the systemic effectiveness and the systemic relevance of their systems to their environment. The two systems approaches, the systems models approach and systems process analysis, enable us to describe EAS's as systems and to analyze and assess their effectiveness.

THE SYSTEMS MODELS APPROACH

Having worked with the three models of the systems models approach in the previous chapters, we need only a brief note here about this approach. The use of the systems models approach—introduced in this book—enables people in the system and in their systemic environment to have a clear understanding of what type their system is and what its systemic characteristics are, how it operates in the environment, and how it does its work and lives its life. It helps them to understand how the components of their EAS are interrelated, what their pattern of interaction is, how they are woven into a web of interdependence, and how they comprise jointly the whole that we call an educational activity system. The use of the same three systems models enables a broad-based "macro-analysis" of an EAS, and the assessment of the systemic adequacy and environmental/societal relevance of the EAS. The three models are also used in representing the design of EAS's.

SYSTEMS PROCESS ANALYSIS

While the three models help us to conduct a "macro-analysis" of an EAS, the application of systems process analysis (SPA) makes it possible for us to carry out a "micro-analysis," and assess the organizational effectiveness of an EAS. SPA is derived from LIVING SYSTEMS THEORY (see Note 1). The theory postulates that all living systems—from a cell to the global system—maintain their effectiveness by processing information, matter, and energy. The degree to which these systems effectively use information and matter/energy determines their organizational health and their success in evolving and developing their potential and attaining their purposes. The methodology enables us to examine simultaneously a number of variables and assess the interactive effects of their key organizational arrangements and functions. SPA focuses on the assessment of processes by which systems acquire and screen information; transform information for use by the system; communicate, store, and retrieve information; analyze and use it for making decisions, and present information to the environment. The same kind of process stream is used in assessing the system's effectiveness in using matter/energy. The effectiveness of these processes is measured on such variables as volume, cost, clarity, accuracy, relevance, usefulness, and timeliness. We introduced SPA in the educational settings, and our research clearly indicated that SPA is a useful methodology and offers a unique potential for analyzing the effectiveness of EAS's in a way that provides us information not only on whether or not an EAS is effective, but also—more significantly—WHY it is or is not effective. Currently available methods of educational effectiveness are based on input output measures. Thus, there is a "black box" between input and output that "hides" the evidence (of effectiveness or lack of it). SPA allows us to open up the "black box" so that we can see what happens in between (input and output); it makes the system transparent; it transforms the box into a "glass box." (See Note 2.)

SYSTEMS DESIGN OF EDUCATIONAL ACTIVITY SYSTEMS

The central and dominant idea of systems design in the context of human activity systems in general—and educational activity systems in particular—is that we can give direction to the evolution of our systems and thus take charge of our future, provided we create an image of the future we aspire to attain, and engage in disciplined inquiry by which we can realize that image by systems design and bring it to life by systems development that implements the design.

The systems design of EAS's is a future-creating, disciplined inquiry that brings together various groups from the community—all those who are involved and interested in, have a stake in, and are affected by the EAS. These groups are organized into the systemic arrangements of a designing organization. In the course of their work, positions are developed, and core values and guiding ideas are formulated by intensive dialogues and negotiations. The process of arriving at decisions is not one of "optimization" but one that arrives at "satisfying" solutions based on collective formulations of consensus positions. The specific methods of design inquiry are selected or developed so that they match the characteristics of the type of system that designers wish to create, and which can respond to the uniqueness of the design situation. (The systems design of EAS was described in my earlier work, see Note 3.) Here, I only outline the major design stages and indicate their relationship to the other domains of the comprehensive inquiry.

* **FRONT-END ANALYSIS**. Activities include: (a) clarify reasons for engaging in design, (b) formulate organizing perspectives for the design process, (c) diagnose and describe a "rich picture" of the design problem situation, and the system and its systemic environment in which the problem situation is embedded. Here we are making use of the three systems models described in this book.

* **CREATE THE GUIDING IMAGE**. Image creation challenges designers to "leap-out" from the constraints of their existing system, and to (a) explore the educational implications of emerged societal characteristics in terms of the societal functions of education and the learnings that are desired, (b) articulate core values and ideas that emerge from the exploration and from their own beliefs and—as an outcome—(c) create an image of the future system that will guide the design.

* **DESIGN THE SYSTEM OF FUNCTIONS**, namely: (a) formulate a core definition of the future system (mission, purposes, and systems characteristics); (b) set the boundaries of the system, (c) generate, devise, and describe alternative configurations of functions that are to be carried out by the system in order to attain the mission/purposes and the desired systems characteristics, (d) establish criteria by which to evaluate the alternatives, and (e) select and describe the most promising alternative. A description of the selected system of functions represents the first model of the future system.

* **DESIGN THE ENABLING SYSTEM**: (a) design the guidance/management system that has the capability to oversee the accomplishment of functions and acquire the resources needed, and (b) design the educational activity system that has the organizational capacity and staff capability to carry out the functions and thus attain the mission and purposes.

* **GENERATE A COMPREHENSIVE DESCRIPTION** of the new system, by the use of the three systems models, and formulate a plan for the development of the new system.

The stages introduced above are carried out in iterative cycles in a "spiralling" mode as we work in five "spaces": (a) the contextual/design-genesis space, in which we initiate the design and conduct the front-end analysis; (b) the design solution phase, where we create the image of the future system, formulate the core definition, set the boundaries, and design the system of functions and the enabling systems; (c) the knowledge space, where we organize and display the information/knowledge required to conduct the design; (d) the experience space, where we test the various alternatives; and (e) the space of the future system, where we display the comprehensive description or model of the future system and present the plan for the development of the new system.

SYSTEMS DEVELOPMENT

The comprehensive description or model of the system is the "blueprint," based on which we develop the system. But it is hard to say where design leaves off and development begins; they blend into each other. Let me explain. As we develop/build the first working representation of the design, we may call this the "prototype form" of the new system that brings the design "to life." We test this prototype against our stated purposes and systems characteristics and develop information that may indicate a need for some changes in the design. The changed/revised design again becomes the blueprint for building the improved version of the system, which we may call the "performance form" of the system. There is a significant difference between the functions of the two forms. In developing the prototype form of the system, our interest focuses on the question: Does the system work at all? In developing the performance form we ask: How well does it work? How well does the system perform? As we test these developmental forms, we are applying the approaches described in the process/behavioral model of the EAS. We activate the processes of assessing the output of the system, we identify potential discrepancies, we develop adjustment models and test these, and implement the adjustment. We continue this process until we gain enough confidence in the new system so that we shall fully implement and institutionalize it. We are not taking any risk, inasmuch as we have built into the system the capability to guide itself: to change, redesign, and renew itself whenever such is called for from within the system or indicated by the environment. I will briefly describe this self-guiding/changing in the next section.

SYSTEMS GUIDANCE AND MANAGEMENT

Systems guidance and management were already described in detail in Chapter Four, where we worked with the process/behavioral model of the EAS. We discussed in some detail processes by which we monitor and assess systems operations as well as consider major systems change. I will briefly describe here the change function of systems guidance, when this domain of the comprehensive systems inquiry becomes involved in the delivery and institutionalization of systemic change.

A systems view of change has helped us to see the issue of change in a very different light. The systems view has helped us to understand that there is a whole set of connected functions—and systems carrying out those functions—that have to be activated in order for change to be set in place and be sustainable. The complex of those functions and the systems carrying out those functions constitute the systems complex of introducing and institutionalizing change. A change system should address three major sets of functions. The FIRST is a definition functions-set that characterizes: (a) the system in which the change will be infused, (b) the genesis or reason for the change, (c) the change itself (the design of the change) that is contemplated, (d) the organizational capacities and staff capabilities required to implement the change, and (e) the resources needed to support and sustain the change. The SECOND set of functions includes: (a) the specification of processes, methods, and arrangements, and the utilization of resources in infusing or "mapping in" the intended change; and (b) the formulation of a plan for introducing and implementing the change. The THIRD set is an implementation and guidance functions-set that includes: (a) the development of the organizational capacity and staff capability to implement the change, (b) making available the required resources, (c) activating the systems change, and (d) monitoring and guiding the activation and institutionalization. (Note 4 refers to a portrayal of the change system complex that carries out these functions.)

REFLECTIONS

The figure in this chapter (5.1) and the text above have presented the overall context of a comprehensive system of disciplined inquiry in the educational arena. As we have seen, the four domains are in recursive relationship, and the three models described in this book play an important function in all of the domains. The inquiry system described in this chapter is not yet manifested in the mainstream thinking and functional practice of the educational community. Nor is this kind of comprehensive inquiry yet part of the preparation program of educational professionals. The lack of such a program and the lack of a use of the inquiry system described here are some of the core reasons for the inadequacy of recent educational improvement programs and efforts.

NOTES

(1) The source is James Miller's *Living Systems* (1978). McGraw-Hill, New York.

(2) A brief report on the application of Systems Process Analysis is presented by B.H. Banathy (June, 1988) in: "Systems Inquiry in Education." *Systems Practice.*

(3) Systems design in the context of education is described in my earlier work: *Systems Design of Education: A Journey to Cre-*

ate the Future (1991). Educational Technology Publications, Englewood Cliffs, NJ.

(4) A strategy for institutionalizing change is described by B.H. Banathy (1986) in "A Systems View of Institutionalizing Change in Education" in the *1985-86 Proceedings of the National Association of Academics of Science*, Columbus, Ohio, Academy of Science.

Glossary

The systems concepts that were used in presenting the three models of human activity systems are now developed in this glossary as systems ideas that are the "stuff" of systems thinking. You might transform the general definitions introduced here into systems ideas that characterize an educational activity system of your choice.

ACCOMMODATION is an environment-system interaction, implemented by a process in which the environment provides resources that satisfy systems requirements.

ACTIVATION OPERATIONS constitute the last stage of input operations that introduce the processed input for use by the transformation operations.

ADAPTATION is a system-environment interaction, implemented by a process in which the system adjusts itself to changes in the environment.

ADAPTIVE SYSTEMS are capable of adjusting themselves to environmental changes.

ADJUSTMENTS are changes that a system brings about in order to modify its behavior, its functions and/or structure, and its characteristics so that it can generate an improved system's state and produce improved output.

BEHAVIORAL SYSTEMS MODEL (also Process Model) describes the behavior of a system through time and displays systems concepts and principles that characterize the operations of the system.

BOUNDARIES of a system delimit and define the systems space and set aside the system from its environment.

BOUNDARY JUDGMENT involves making decisions about both: what constitutes a boundary and what is included or excluded from being within the system.

CENTRALIZED RELATIONSHIP indicates that within a system one of the subsystems plays a central and coordinating role so that other subsystems are arranged around it.

CLOSED SYSTEM refers to a state of being isolated from the environment. It is a state in which the system is sealed off from its environment by its boundaries. There is no interchange between the system and its environment. Human activity systems cannot be completely closed; we can speak only of various degrees of closure.

CLOSURE BY CONTROL is a process by which the system adjusts the breaks in its boundaries in order to regulate input and output.

COMPLEXITY as a systemic characteristic stands for a large number of densely connected parts and multiple levels of embeddedness.

COMPONENTS are integral parts of a system. They are selected and employed by the system based on their potential to carry out functions that are necessary to attain the purpose(s) of the system. Their relational arrangement provides the structure of the system and it is from their interaction that emerge those systems properties that define the system and characterize the wholeness of the system.

CONCLUSION-ORIENTED DISCIPLINED INQUIRY indicates a rigorous exploration and description of WHAT IS. It is knowledge production about phenomena of all kinds. It is the domain of the scientific disciplines and takes the form of research.

CONSTRAINTS are limitations and restrictions imposed upon the system, either from the environment or from within, that might curtail the use of resources or delimit the carrying out of operations.

COST BENEFIT is a consideration of what costs (resources or efforts) can we (or should we) employ that attain outcomes that we consider to be beneficial to the system and/or to the environment.

COST EFFECTIVENESS is a consideration of what degree of system or product effectiveness can be attained at what cost; or given a defined level of cost, how much effectiveness can be attained for it.

DECISION-ORIENTED DISCIPLINED INQUIRY is a rigorous exploration of WHAT SHOULD BE. It produces propositions for decision making. It is prescriptive in nature. Its main forms include design and problem solving.

DECODING is a process by which input (information/resources) coming from the environment is interpreted for its usefulness in accordance with the model of the system and is (re)formulated in the "language" of the system.

EDUCATIONAL ACTIVITY SYSTEMS are social/human activity systems that provide resources, opportunities, arrangements, and situations for learning and human development.

EGALITARIAN RELATIONSHIP indicates equality status among subsystems (of a given system). In this kind of relationship none of the peer subsystems play a dominant or central role.

EMBEDDEDNESS is a state in which one system is nested in another system.

EMERGENCE is a process by which, from the interaction and integration of parts of a system, novel properties come forth that are characteristics of the systems as a whole but are not characteristics of the parts.

ENABLING SYSTEMS have the organizational capacity and human capability to carry out the defined functions of a system.

ENTITY is another term that can be used in general for denoting a system or an element (component) of a system.

ENVIRONMENT is the context within which a system exists. It is composed of all things that surround the system, and it includes everything that may affect the system and may be affected by it. (For a distinction between general and systemic environment see their definitions later.)

EXPANSIONISM, the opposite of reductionism, is a process by which we seek meaning and understanding by enlarging and extending our exploration.

EXPLORATION involves an active search of the environment with the purpose of understanding its systems-relevant characteristics and requirements and interpreting their implications for the system.

FEEDBACK is a process by which information concerning the adequacy of the system, its operations, and its output are introduced into the system.

NEGATIVE FEEDBACK tells us that there is a discrepancy between what the system produces and what it should produce. It tells us that we should change something IN the system so that we can reduce the deviation from the norms stated in the output model of the system.

POSITIVE FEEDBACK, on the other hand, tells us that the whole system should change, that we should increase the deviation from the present system state, and change the output model.

FEEDBACK AND ADJUSTMENT provide for the analysis and interpretation of information generated about the adequacy of the output and the operations of the system. The interpretation is used for designing and introducing adjustments (into the system) in order to bring about adequate output and improved system operations.

FUNCTIONS denote actions that have to be carried out in order to meet systems requirements and attain the purpose(s) of the system.

FUNCTIONS/STRUCTURE MODEL is a systems model that organizes in relational arrangements systems concepts and principles that present an image of a system in a given moment of time. A metaphor for this model is a "still-picture" or "snapshot."

GENERAL ENVIRONMENT is everything that is outside of the boundaries of the system; it constitutes the largest definable context of the system.

GENERAL SYSTEMS FUNCTIONS are characteristics of all kinds of living systems.

GENERAL SYSTEMS MODELS are abstract constructions that represent systems in general. They are developed from a relational arrangement of general systems concepts and principles.

GENERAL SYSTEMS RESEARCH is a conclusion-oriented disciplined inquiry aimed at the identification of concepts and principles that are common to all systems. It develops and tests models that represent systems in general.

GENERAL SYSTEMS THEORY identifies concepts, principles, and models that are common to all kinds of systems and identifies isomorphes between and among various types of systems.

HIERARCHY denotes a vertical arrangement of entities (systems and their subsystems).

HIERARCHICAL RELATIONSHIP is one in which one entity is subordinated to another.

HUMAN ACTIVITY SYSTEMS are designed social systems organized for a purpose, which they attain by carrying out specific functions.

IDENTIFICATION OPERATIONS are part of input processing (see later). They interpret the input received from the point of the system, qualify, and, if possible, quantify its value to the system.

INDEPENDENCE of components or subsystems within a system means a lack of integration. A change in one component/subsystem may not bring about change in others.

INPUT has a meaning as a "noun" and as a "verb." In its "noun sense" it denotes information, people, energies, materials, and other resources that enter into the system from the environment. Its meaning as a "verb" denotes action by which input is entered into the system. (See input processing.)

INPUT MODEL describes in an organized and relational way (1) all elements of input that are required by the system, and (2) the operations by which the input is processed.

INPUT PROCESSING refers to systems operations that provide for (1) the interaction between the system and its environment, (2) the identification of systems-relevant input, and (3) the introduction of system-relevant input (into the system) that is required for transformation processing.

INSTITUTIONALIZATION is a process by which a system becomes an established human activity system within a specified systemic environment, with all the resources and policies provided that are necessary for its existence and maintenance.

INTEGRATION OPERATIONS intend to make the components of the system increasingly more interactive, interdependent, and fused.

INTERACTION OPERATIONS are the frontal part of input processing. They enable the system to seek, receive, decode, verify, and register input signals and input elements coming from the environment.

INTERDEPENDENCE of components within a system means mutual reliance and signifies that change in one component brings about change in others.

MODEL—as used in the text—means an abstract representation of: (1) an existing system (or part of it), (2) a possible (future) system, and (3) an expected outcome/output state.

MODEL OF ADJUSTMENT is a (conceptual) representation of changes and measures that can be taken in order: (1) to correct for a discrepancy between the expected and actual output, and (2) to alter systems operations that would lead to improved system performance.

MODEL BUILDING is a disciplined inquiry by which a conceptual (abstract) representation of a system is constructed or a representation of expected outcomes/output is portrayed.

MOTION-PICTURE MODEL is a metaphor to illustrate the behavior of a human activity system over time, and it elaborates the systems concepts and principles that are relevant to such behavior.

MULTIPLE CAUSALITY indicates that the interplay of several factors/variables brings about a given state. (Opposite of single causality.)

MULTISYSTEM is a complex of several related systems.

MUTUAL (RECURSIVE) CAUSALITY indicates that "A" affects "B" as well as "B" affects "A."

OPEN refers to a state and characteristics of that state in which a system continuously interacts with its environment.

OPEN SYSTEM is one that maintains the state and exhibits the characteristics of openness described above.

ORGANIZATIONAL LEARNING is a process of developing organizational capacity and human capability to articulate and continuously examine the purposes, underlying perspectives and assumptions, and individual and organizational values in view of the (a) performance of the organization, and (b) the changing characteristics and expectations of the environment(s) in which the organization is embedded.

ORGANIZING PERSPECTIVES include core ideas, core values, images, and approaches that guide our systems inquiry.

OUTPUT is whatever the system is producing and entering into its environment.

OUTPUT MODEL is an organized and relational description of the intended/expected state and characteristics of the outcome of systems operations or the product of the system.

OUTPUT PROCESSING refers to operations that identify and assess systems-relevant output and that introduce output into the environment.

PEER SYSTEMS are components of a system in which they are embedded.

PERFORMANCE-EFFECTIVENESS is a dimension of monitoring and evaluating the extent to which the system meets performance expectations.

PERFORMANCE MODEL displays the desired way that a system should behave and carry out its operations.

PROCESS MODEL is an organized arrangement of systems concepts and principles that portray the behavior of a system through time. Its metaphor is the "motion-picture" model.

PROGRESSIVE INTEGRATION is a process by which components of the system become increasingly more interactive, interdependent, and fused.

PROGRESSIVE SEGREGATION comes about as components of a system become increasingly more independent, exhibit less interaction, and become more and more isolated from each other.

REDUCTIONISM is a scientific orientation that seeks to understand phenomena by breaking them down into their smallest possible parts.

RESOURCES are information, knowledge, people, materials, money, facilities, etc., that are placed at the disposal of a system.

SELF-REGULATING systems are able to modify their own behavior and operations in order to enhance the attainment of their purpose(s).

SIMPLE OR LINEAR CAUSALITY indicates that "A" affects "B."

SOCIAL SYSTEMS are human activity systems organized from interacting and interdependent components that are engaged in carrying out functions by which they attain their purpose(s). They are open to and interact with their environment, from which they receive input required for their existence.

SPECIFIC-TO-SYSTEM FUNCTIONS are those activities that serve the unique characteristics/requirements of a given system.

STILL PICTURE MODEL (or a "snapshot" model) is a metaphor for a model that depicts a system at a given moment of time. It organizes systems concepts and principles in relational arrangement to represent a functional/structural image of the system.

SUBJECT(S) (of a system) is the entity or entities around which the system is organized and which is transformed by the system from the initial (input) state into the desired (output) state.

SUBSYSTEM is a major component of a system. It is made up of two or more interacting and interdependent components. Subsystems of a system interact in order to attain their own purpose(s) and the purpose(s) of the system in which they are embedded.

SUPRASYSTEM is made up of a number of component systems organized in interacting relationships in order to serve their embedding suprasystem.

SYSTEM is comprised of a set of relationally arranged and interdependent components organized as a definable entity in a given environment in order to attain its specified purpose. Components interact and are united according to some organizing idea represented by the design of the system.

SYSTEM CONCEPT defines a unit of "systemness," or systemic property, such as "input," "transformation," "output," etc.

SYSTEM CONTROL is a process by which the system regulates itself or by which the behavior and operations of the system are regulated.

SYSTEM DESIGN is a decision-oriented disciplined inquiry that aims at the construction of a model that is an abstract representation of a future system.

SYSTEM DEVELOPMENT brings a system design to life. It involves the implementation of the design in the real-world setting, its testing (potential revision), and validation.

SYSTEM-ENVIRONMENT COACTIONS are processes by which the system adjusts—or changes itself—to changes in the environment, and the environment accommodates the changing requirements of the system and/or is changed/shaped by the system.

SYSTEM-ENVIRONMENT COEVOLUTION indicates the mutual shaping and development of the system and the environment.

SYSTEM-ENVIRONMENT MODEL examines and defines a system in its context and organizes systems concepts and principles that are relevant to system-environment interaction.

SYSTEM OF FUNCTIONS is a systemic arrangement of interrelated functions and subfunctions that have to be carried out in order to attain the purpose(s) of the system.

SYSTEM SPACE is a domain that a system occupies as defined by its boundaries, which separate the system from its environment.

SYSTEMIC ENVIRONMENT is that part of the general environment of a system with which the system is constantly and regularly interacting.

SYSTEMIZATION is part of the transformation process by which components of a system become increasingly more "system-like" by taking on the characteristics of the whole (system).

SYSTEMIZATION-INTEGRATION operations (of transformation) are complementary operations that make components of the system not only more "system-like" but also increasingly more integrated.

SYSTEMS ANALYSIS has several contextual meanings. (1) It can undertake the inquiry of what and how a system is constructed, leading to a systems description. (2) It can lead to an evaluation of a system by asking (a) how systemic it is (how it operates as a system), or (b) how effective it is and how well it performs against stated criteria. (3) It can be part of systems design as its initial or "front-end" exploration, leading to a formulation of a statement of the problem situation that the design is to address.

SYSTEMS APPROACH views perceived phenomena as a system and deals with problem situations and opportunities that emerge by the application of systems inquiry.

SYSTEMS INQUIRY is a disciplined approach by which we can apply systems theory, systems philosophy, and systems methodology (grounded in theory and philosophy) in a variety of functional contexts and systems types.

SYSTEMS LEVELS portray a vertical arrangement of embeddedness (of systems), each level referencing a system organized/existing at that level.

SYSTEMS METHODOLOGY (1) studies methods by which to pursue systems scholarship and produce systems knowledge (as a domain of conclusion-oriented disciplined inquiry); and (2) develops and describes a range of approaches, methods, strategies, and tools for applying systems theory and philosophy in the analysis, description, design, development, and management of a variety of systems types (as a domain of decision-oriented disciplined inquiry).

SYSTEMS MODELS are relational presentations of systems concepts and principles organized according to a stated purpose and presented in a comprehensive scheme.

SYSTEMS MODELS APPROACH makes use of systems models in the analysis, design, development, and management of human activity systems.

SYSTEMS OPERATIONS are components of such major system processes as input, transformation, output, feedback-adjustment, and systems change.

SYSTEMS PHILOSOPHY is in contrast to the analytic, reductionist, linear, single cause-and-effect, and mechanistic view of the philosophy of traditional science; systems philosophy brings forth a reorganization of ways of knowing and thinking about perceived reality. It has created a new world-view manifested in synthetic, expansionist, dynamic, multiple/mutual/recursive causality modes of thinking and inquiry.

SYSTEMS PRINCIPLES are constructed of related systems concepts. They display the laws by which systems behave. For example, the more complex the input, the more complex the output.

SYSTEMS PROCESS ANALYSIS is based on living systems theory and probes into the health/pathology of systems by the application of a methodology that evaluates the effectiveness of systems on multiple dimensions.

SYSTEMS REQUIREMENTS are specific expectations, demands, and conditions that a system is to satisfy.

SYSTEMS RESEARCH is a study of the characteristics, properties, organization, and behavior of systems of various kinds, and tests generalizations derived from such studies.

SYSTEMS SPECIFICATIONS are derived from and elaborate the stated mission and purposes of the system and answer such questions as: (1) Who are the clients of the system? What services should be offered to them? What characteristics should those services have? Where, when, and how should those services be provided? (2) Who should own the system? How should we distribute ownership? What rights and responsibilities should owners have?

(3) What kinds of responsibilities and relationships should the system have toward other systems, the community, and the larger society?

SYSTEMS STRATEGIES are components of the systems models approach applied in the analysis, design, development, and management of human activity systems.

SYSTEMS THEORY presents concepts, principles, and models applicable to the description, organization, and the behavior of systems.

SYSTEMS THINKING is an internalized manifestation (in the thinking of individuals or social systems) of systems concepts, systems principles, and systems models.

SYSTEMS TYPES are members of a set of classifications that arrange types of human activity systems according to how open-closed, mechanistic-systemic, unitary-pluralistic, or restricted-complex they are. Differentiated on the four-fold continua, systems types include rigidly controlled, deterministic, purposive, heuristic, and purpose-seeking.

SYSTEMS VIEW is a manifestation of systems thinking in the various domains of disciplined inquiry and experiential contexts.

TRADEOFF is an exchange of one aspect for another, and TRADE-OFF ANALYSIS is the consideration of the effects of such exchange.

TRANSFORMATION is the process by which the input is changed into output.

TRANSFORMATION CONTROL AND ADJUSTMENT are component operations of the transformation process. They monitor transformation, gather information on its effectiveness, and analyze and interpret the information, in order to introduce adjustments by which to improve the transformation process.

TRANSFORMATION FACILITATION is comprised of a set of operations aimed at the continuous energizing and maintenance (in good operational order) of all components that participate in the transformation process.

TRANSFORMATION PROCESSING includes the integrated operations of transformation production, systemization-integration, transformation facilitation, and transformation control.

TRANSFORMATION PRODUCTION is a set of operations in which the subject(s) of the system and other systems components are engaged in, interact, and use resources in order to accomplish the purposed transformation (of the subject(s)) of the system, and thus achieve the goal of the system.

TRANSFORMATION MODEL is a conceptual representation of a systemic arrangement of operations by which the input is changed to output.

WHOLENESS (of systems) refers to the integrated/fused state of the components of a system, exhibiting the indivisible nature of systems.

Index

F

G

H

J

L

M

N

O

P

About the Author

Bela H. Banathy is a researcher, educator, and author. He is a graduate of the Hungarian Royal Academy, and has a master's degree in counseling psychology with postgraduate work in psycholinguistics at San Jose State University and a doctorate in education with a minor in linguistics from the University of California, Berkeley.

Until his recent retirement, he was Senior Research Director at the Far West Laboratory for Research and Development, where he directed some fifty R&D projects in the course of the last two decades. During the 60s and 70s, he taught graduate courses and seminars at San Jose State University and at the University of California, Berkeley. In the 80s, he developed and directed the systems science program of the Saybrook Graduate School, where he is now Emeritus Professor. Both his R&D work and teaching have focused on the application of systems and design theories and methodologies in social and educational systems. He is president of the International Systems Institute, a nonprofit scientific and educational agency. In the 50s and 60s he was on the faculty of the US government's foreign language program in Monterey, California as Chair of the Hungarian Department and later as Dean of the East-Europe Middle-East Division.

A Past-President of the International Society for the Systems Sciences, he is now on the Board of Trustees of the Society, and chairs the Society's Commission on Education. Since 1981 he has served on the Board of Directors of the International Federation of Systems Research. He is on the International Editorial Boards of four journals: *Systems Research, Systems Practice, World Futures,* and *Asia Pacific Business Review*. He is Contributing Editor of *Educational Technology*, an international journal. During the last decade he has coordinated systems research conferences held in seven different countries. He recently co-chaired a NATO Advanced Research Workshop on Comprehensive Systems Design in Education. He is a co-founder of the General Evolutionary Research Group and a fellow at the Vienna Academy for the Study of the Future.

He has authored several books, chapters in books, and over one hundred articles and research reports. Over the years, he has edited a number of compendia and conference proceedings and chaired meetings of various professional societies. During the last several years he has focused his research and publications on the comprehensive design of social and educational systems.